Duncan Petersen's

Charming Small Hotel Guides

Italy

Duncan Petersen's

CHARMING SMALL HOTEL GUIDES

Italy

Fiona Duncan & Leonie Glass

DUNCAN PETERSEN

19th expanded edition

Conceived, designed and produced by
Duncan Petersen Publishing Ltd,
C7 Old Imperial Laundry, Warriner Gardens, London SW11 4XW

Editorial director Andrew Duncan
Editors Fiona Duncan, Leonie Glass and Nicky Swallow
Contributing editors George Pownall, Louise Brealey
Production editors Hermione Edwards, Jacqui Sayers
Designer Barbara Mercer
Cover design Lizzie Ballantyne
Maps Map Creation Ltd

A CIP catalogue record for this book is available
from the British Library

ISBN 978-1-903301-48-7

DTP by Duncan Petersen Publishing Ltd
Printed by Printer Portuguesa, Portugal

Contents

In this introductory section:

Our selection criteria 8

Types of accommodation 9

How to find an entry 11

Reporting to the guide 14

Maps 15-25

Welcome to this new edition of *Charming Small Hotel Guides Italy*. It features some big changes which we believe will make the guide more popular than ever with our readers.

• *Most hotels now have two colour photographs rather than one – often giving an inside as well as an outside view of the hotel.*

• *The layout has been changed in order to take you more quickly to essential booking information.*

We believe that these have proved to be real improvements, rather than change for its own sake. In all other respects, the guide remains true to the values and qualities that make it unique (see opposite), and which have won it so many devoted readers. This is the nineteenth new edition (including the first edition) since it was first published in 1986. It has sold hundreds of thousands of copies in the U.K., U.S.A. and in five European languages.

Why are we unique?

This is the only independently-inspected (no hotel pays for an entry) UK-originated accommodation guide that:

• has colour photographs for every entry;

• concentrates on places that have real charm and character;

• is highly selective;

• is particularly fussy about size. Most hotels have fewer than 20 bedrooms; if there are more, the hotel must have the feel of a much smaller place. We have found that a genuinely warm welcome is much more likely to be found in a small hotel;

• gives proper emphasis to the description, and doesn't use irritating symbols;

• is produced by a small, non- bureaucratic company with a dedicated team of like-minded inspectors.

See also 'So what exactly do we look for?', page 8.

So what exactly do we look for?
Our selection criteria

• A peaceful, attractive setting. Obviously, if the entry is in an urban area, we make allowances.

• A building that is handsome, interesting or historic; or at least with real character.

• Adequate space, but on a human scale. We don't go for places that rely too much on grandeur, or with pretensions that could be intimidating.

• Good taste and imagination in the interior decoration. We reject standardized, chain hotel fixtures, fittings and decorations.

• Bedrooms that look like real bedrooms, not hotel rooms, individually decorated.

• Furnishings and other facilities that are comfortable and well maintained. We like to see interesting antique furniture that is there to be used, not simply revered.

• Proprietors and staff who are dedicated and thoughtful, offering a personal welcome, but who aren't intrusive or overly effusive. The guest needs to feel like an individual.

• Interesting food. In Italy, it's increasingly the norm for food to be above average. There are few entries in this guide where the food is not of a high standard.

• A sympathetic atmosphere; an absence of loud people showing off their money; or the 'corporate feel'.

Introduction

A fatter guide, but just as selective

In order to accommodate most entries with a whole-page description and colour photograph, we've had to print more pages. But we have maintained our integrity by keeping the selection to around 300 entries.

Over the years, the number of charming small hotels in Italy has increased steadily – not dramatically. We don't believe that there are presently many more than about 350 truly charming small hotels in Italy, and that, if we included more, we would undermine what we're trying to do: produce a guide which is all about places that are more than just a bed for the night. Every time we consider a new hotel, we ask ourselves whether it has that extra special something, regardless of category and facilities, that makes it worth seeking out.

Types of accommodation in this guide

Despite its title, the guide does not confine itself to places called hotels or places that behave like hotels. On the contrary, we actively look for places that offer a home-from-home (see page 10). We include small and medium-sized hotels; plenty of traditional Italian guesthouses (pensioni) – some offering just bed and breakfast, some offering food at other times of day, too; restaurants with rooms; agriturismi, which are usually bed-and-breakfasts on farms or working rural estates; and some self-catering apartments, in town and country houses, provided they offer something special.

No fear or favour

To us, taking a payment for appearing in a guide seems to defeat the object of producing a guide. If money has changed hands, you can't write the whole truth about a hotel, and the selection cannot be nearly so interesting. This self-evident truth seems to us to be proved at least in part by the fact that pay guides are so keen to present the illusion of independence: few admit on the cover that they take payments for an entry, only doing so in small print on the inside.

Not many people realize that on the shelves of British bookshops there are many more hotel guides that accept payments for entries than there are independent guides. This guide is one of the few that do not accept any money for an entry.

Introduction

Home from home

Perhaps the most beguiling characteristic of the best places to stay in this guide is the feeling they give of being in a private home – but without the everyday cares and chores of running one. To get this formula right requires a special sort of professionalism: the proprietor has to strike the balance between being relaxed and giving attentive service. Those who experience this 'feel' often turn their backs on all other forms of accommodation – however luxurious.

The Italian hotel scene

Our latest survey of Italian hotels for this new edition of the guide has left us in little doubt about just how much we like them, and how much we enjoy to stay in them. Quite apart from the fact that many of them are in wonderful buildings and beautiful locations, their standards of welcome, ambience, cleanliness, attention to detail and food are – on the whole – above average. Perhaps the main quality that sets them apart from other European hotels is the genuinely relaxed, informal yet sophisticated, atmosphere that you find in even the smartest places. It's easy to feel at ease; there's much less talking in hushed tones in sepulchral public rooms than elsewhere, and staff are, by and large, warm and friendly. They won't snigger (as the French might) at a guest's attempt to speak their language, however botched, although many Italian hoteliers and their staff have several languages. Standards, once set, tend to be maintained: there's much less fluctuation than in, say, English hotels, since the majority remain in the family for generations, even these days. Yet despite this reassuringly old-fashioned characteristic, Italian hoteliers have been quick to take up new technology and the vast majority, even very simple ones, have e-mail and their own excellent websites.

The food is another bonus of Italian hotels. While you won't find many dining rooms presenting culinary fireworks, you will find it hard not to eat at least adequately and at best extremely well in all the hotels included in this guide. You will come across little international food on the menu: the emphasis is on regional, seasonal dishes using fresh local ingredients.

Check the price first

In this guide we have adopted the system of price bands, rather than giving actual prices as we did in previous editions. This is because prices were often subject to change after we went to press. The price bands refer to the approximate price of a standard double room (high season rates) with breakfast for two people. They are as follows:

€	under 110 Euros
€€	110-180 Euros
€€€	180-260 Euros
€€€€	260-350 Euros
€€€€€	more than 350 Euros

To avoid unpleasant surprises, always check what is included in the price (for example, VAT and service, breakfast, afternoon tea) when making the booking.

How to find an entry

In this guide, the entries are arranged in geographical groups. First, the whole of Italy is divided into three major sections; the book starts with Northern Italy, then proceeds to Central Italy and lastly Southern Italy. Within these sections, the entries are grouped by regions. Some of these regions correspond to the administrative regions of the country (Tuscany and Emiglia Romana, for example). Some are combinations of these regions (Lazio and Abruzzo, for example). Some are broader – the North-West or the North-East, for example.

Within each regional section the entries follow a set sequence: first comes an:

Area Introduction – an overview of the accommodation scene in that region, together with extra addresses of places which didn't quite deserve a full entry, or of places which we have heard good things about but have not yet been able to inspect and which might be useful if our main choices are booked up. Next come the full entries themselves, arranged alphabetically by city, town or nearest village. If several occur in or near one town, entries are arranged in alpha order by name of hotel.

To find a hotel in a particular area, use the maps following this introduction to locate the appropriate pages.

To locate a specific hotel, whose name you know, or a hotel in a place you know, use the indexes at the back, which list entries both by name and by nearest place name.

HOW TO READ AN ENTRY

Postal address and other key information.

Places of interest within reach of the hotel

This sets the hotel in its geographical context and should not be taken as precise instructions as to how to get there; always ask the hotel for directions.

Rooms described as having a bath usually also have a shower; rooms described as having a shower only have a shower.

This information is only an indication for wheelchair users and the infirm. Always check on suitability with the hotel.

Essential booking information.

SARDINIA   SOUTHERN ITALY

Alghero

Lungomare Valencia 1, 07041
Alghero, Sassari

Tel 079 981818
e-mail info@hotelvillalas-tronas.it
website www.hotelvillalas-tronas.it

Nearby Maria Pia, the best nearby beach, is 4 km north.
Location in modern Alghero, 800 m S of old Alghero; with car parking
Food breakfast, lunch, dinner
Price ©©©©
Rooms 25; 20 double and 5 suites with bath; all rooms have phone, TV, air conditioning, minibar, hairdrier
Facilities sitting room, dining room, bar, sea-water swimming pool, gym, bicycles **Credit cards** AE, DC, MC, V
Disabled not suitable
Pets accepted
Closed never
Manager Maria Teresa Masia

Villa Las Tronas
Seaside hotel

This castellated, 19thC folly lords it over its own bare, rocky promontory, and it stands aloof from the blocks of flats that otherwise characterize this unattractive part of modern Alghero. The interior – all marble floors and ornate chandeliers – is as grand as you might expect of somewhere that was a holiday retreat for Italian royalty until the 1940s. Yet the unstuffy and businesslike staff ensure it is not intimidatingly formal.

Antiques abound, including in the luxurious bedrooms, which feature brass or sleigh beds and grand canopies, along with swanky marble bathrooms. Those billed as having garden views in reality overlook Alghero's apartment blocks. You pay extra to open the shutters on a view across the bay to the awesome cliff of Capo Caccia; the priciest sea-facing rooms come with balconies. Rooms were revamped in 2000.

There are no beaches in this part of Alghero, but the hotel has a pool, and many guests swim off the rocks and from an old dockyard.

When we inspected, breakfast was dire. For food, you may be better off making the five-minute stroll along the seaside promenade into the magical backstreets of old Alghero, where you'll find a wide choice of restaurants. Bicycles are provided free.

300

Introduction

City, town or village, and
region, in which the hotel
is located.

Name of hotel

Type of
establishment

Description – never
vetted by the hotel

Breakfast, is normally
included in the price of
the room. We have not
quoted prices for lunch
and dinner. Other meals,
such as afternoon tea, may
also be available. 'Room
service' refers to food and
drink, either snacks or full
meals, which can be
served in the room.

Always let the hotel know in
advance if you want to bring
a pet. Even where pets are
accepted, certain restrictions
may apply, and a small charge
may be levied.

Telephoning Italy from abroad
To call Italy from the U.K., dial 00, then
the international dialling code 39, then
dial the number, including the initial 0.
From the U.S., dial 001 39.

Smoking
Some or all the public rooms and
bedrooms in an increasing number
of hotels are now non-smoking.
Smokers should check the hotel's
policy when booking.

Children
Children are almost always accepted,
usually welcomed, in Italian hotels.
There are often special facilities, such
as cots, high chairs, baby listening and
early supper. Check first if they may
join parents in the dining room.

**We list the following
credit cards:**
AE   American Express
DC   Diners Club
MC   Mastercard
V   Visa

Tipping
Italian waiters do not rely on tips
in the same way as in some other
European countries (if lucky, they
will get a share of the profits).
However, Italians usually round
up the bill if pleased with service.

Reporting to the guide

Please write and tell us about your experiences of small hotels, guest houses and inns, whether good or bad, whether listed in this edition or not. As well as hotels in Italy, we are interested in hotels in France, Spain, Austria, Germany, Switzerland and the U.S.A. We assume that reporters have no objections to our publishing their views unpaid.

Readers whose reports prove particularly helpful may be invited to join our Travellers' Panel. Members give us notice of their own travel plans; we suggest hotels that they might inspect, and help with the cost of accommodation.

The address to write to us is:

Editor, *Charming Small Hotel Guides*
C7 Old Imperial Laundry, Warriner Gardens, London SW11 4XW

Checklist

Please use a separate sheet of paper for each report; include your name, address and telephone number on each report.

Your reports will be received with particular pleasure if they are typed, and if they are organized under the following headings:

Name of establishment
Town or village it is in, or nearest
Full address, including postcode
Telephone number
Time and duration of visit
The building and setting
The public rooms
The bedrooms and bathrooms
Physical comfort (chairs, beds, heat, light, hot water)
Standards of maintenance and housekeeping
Atmosphere, welcome and service
Food
Value for money

We assume that in writing you have no objections to your views being published unpaid, either verbatim or in an edited version. Names of major outside contributors are acknowledged, at the editor's discretion, in the guide.

Hotel location maps

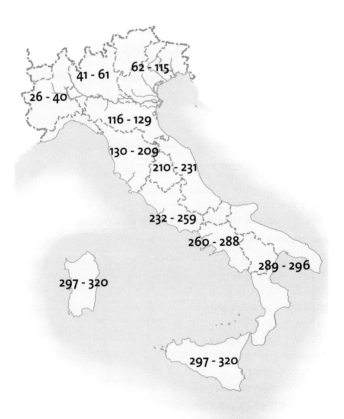

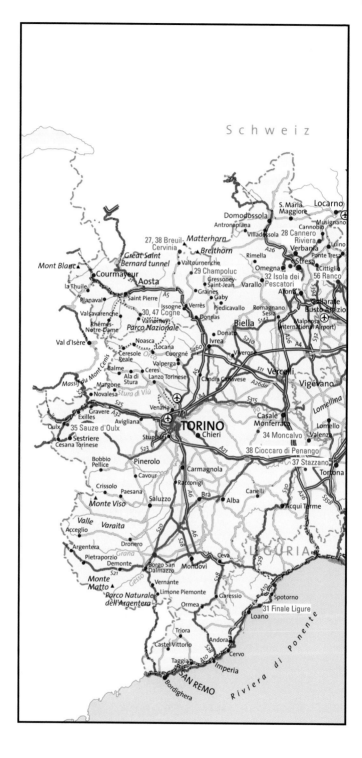

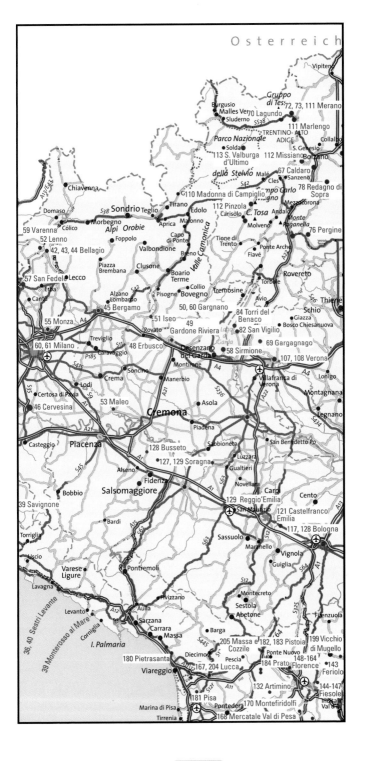

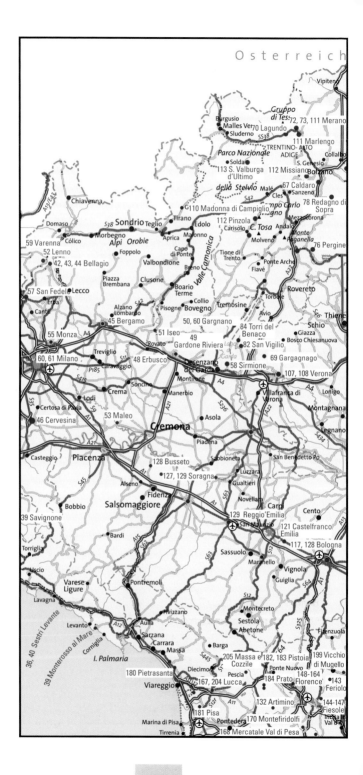

Osterreich

Vipiteno

Burgusio
Malles Ver 70 Lagundo   Gruppo
    Sluderno   S538   di Tes 72, 73, 111 Merano

                                    111 Marlengo
                             TRENTINO- ALTO
Parco Nazionale   ADIGE   Collalbo
    Solda   S. Genesio
113 S. Valburga   112 Missiano Bolzano
    d'Ultimo
                                67 Caldaro
della Stelvio   Malè Cles   Sanzeno
                                     78 Redagno di
                 G110 Madonna di Campiglio po Carlo Sopra
Chiavenna   gno   Mezzocorona
                 Tirano Edolo   C. Tosa Andalo
Domaso   S38 Sondrio Teglio 112 Pinzola   Monte
                     Aprica Carisolo   Molveno Paganella
59 Varenna Cólico Morbegno Malonno   76 Pergine
52 Lenno   Alpi Orobie   Capo   Tione di
       Foppolo   di Ponte   Trento
42, 43, 44 Bellagio Valbondione Breno   Ponte Arche
           Piazza   Clusone   Fiavè
57 San Fedele Brembana   Torbole
           Lecco   Boario   Rovereto
Erba   Terme
Cantù   Alzano   Collio   Avio
         Lombardo Pisogne Bovegno Tremosine   Schio
45 Bergamo   50, 60 Gargnano   Giazza Thie
55 Monza A4 51 Iseo 49   84 Torri del Bosco Chiesanuova
         Rovato   Benaco
60, 61 Milano Treviglio   Gardone Riviera 82 San Vigilio
       Caravaggio S11 48 Erbusco Desenzano 69 Gargagnago
          Pt85   del Garda
       Soncino   Montirone 58 Sirmione 107, 108 Verona
   Lodi Crema   A4   Villafranca di A4 Lonigo
Certosa di Pavia Manerbio   Verona   Montagnana
46 Cervesina   53 Maleo   Asola   Legnano
                    Cremona
Casteggio Piacenza Piadena
                128 Busseto Sabbioneta San Benedetto Po
       Alseno 127, 129 Soragna Luzzara
Bobbio   Fidenza Gualtieri
       Salsomaggiore Novellara Carpi
39 Savignone   129 Reggio'Emilia Cento
         Bardi   San Maurizio 121 Castelfranco
Torriglia   Emilia
                  Sassuolo   117, 128 Bologna
Uscio   Maranello
   Varese   Pontremoli   Vignola
   Ligure   Guiglia S64
Lavagna   S12
       Levanto Aulla   Montecreto
       Sarzana   Sestola   Firenzuola
Corniglia Carrara   Abetone
   I. Palmaria Massa Barga   205 Massa e 182, 183 Pistoia 199 Vicchio
                Diecimo Cozzile Ponte Nuovo di Mugello
180 Pietrasanta Pescia 184 Prato 143
   Viareggio 167, 204 Lucca   Florence Feriolo
                132 Artimino   144-147
                          Fiesole
181 Pisa   170 Montefiridolfi Val 8
Marina di Pisa Pontedera
Tirrenia 168 Mercatale Val di Pesa

18

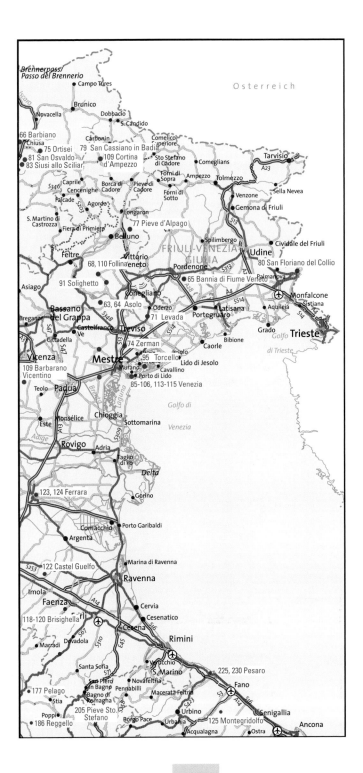

Brennerpass/
Passo del Brennerio
Campo Tures

Osterreich

Brunico
Novacella
Dobbiaco
S. Candido

66 Barbiano
Chiusa
75 Ortisei
81 San Osvaldo
83 Siusi allo Sciliar
Carbonin
79 San Cassiano in Badia
Comelico Superiore
109 Cortina d'Ampezzo
Sto Stefano di Cadore
Comeglians
Tarvisio
A23

Caprile
Cencenighe
Falcade
Agordo
Borca di Cadore
Pieve di Cadore
Forni di Sopra
Ampezzo
Tolmezzo
Forni di Sotto
Venzone
Sella Nevea
Gemona di Friuli

S. Martino di Castrozza
Fiera di Primiero
Longaron
77 Pieve d'Alpago
Belluno
Spilimbergo
Cividale del Friuli

Feltre
Vittorio
68, 110 Follina Veneto
FRIULI-VENEZIA GIULIA
Udine
80 San Floriano del Collio

91 Solighetto
Pordenone
Palmanova

Asiago
Conegliano
63, 64 Asolo
65 Bannia di Fiume Veneto
Monfalcone
Sistiana

Bassano del Grappa
Breganze
Castelfranco Ve
Oderzo
71 Levada
Latisana
Portegruaro
Aquileia
SS14

Cittadella
Treviso
74 Zerman
Bibione
Grado
Golfo
Trieste

Vicenza
Mestre
95 Torcello
Jesolo
Lido di Jesolo
di Trieste

109 Barbarano Vicentino
Murano
Cavallino
Porto di Lido
85-106, 113-115 Venezia

Teolo
Padua

Monsélice
Chioggia
Golfo di

Este
Sottomarina
Venezia

Rovigo
Adria

Taglio di Po

Delta

123, 124 Ferrara
Gorino

Comacchio
Porto Garibaldi

Argenta

122 Castel Guelfo
Marina di Ravenna

Imola
Ravenna

Faenza
Cervia

118-120 Brisighella
Forlì
Cesenatico

Marradi
Dovadola
Cesena
Rimini

Santa Sofia
Verucchio
225, 230 Pesaro

177 Pelago
San Piero in Bagno
Bagno di Romagna
Novafeltria
Pennabilli
S. Marino
Fano

Stia
Macerata Feltria

Poppi
205 Pieve Sto. Stefano
Borgo Pace
Urbino
125 Montegridolfo
Senigallia

186 Reggello
Urbania
Acqualagna
Ostra
Ancona

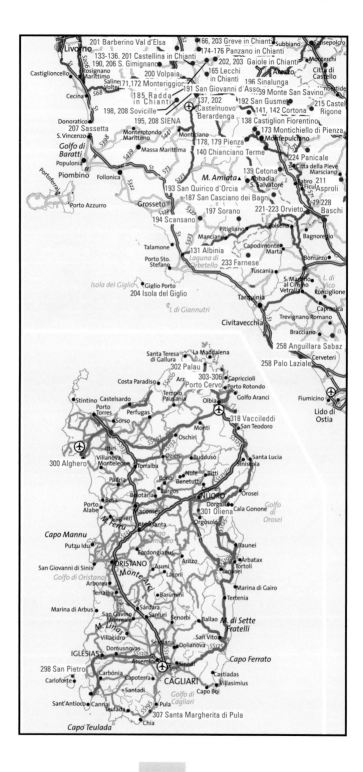

Livorno
201 Barberino Val d'Elsa
166, 203 Greve in Chianti
Subbiano
Sansepolcro
133-136, 201 Castellina in Chianti
174-176 Panzano in Chianti
Monterchi
190, 206 S. Gimignano
202, 203 Gaiole in Chianti
Città di
Castello
Rosignano
Marittimo
165 Lecchi
in Chianti
Arezzo
Castiglioncello
Saline di
Volterra
71,172 Monteriggioni
196 Sinalunga
Umbertide
Cecina
185 Radda
in Chianti
191 San Giovanni d'Asso
59 Monte San Savino
137, 202
192 San Gusme
215 Castel
Rigone
198, 208 Sovicille
Castelnuovo
Berardenga
141, 142 Cortona
Donoratico
195, 208 SIENA
138 Castiglion Fiorentino
207 Sassetta
173 Montichiello di Pienza
S. Vincenzo
Monterotondo
Marittimo
Monticiano
178, 179 Pienza
Montepulciano
Golfo di
Baratti
Massa Marittima
140 Chianciano Terme
224 Panicale
Populonia
139 Cetona
Città della Pieve
Marsciano
Portoferraio
Piombino
Follonica
M. Amiata
Abbadia
S. Salvatore
Fabro
Ficulle
211
Asproli
Porto Azzurro
193 San Quirico d'Orcia
79 228
Baschi
Grosseto
187 San Casciano dei Bagni
221-223 Orvieto
194 Scansano
197 Sorano
Pitigliano
Bolsena
Manciano
Bagnoregio
Talamone
131 Albinia
Capodimonte
Marta
Bomarzo
Porto Sto.
Stefano
Laguna di
Orbetello
233 Farnese
Tuscania
S. Martino
al Cimino
Vetralla
L. di
Vico
Ronciglione
Isola del Giglio
Giglio Porto
204 Isola del Giglio
Tarquinia
Capranica
I. di Giannutri
Trevignano Romano
Civitavecchia
Bracciano
258 Anguillara Sabaz
Santa Teresa
di Gallura
La Maddalena
Cerveteri
302 Palau
258 Palo Laziale
Costa Paradiso
Arz
303-306 Capriccioli
Porto Cervo
Porto Rotondo
Tempio
Pausania
Golfo Aranci
Fiumicino
Stintino
Castelsardo
Olbia
Porto
Torres
Perfugas
Lido di
Ostia
Sorso
318 Vaccileddi
Monti
San Teodoro
Oschiri
Ittiri
Ozieri
Budduso
Santa Lucia
300 Alghero
Villanova
Monteleone
Torralba
Siniscola
Bono
Nule
Bitti
Padria
Benetutti
Burgos
Orosei
Bosa
Bolotana
NUORO
Porto
Alabe
Macomer
Dorgali
Cala Gonone
Golfo
di
Orosei
Cuglieri
301 Oliena
M. Ferru
Abbasanta
Orgosolo
Capo Mannu
Lago
Omodeo
Putzu Idu
Baunei
Fordongianus
San Giovanni di Sinis
ORISTANO
Aritzo
Arbatax
Tortoli
Golfo di Oristano
Monte Arci
Asuni
Lanusei
Arborea
Laconi
Terralba
Barumini
Marina di Gairo
Tertenia
Marina di Arbus
Sardara
San Gavino
Monreale
Sanluri
Senorbi
Ballao
M. di Sette
Fratelli
M. Linas
Villacidro
San Vito
Domusnovas
Seulana
Dolianova
IGLESIAS
Assemini
Sinnai
Capo Ferrato
298 San Pietro
Carbonia
Castiadas
Carloforte
Capoterra
CAGLIARI
Villasimius
Santadi
Golfo di
Cagliari
Capo Boi
Sant'Antioco
Cannai
Teulada
Pula
307 Santa Margherita di Pula
Chia
Capo Teulada

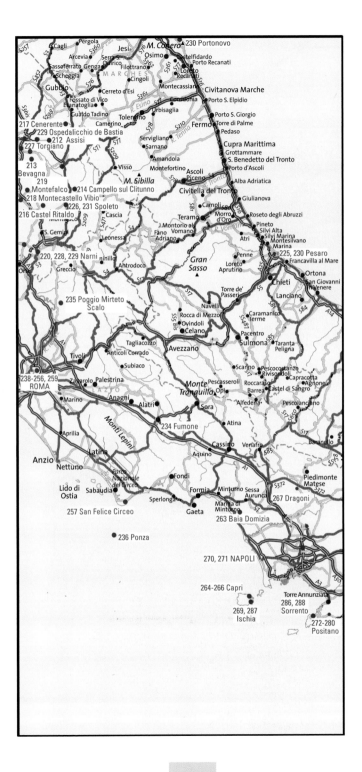

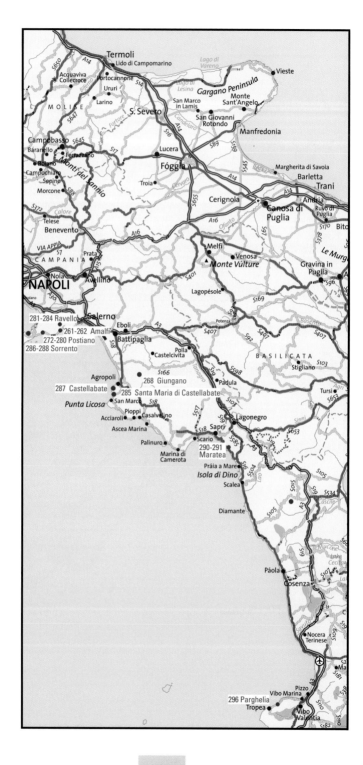

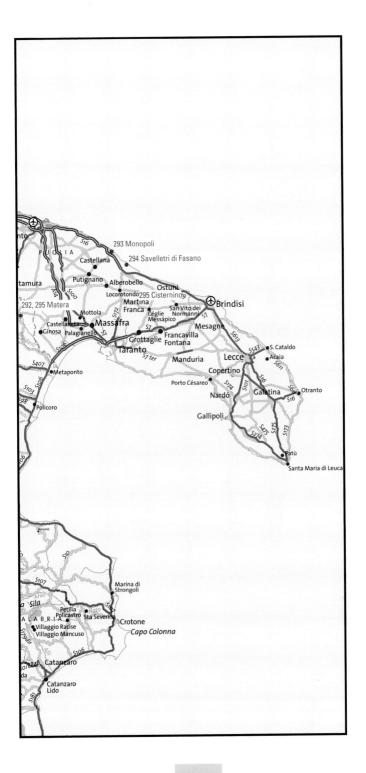

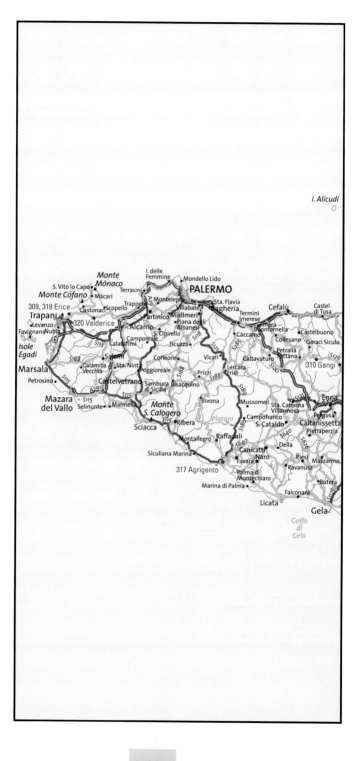

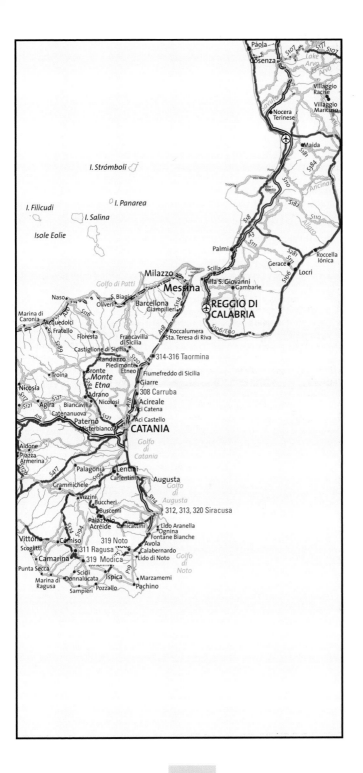

North-west Italy offers three contrasting regions: the land 'at the foot of the mountains', Piedmont; the mountainous Valle d'Aosta; and the coastal Liguria. Piedmont (Piemonte) does, no doubt, have its attractions, but they do not impress themselves on many foreign visitors, who tend to hurry across this large region on their way to the recognized glories of Italy to the east and south. To the traveller, as to the resident, the region is dominated by the city lying at its heart – Turin. Of the swish hotels, the most attractive (and not quite the most expensive) is the **Jolly Hotel Ligure** (tel 011 55641). Of the more modest places, the **Genio** (tel 011 6505771) and the stylish **Victoria** (tel 011 5611909) are smartly modern, of moderate size and central, the former particularly handy for the station.

A little further away from the middle is the cheaper **Piedmontese** (tel 011 6698101). Within easy reach of Turin, we can recommend the **Salzea** (tel 011 6497809) at Trofarello, the **Panoramica** (tel 0125 669966) at Loranze, and the **Locanda del Sant' Uffizio**, featured on page 38. Recent entries to this edition include **Cascina Orsolina** (page 34), and **La Traversina** (page 37). In addition, readers recommend two places, **Locanda del Pilone** (tel 0173 366616) at Madonna di Como near Alba, and **Tra Arte e Querce** (tel 0173 792156) at Monchiero, south of Barolo – a 'fantastic' family-run restaurant-with-rooms 'in the middle of nowhere' specialising in truffles. In the region of the Italian Lakes, **Hotel Cannero** at Cannero Riviera on Lake Maggiore is a great favourite (p 28), as well as the **Verbano** on Isola dei Pescatori (see p 32).

To the north of Turin is the mainly French-speaking Valle d'Aosta, a steep-sided valley surrounded by some of the highest peaks in the Alps, and best known for its mountain scenery and winter sports facilities. It borders France to the west, where Monte Bianco (Mont Blanc) is the highest peak in Europe, and Switzerland to the north, where the Cervino (the Matterhorn) and Monte Rosa also tower well above 4,000 m. In this area we have chalet-style hotels to recommend in Champoluc (p 29) and Breuil-Cervinia (p 27). We can also recommend a new boutique hotel in Entreves near Courmayeur, **Auberge de la Maison** (tel 0165 869811), an adjuct of the highly regarded restaurant, **La Maison de Filippo**.

To the south is Italy's highest mountain, Gran Paradiso, surrounded by a stunning national park named after it. In the middle of the park, in Cogne, we have another recommendation, **Le Bellevue** (p 30).

The third region is Liguria, a thin strip of mountainous coastline dominated by the Italian Riviera, for which we offer several recommendations. On the Riviera di Levante, south-east of Genoa, we include one hotel in Sestri Levante, one in Levanto, and one in the Cinque Terre village of Monterosso al Mare. We have not yet had the opportunity to visit a new bed-and-breakfast establishment, **Castello di Monleone** in Moneglia (tel 0185 49291) on the same stretch of coast, but it looks lovely, as does **Hotel Villa Edera**, in the grounds of which the Castello stands (tel 0185 49291). We can also recommend an old favourite, **Ca' Peo** at Leivi in the hills, family run with excellent food served in a charming dining room and very simple, dated bedrooms which don't suit everyone (tel 0185 319696). On the Riviera di Ponente, west of Genoa, we feature the **Punta Est** at Finale Ligure.

Breuil-Cervinia

11021 Breuil-Cervinia, Aosta

Tel 0166 948998
e-mail
hermitage@relaischateaux.com
website www.hotelhermitage.com

Nearby golf (500 m); Aosta (50 km).
Location just NE of Breuil-
Cervinia; garage
Food breakfast, lunch, dinner;
room service
Price €€€€
Rooms 36; 18 double and twin, 18
suites, all with bath; all rooms have
phone, TV, minibar, hairdrier, safe
Facilities sitting room, dining room,
meeting room, health and beauty
centre, swimming pool, lift/elevator,
terrace
Credit Cards AE, DC, MC, V
Disabled access difficult
Pets not accepted
Closed May-Jul, Sept-Dec
Proprietors Neyroz family

Hermitage
Mountain chalet

Wake up to a spectacular view of
Monte Cervino (better known as
the Matterhorn) through your bedroom
window, then relax after a hard day's skiing
with a massage, a mud bath or a book in
front of a crackling log fire. This glossy
Relais & Châteaux hotel comes with all
the trimmings: a health and beauty centre,
small indoor pool, a sitting room furnished
with vast deep sofas and chairs, and an elegant dining room, candlelit by night. It even
boasts liveried porters and a heated
garage. A low modern chalet built in traditional style, it has been done up with coun-
try-house furnishings and an appropriately
Alpine flavour. Wood floors and walls,
antique furniture and oak beams abound.
There are as many suites as bedrooms, and
all succeed in being cosy as well as luxurious, with pretty wallpaper, well-placed
lamps, knick-knacks, mirrors and prints
and some particularly handsome pieces of
furniture. Our favourite rooms are the
ones in the attic, which have sloping
beamed ceilings and the most character.

The dining room, whose picture windows frame a blue larch forest, prides itself
on a menu of simple local dishes accompanied by excellent regional wines. The
hotel only accepts children over six.

Lungo Lago 2, 28821 Cannero
Riviera, Verbania

Tel 0323 788046/788113
e-mail info@hotelcannero.com
website
www.hotelcannero.com

Nearby Borromean Islands;
Ascona (21 km), Locarno (25
km).
Location in resort, overlook-
ing lake; car parking
Food breakfast, lunch, dinner
Price €
Rooms 55 double and twin
and single, all with bath or
shower; all have air
conditioning; 10 self-catering
apartments
Facilities sitting room, bar,
dining room, library, lift/eleva-
tor, 2 terraces, garden, swim-
ming pool, tennis, bicycles
Credit cards AE, DC, MC, V
Disabled 10 rooms accessible
Pets by arrangement **Closed**
Nov–mid Mar **Proprietor**
Signora Gallinotto

Cannero
Lakeside hotel

Cannero is one of the quietest resorts on Lake Maggiore and its most desir-able hotels lie right on the shore. Only the ferry landing-stage and a dead-end road separate the Cannero from the waters of Lake Maggiore.

The building was once a monastery, though only an old stone column, a couple of vaulted passageways, a quiet courtyard and a beautifully preserved 17thC well suggest it is anything other than a modern hotel. The emphasis is on comfort and relaxation, and the atmosphere is very friendly, thanks largely to the attention of Signora Gallinotto and her family. Downstairs, big windows and terraces make the most of the setting. The restau-rant focuses on the lake, with an outdoor terrace running alongside. Bedrooms are light and well cared for with adequate bathrooms. Self-catering apartments are also available for families with children.

There are gorgeous views of lake and mountains from front rooms, all with bal-conies. By day this provides a delightful spot to take a dip or hang out under the red parasols. Readers' plaudits are legion: 'please be sure to rate it A+++!'; 'clean as a whistle, exceptional value, wonderful'; 'family and staff the most friendly and help-ful imaginable'.

Champoluc

Via Croues 5, 11020
Champoluc, Monte Rosa,
Aosta

Tel 0125 307128
e-mail hotelannamaria@tis-
cali.it
website www.hotelvillaanna-
maria.com

Nearby Verrès (27 km);
Valtournenche and Gressoney
valleys.
Location off lane to right at
end of village, signposted to
hotel; car parking
Food breakfast, lunch, dinner
Price €€ (half board only in
high season)
Rooms 20 double and twin,
family, 14 with bath or show-
er; all rooms have phone, TV
Facilities sitting room, dining
room, terrace, garden
Credit cards MC, V
Disabled access difficult
Pets not accepted
Closed never
Proprietor Aldo Aquarone

Villa Anna Maria
Mountain chalet

In a quiet wooded hillside setting close to
the village of Champoluc, the main community in a steep-sided valley beneath the
mighty Monte Rosa, this traditional shuttered chalet is as charming in summer, surrounded by mountain flowers as it is deep
in winter snow. Its charm lies in the fact
that hardly anything seems to have
changed since the house was built in 1940
by the eponymous mother and grand-
mother of the present owners. In the rustic dining room, for example, polished
wood covers the floor, ceiling and walls,
bright copper pots gleam from shelves,
and red-and-white gingham curtains frame
the windows. Guests sit at tables with
crisp white cloths, and are served simple
but delicious country fare including *fondu-
ta* with *fontina*, the local cheese fondue.

The cosy bedrooms also have panelled
walls and, whether they look up at the
mountain or down the valley, benefit from
utter peace and quiet, spared from traffic
noise as cars are not allowed up to the
hotel. Guests must park in the private car
park 50 metres or so down the hill, and
then walk up to the chalet through romantic pine woods, while kind staff collect
their luggage. The father and son owners
extend a warm welcome.

Cogne

Rue Grand Paradis 22, 11012
Cogne, Aosta

Tel 0165 74825
e-mail bellevue@relais-
chateaux.com
website www.hotelbellevue.it

Nearby Valnontey Alpine
Garden (3 km); Saint Pierre
(20 km).
Location in centre of Cogne
facing the Glacier; car parking
Food breakfast, lunch, dinner
Price €€€
Rooms 38; 28 double and
twin, 7 suites with fireplace and
Jacuzzi (three with sauna), 3
chalets, all with bath or show-
er; all have minibar, hairdrier
Facilities sitting room, TV
room, playroom, dining rooms,
bars, swimming pool, health
centre, lift/elevator, terrace
Credit cards AE, DC, MC, V
Disabled 2 adapted rooms
Pets accepted **Closed** early
Oct–early Dec **Proprietors**
Jeantet-Roullet family

Bellevue
Mountain chalet

This hotel is aptly named, nestled in the heart of a national park on the flat grassy floor of a valley dominated by Gran Paradiso and other peaks. Its 'beautiful view' stretches across meadows filled with wildflowers to the snow-capped peaks and most of the public rooms and balconied bedrooms reap the benefit. The Bellevue has been owned and run by the same family, with tradition as the keynote, since it was built in the 1920s. The simple decoration combines pale colours with the glow of wood, local artworks and antiques, lace and fresh alpine flowers. Open fires blaze in every grate. Home-baked bread is served with the imaginative regional meals by a cheerful staff, who speak French and wear national costume. In addition to the hotel dining room you can eat at the new Bar à Fromage, Restaurant de Montagne and Jeantet-Roullets' village Brasserie du Bon Bec. Start the day with the generous buffet breakfast to set you up for skiing or hiking. On your return, in the renovated health centre, La Valheureusa, you can try a hay bath or 'peeling on the hot stone'.

The neat comfortable bedrooms and suites, with cosy sitting rooms and fire-places, have ultra-modern bathrooms, some with Jacuzzis. The three chalets are ideal for families.

Finale Ligure

Via Aurelia 1, 17024 Finale Ligure, Savona

Tel 019 600612
e-mail info@puntaest.com
website www.puntaest.com

Nearby Finale Borgo (3 km); Alássio (26 km).
Location E of the historic town; car parking
Food breakfast, lunch, dinner
Price €€€
Rooms 40; 30 double, 4 single, 6 suites, all with bath; all rooms have phone, minibar; some rooms have TV, air conditioning
Facilities sitting room, bar, TV room, meeting room, piano bar, terrace, garden, swimming pool
Credit cards AE, DC, MC, V
Disabled access difficult
Pets not accepted
Closed mid-Oct to late Apr
Proprietors Podestà family

Punta Est
Seaside villa

The Italian Riviera west of Genoa is for the most part disappointing: most of its resorts are dreary, and most of its hotels mediocre. Happily, the Punta Est is an exception. The hotel is converted from a splendid 18thC villa which stands high and proudly pink above the buzz of the main coastal road, overlooking the sea. Signor Podestà, who used to be a sculptor, has acted as resident architect since the hotel was first created in the late 1960s, and with great success. By preserving the original features of the house and adding to it in a sympathetic style, he has managed to preserve the atmosphere of a private villa. The interior is cool and elegant – all dark-wood antiques, fine stone arches, fireplaces and tiled floors. But with such an impressive setting, the focus is on the terraces and gardens, with their lovely views.

Breakfast is taken (off Staffordshire china) in a sort of canopied greenhouse – a lovely sunny spot, surrounded by greenery. Other meals are served in a dining room in the annexe, where stone arches and beams create a vaguely med-ieval setting. You can choose between international and Ligurian dishes, including bass cooked with strong aromatic local herbs. The beach is only a couple of minutes' walk down the hillside.

Isola dei Pescatori

Via Ugo Ara 2, Isola dei
Pescatori, 28838 Stresa,
Verbania

Tel 0323 30408/32534
e-mail hotelverbano@tin.it
website www.hotelverbano.it

Nearby Isola Bella; Stresa;
Pallanza; Baveno.
Location on tiny island in
Lake Maggiore; regular boats
from Stresa, where there is
ample car parking space
Food breakfast, lunch, dinner
Price €€
Rooms 12 double and twin, 8
with bath, 4 with shower; all
rooms have phone, hairdrier
Facilities sitting room, dining
room, bar, terrace
Credit cards AE, DC, MC, V
Disabled no special facilities
Pets accepted
Closed mid-Nov to mid-Feb
Manager Signor Alberto
Zacchera

Verbano
Lakeside guesthouse

The Isola dei Pescatori may not have the *palazzo* or gardens of neighbouring Isola Bella (unlike the other islands, it has never belonged to the wealthy Borromeo family), but it is just as charming in its own way. The cafés and the slightly shabby, painted fishermen's houses along the front are, perhaps, reminiscent of a Greek island – though not an undiscovered one.

The Verbano is a large russet-coloured villa occupying one end of the island, its garden and terraces looking across Lake Maggiore to Isola Bella. It does not pretend to be luxurious, but it does offer plenty of character and local colour. There are beautiful views from the bedrooms, and 11 of the 12 have balconies. Each room is named after a flower; most are prettily and appropriately furnished in old-fashioned style, with painted furniture; those which were a little tired-looking have been refurbished, and more refurbishment has been undertaken since a change of ownership. The quietest rooms are those away from the terrace.

But the emphasis is really on the restaurant, with home-made pastas a speciality. If weather prevents eating on the terrace, you can still enjoy the views through the big windows of the dining room. 'Excellent food, friendly staff,' says a visitor. Reports would be welcome.

Levanto

Loc. Villanova, 19015 Levanto, Spezia

Tel 0187 802517
e-mail info@agriturismovillanova.it
website www.agriturismovillanova.it

Nearby Levanto (1 km); Cinque Terre.
Location on private estate about 1 km outside Levanto; car parking
Food breakfast
Price €–€€€
Rooms 11; 3 double, 3 triple, 2 suites, 3 self-catering apartments, all with bath or shower; all rooms have phone, TV, minibar, hairdrier
Facilities breakfast room, terrace, garden,
Credit cards AE, MC, V
Disabled no facilities
Pets not accepted
Closed 8th Jan-8th Feb
Proprietor Barone Giancarlo Massola

Agrit. Villanova
Country villa

The lovely old red and cream Villa Villanova is where Barone Giancarlo Massola's ancestors spent their summers in the 18th century. Set in a sunny clearing at the end of a long drive, the property is surrounded by vines, fruit and olive trees, from which the family produces olive oil, wine and homemade jams. 'We so enjoyed our visit that we plan to return' a satisfied guest wrote to tell us. And so they did, enthusing on both occasions about their charming and rustic-elegant room with comfortable bed dressed in embroidered cotton sheets and small but stylish, well-designed bathroom. 'The buffet breakfast was delicious, including homemade fruit compote, preserves and bread as well as ham and cheese. There were lovely views from our room and the atmosphere was one of comfort and peace. The staff could not have been more helpful.'

Barone Massola has converted his villa and the small farmhouse behind to include eight bedrooms and suites and three self-catering apartments, each with its own entrance and terrace. There are no public rooms, but a communal terrace for breakfast and an indoor breakfast room for use during inclement weather. The youthful atmosphere is very much set by Barone Massola himself, who wears jeans and has a wispy beard.

Via Caminata 28, 14036
Moncalvo, Asti

Tel 0141 921180
e-mail welcome@cascinaor-
solina.it
website
www.cascinaorsolina.net

Nearby Asti (21 km); vine-
yards.
Location one km SW of
Moncalvo, in own grounds; car
parking
Food breakfast
Price €€
Rooms 9 double and twin, all
with bath or shower; all rooms
have TV, hairdrier
Facilities sitting rooms, break-
fast room, terrace, garden,
swimming pool, sauna, Turkish
bath, small gym
Credit cards AE, DC, MC, V
Disabled one specially adapted
room
Pets accepted
Closed Jan
Proprietor Daniela Cortassa

Cascina Orsolina
Country guesthouse

In spite of the increase in tourism in this
gentle part of Piemonte, there is still a
dearth of nice places to stay, so it was a
real pleasure to stumble on this delightful
guest house. Around here, a *cascina* is a
large, L-shaped rural building surrounded
by its own vineyards; Daniela Cortassa's
family has produced wine for several generations, but she only opened her house
to guests in 2002.

Situated in rolling countryside just outside the small town of Moncalvo d'Asti,
the origins of the building can still be seen
in the two floors of tall arched windows
which once housed the granary but which
today allow sunlight to come flooding in.
Inside, a tasteful, up-market country style
predominates, starting with gorgeous
blond wood floors. The huge ground floor
living room has a big stone fireplace at one
end and comfortable sofas and armchairs
grouped around low tables; the breakfast
room also has a open fire for cool weather. The bedrooms are beautifully and individually furnished with antiques, pretty fabrics and personal objets. Soft lighting gives
everything a warm glow while Mexican
wall hangings and oriental carpets add
colour to the rooms.

A well-furnished terrace, overlooking
the pretty garden and lily pond, offers a
peaceful spot for outdoor relaxation.

Sauze d'Oulx

Case Sparse 21, Le Clotes,
10050 Sauze d'Oulx, Torino

Tel 0122 850273
website www.chaletilcapri-
corno.it

Nearby Susa (28 km);
Briançon, France (28 km).
Location above and 2 km E of
town; car parking in summer
Food breakfast, lunch, dinner
Price €€
Rooms 7 double and twin with
bath; all rooms have phone,
TV, hairdrier
Facilities bar, dining room,
terrace
Credit cards MC, V
Disabled access difficult
Pets not accepted
Closed May to mid-Jun, mid-
Sep to Dec
Proprietors Carlo and
Mariarosa Sacchi

Il Capricorno
Mountain chalet

This typical wooden chalet has a fairy-tale setting surrounded by pine trees on the slopes above the busy ski resort of Sauze d'Oulx and can only be reached by a steep, winding dirt track. In summer you can drive right up to the hotel, but in winter, you must park in town and be collected by snowmobile. Inside, it is as spick-and-span and cosy as a chalet should be: the snug rooms, brightened by fresh flowers, log fires and traditional wooden furniture, mostly handmade by Carlo himself. The dining room, beyond a tiny bar, is especially cheerful with its burnished copper pots and kettles, neat pile of logs beside the hearth and pretty blue-and-white tablecloths. The seven spotless bedrooms and bathrooms have recently been updated, and there are balconies for a select few.

In winter you can ski down the hill from the front door; in summer there are mountain hikes that beckon in all directions. Because they have so few guests (there are only seven rooms), the Sacchis go to great lengths to indulge them, not least with the delicious meals that Mariarosa produces every day.

After a long day's skiing or walking, this is the perfect place to return to. And as more people are beginning to realize this, you must book early.

35

Sestri Levante

Via Cappuccini 43, 16039
Sestri Levante, Genova

Tel 0185 43048/41175
e-mail
helvetia@hotelhelvetia.it
website www.hotelhelvetia.it

Nearby Portofino (28 km);
Genoa (50 km).
Location at end of small 'Bay
of Silence' beach; limited car
parking and garage
Food breakfast
Price €€
Rooms 21 double and twin
with shower; all rooms have
phone, TV, video, minibar,
hairdrier, safe
Facilities sitting room,
TV/video room, dining room,
bar, lift/elevator, terrace, gar-
den, table tennis
Credit cards AE, MC, V
Disabled no special facilities
Pets not accepted
Closed Nov to Feb
Proprietor Lorenzo Pernigotti

Helvetia
Seaside hotel

The Helvetia's claim that it has 'the quietest and most enchanting position of
Sestri Levante' is no exaggeration: it stands
at one end of the appropriately named
Baia del Silenzio. The hotel is distinguished
by its spotless white façade, and the yellow
and white canopies that shade its balconies and terrace.

Lorenzo Pernigotti devotes himself
wholeheartedly to his guests and provides
the sort of extras – including 15 gleaming
yellow bikes – that you might expect to
find in a four-star hotel; but the Helvetia
remains small and personal; one satisfied
guest says he 'felt just like part of the family'. (the hotel was opened by Signor
Pernigotti's parents in what was their own
seaside villa.) Another was delighted by
the sophisticated key system which controls the lights and music in the bedrooms.
The sitting room/bar has the air of a private home – antiques, coffee-table books,
newspapers, potted plants – and the
breakfast room is lovely, with views of the
bay. Bedrooms are light and airy, overlooking either the bay or the gardens. The day
starts on the terrace, with an unusually liberal help-yourself breakfast. Luxuriant gardens climb up the hillside, with tables in
the shade. Serious sun-bathers can take to
sunbeds. And there's a tiny pebble beach
just across the road.

Stazzano

Cascina La Traversina 109,
15060 Stazzano, Alessandria

Tel 0143 61377
e-mail latraversina@latraversina.com
website www.latraversina.com

Nearby Marengo; Asti;
Albugnano; Milan-Genoa
autostrade.
Location on hillside 2 km
from Stazzano; in Stazzano
follow sign for 2 km on
unpaved road; in own grounds;
parking
Food breakfast, dinner
Price €–€€
Rooms 5: 2 doubles, 3 apart-
ments (each for 2 persons);
all with shower
Facilities breakfast room,
conservatory, terrace, garden,
swimming pool **Credit cards**
MC, V **Disabled** not suitable
Pets not accepted
Closed never
Proprietors Rosanna and
Domenico Varese

Agrit. La Traversina
Country villa

What a lovely place. You can hardly make out a building behind the great swathe of creepers, climbers, roses and geraniums that smother this delightful old farmhouse, set on a thickly wooded hillside, that has belonged to Rosanna Varese's family for 300 years or so. Shuttered windows peak out through the foliage and look down on rows of potted plants, cats sleeping in the sun, and flowers everywhere. In the garden there is a small, inviting swimming pool, surrounded by more trees, flowering shrubs and roses (180 varieties , plus 50 varieties of irises and 70 of hostas). In the lovely garden, best in late May, there are plenty of spots to find some shade and relax with a book.

Rosanna (formerly an architect) and Domenico warn visitors what to expect on their website, so no one is left in any doubt. Do you love dogs and cats? Do you mind not smoking in the bedrooms? Do you mind no television in the bedrooms (there are plenty of books and magazines)? And last, but not least, would you enjoy eating together with us and other guests in the evening? If the answers are yes, then La Traversina is for you. The hosts are warm and welcoming, bedrooms are homely and attractive, and Rosanna's home cooking, eaten on the terrace or in the conservatory, is superb.

Breuil-Cervinia

Frazione Cret-Perrères, 11021
Breuil-Cervinia, Aosta

Tel 0166 948775
e-mail info@lesneigesdantan.it
website
www.lesneigesdantan.it
Food breakfast, lunch, dinner
Price €€ **Closed** early May
to late Jun, Oct-Nov or mid-
Sep to Dec
Proprietors Bich family

Neiges d'Antan
Mountain chalet

It is the warmth and generosity of the hands-on owners that make this hotel in the shadow of Monte Cervino (the Matterhorn) a great place. From the outside, you couldn't call the chalet beautiful, but the rustic interior is welcoming, and recent renovation has made staying here a more than comfortable experience: new features include a sauna and a cosy wood burning stove in the living room. Signora Bich is the chef, expert at reviving old family recipes, and her son is the *sommelier*: in addition to a carefully-chosen cellar, he oversees an impressive range of *grappa* in the snug wood-panelled and rough-stone bar. Ideal for families, and visitors all say that it is excellent value for money.

Cioccaro di Penango

14030 Cioccaro di Penango,
Asti

Tel 0141 916292
e-mail santuffizio@thi.it
website www.thi.it
Food breakfast, lunch, dinner
Price €€€–€€€€€€
Closed Jan, Feb
Manager Vito Andresini

Loc. del Sant' Uffizio
Converted monastery

Set in a glorious landscape of vineyards and hills, the *locanda* impresses from the moment you catch sight of its mellow-brick exterior and, when you step through the door, the interior does the same. Original features, including frescoed ceilings, have been preserved, and furnishings are a blend of antique and chic modern. Try to secure one of the bedrooms in the old cloisters. These have a small terrace or balcony overlooking the inviting pool and mature garden. Readers have in the past been impressed by the food, although a recent guest reported slipped standards in the kitchen (it no longer has a Michelin star) as well as housekeeping, since the owners sold to Turin Hotels International. Reports would be welcome.

Monterosso al Mare

Via Corone 1, 19016
Monterosso al Mare, La Spezia

Tel 0187 817502
e-mail portoroca@portoroca.it
website www.portoroca.it
Food breakfast, lunch, dinner
Price €€–€€€€€
Closed 5th Nov-31st Mar
Proprietors Jacazzi family

Porto Roca
Seaside hotel

Perched above a spectacular, almost inaccessible stretch of coastline, Monterrosso is the largest of the charming, relatively undiscovered Cinque Terre villages. This, their best hotel, clings precariously to a rocky headland. It's a steep climb up from the beach, but the location is all-important here, with sweeping views of the rugged coast and clear sea. When you book, be sure to ask for a room with a sea view. The ones at the back are desperately disappointing. Inside, the furnishings are dated but comforting. The bedrooms (at least the ones at the front) are fresher and brighter, and most have balconies.

Savignone

Piazza della Chiesa 14, 16010
Savignone

Tel 0109 360063
e-mail fieschi@split.it
website www.palazzofieschi.it
Food breakfast, lunch, dinner
Price €–€€
Closed 5th Nov-31st Mar
Proprietors Caprile family

Palazzo Fieschi
Town hotel

Savignone is one of those small Italian towns where even the dogs yawn. The Palazzo Fieschi dominates its little square. Magnificent public rooms with Murano chandeliers and painted ceilings, a restaurant serving a full menu of interesting country dishes, the cool and quiet of thick stone walls and a pleasant garden make up in some measure for rather tired furniture and decoration in the bedrooms. The owner/manager is kind and helpful. A lift and small conference room nod towards modernity, but the Palazzo would best suit visitors who want a calm base from which to explore the district – perhaps on foot – and who like to come back to old-fashioned provincial grandeur and a generous dinner at the end of the day.

Sestri Levante

Via Penisola 26, 16039 Sestri
Levante, Genova

Tel 0185 487020
e-mail
info@hoteldeicastelli.com
website
www.hoteldeicastelli.com
Food breakfast, lunch, dinner
Price €€€
Closed mid-Oct to late Apr
Manager Anselmo Maurizio

G. Hotel dei Castelli
Converted castle

With a splendid location high up on Sestri Levante's wooded peninsula, Grand Hotel dei Castelli has been highly recommended to us by a recent visitor. 'From arrival at the gate onwards, there were no disappointments. The whole complex has been beautifully restored to a very high standard. The gardens and wooded areas are most attractive and beautifully kept with extensive views of the town and coastline. The staff were welcoming and helpful, especially in the restaurant…The food was excellent and good value, and the breakfast terrace had superb views.' Two lifts take guests down to the private beach.

Area introduction

Lombardy is an enormous region, stretching from the high Alps bordering Switzerland almost as far as the Adriatic and Ligurian seas. It contains Lake Como, with Lakes Maggiore and Garda forming its boundary in the west and east respectively, and has at its heart the glossy economic and industrial centre of Italy: Milan. Despite Milan's considerable heritage – notably a marvellous cathedral, important art collections and the world's most famous opera house – Milan's hotels are business-oriented and as big and glossy as the city itself. Surprisingly though, we have been able to find a clutch of excellent small hotels and in addition to these we can recommend **Antica Locanda Solferino** (tel 02 6570129).

Our main lakeside recommendations concentrate on Lake Como and Lake Garda. Bellagio is the main resort on Lake Como and the location of most of our hotels, with Menaggio a close second. As we don't have any recommendations here, try the **Bellavista** (tel 0344 32136) in Menaggio itself, or the **Loveno** (tel 0344 32110) in the village of Loveno 2 km away – a 13-room hotel with a garden and views of the lakes and mountains. In Argegno is **Villa Belvedere**, now run on bed and breakfast lines by the Cappelletti family, with wonderful views (tel 031 821116).

On Lake Lugano, try the **Stella d'Italia** at San Mamete Valsolda (tel 0344 68139) and on tranquil Lake Orta the exotic 1879 **Villa Crespi**, now a beautifully restored luxurious hotel with health spa (tel 0322 911902). On tiny Lake Mergozzo, an extension of Lake Maggiore, **La Quartina** is a simple hotel with good food (tel 0323 80118).

As for Lake Garda, the main resort for the southern end is Sirmione, beautifully situated, with the massive Castle of the Scaligers, Roman remains and lovely gardens to visit, but also very conveniently placed for the main Milan-Venice motorway and therefore very busy during the day with trippers trying to 'see' Lake Garda, Verona and Venice in a day. (For our recommendations on the eastern shore of the lake, see our North-East section.) In Sirmione, you'll find the **Grifone**, a modestly-priced stalwart of the guide. Further north, on the lakes's western shore, there are more recommendations at Gardone Riviera and Gargnano. The latter has seen the opening of one of the most lavish new hotels in Italy, **Villa Feltrinella**, with a peerless waterside location and a wonderful Belle Epoque interior (tel 0365 798000). At Riva del Garda, surrounded by vineyards, is **Albergo al Maso**, a reader's recommendation (tel 0464 521514). On the smaller neighbouring Lake Iseo is another stalwart of the guide, **I Due Roccoli**, while a smart new hotel, **Relais Mirabella at Clusane sul lago** (tel 030 9898051) may also merit investigation.

In Mantua, south of Garda, we have one recommendation, the **San Lorenzo**, and south of that **Il Leone** at Pomponesco. In Bergamo we also have one entry, **Il Gourmet**, and in addition can recommend **Il Sole**, a restaurant-with-rooms in the walled upper town (tel 035 218238); and not far away in Capriate San Gervasio, **Il Vigneto** (tel 02 90939351). In countryside north-west of Bergamo is a new 10-room eco-friendly hotel, **Casa Clelia**, with much rustic character (tel 035 799133).

Two lovely new entries to this edition are **La Barme** in Cogne and **Albergo Milano** in Varenna (pages 47 and 59).

Piazza Mazzini, 22021
Bellagio, Como

Tel 031 950342
e-mail hotflore@tin.it
website www.bellagio.co.nz

Nearby Villa Serbelloni;
Madonna del Ghisallo (37 km).
Location on main *piazza* over-
looking lake; garage
Food breakfast, lunch, dinner
Price €€
Rooms 34; 32 double and
twin, 2 suites, all with bath; all
rooms have phone, TV, mini-
bar, hairdrier, safe
Facilities dining room, bar,
reading/TV room, terrace
Credit cards AE, MC, V
Disabled not suitable
Pets accepted
Closed late Oct to mid-Apr
Proprietors Ketzlar family

Florence
Lakeside hotel

Bellagio is the pearl of Lake Como. It
stands on a promontory at the point
where the lake divides into two branches,
and the views from its houses, villas and
gardens are superb. The Florence is a
handsome 18thC building occupying a
prime position at one end of the main
piazza, overlooking the lake. A terrace
under arcades, where drinks and snacks
are served, provides a welcoming entry to
the hotel and the interior is no less
appealing. Whitewashed walls, high vaulted
ceilings and beams create a cool, attractive
foyer; to one side, elegant and slightly
faded seats cluster round an old fireplace.

Bedrooms have the same old-fashioned
charm as the public rooms, furnished with
cherry-wood antiques and attractive fabrics; the most sought after, naturally, are
those with balconies and views over the
lake. Meals can be taken on a delightful terrace under shady trees across the street
from the hotel, watching the various craft
ply across the lake. The hotel has been in
the same family for 150 years, and is now
in the hands of brother and sister, Ronald
and Roberta Ketzlar; they both speak
good English, and have created a gourmet
restaurant and two new suites. A recent
visitor was thoroughly enchanted.

Bellagio

Piazza Mazzini 32, 22021
Bellagio, Como

Tel 031 950320
e-mail dulac@tin.it
website www.bellagio.info

Nearby Villa Serbelloni;
Madonna del Ghisallo (37 km).
Location on main piazza over-
looking lake; car parking
Food breakfast, lunch, dinner
Price €€
Rooms 42; 38 double and
twin, 4 single, all with bath or
shower; all rooms have phone,
TV, air conditioning, minibar,
hairdrier
Facilities restaurant, bar,
terrace
Credit cards MC, V
Disabled not suitable
Pets accepted
Closed end Oct-April;
restaurant Tue
Proprietors Leoni family

Hotel du Lac
Lakeside hotel

Smack in the middle of Bellagio's waterfront, the Hotel du Lac's stunning view
of Como is matched by the Leoni family's
pretty faultless performance in all depart-
ments. If you want to be picky you might
say that one or two of the rooms are on
the small side, or that the decoration in
some of the bathrooms is a little dated,
but there your list would have to stop. The
smart marble-floored reception hall runs
off an arcade where the café's wicker
chairs offer a comfy spot from which to
keep an eye on Bellagio's pavement socie-
ty. The bright and inviting bar is also on the
ground floor but the staff will bring you a
drink (they have an impressive selection of
cocktails) anywhere in the hotel.

On the first floor the windows in the
unfussy restaurant run the width of the
building to make the most of the
panoramic view and the inventive menu
offers a broad choice of excellent dishes –
with cheeses and wines to match. The
impeccably maintained bedrooms are simply decorated, the beds comfortable and, it
ought to go without saying, the best have
views of the lake. The rooftop terrace
offers another vantage point, with
deckchairs for sunbathing and awnings for
those who prefer some shade. Staff are
friendly, professional and helpful.

Bellagio

Piazza del Porto, 4 - 22021
Bellagio

Tel 031950263
e-mail info@lapergolabella-
gio.it **website** www.lapergola-
bellagio.it

Nearby Villa Serbelloni;
Madonna del Ghisallo (37 km).
Location in village of Pescallo
just SW of Bellagio, overlook-
ing lake; public car parking
Food breakfast, lunch, dinner
Price €€
Rooms 11; 5 double, 4 twin, 2
with bath, 7 with shower, 2 sin-
gle with shower; all rooms have
phone, TV, safe
Facilities restaurant, terrace
Credit cards AE, DC, MC, V
Disabled no special facilities
Pets accepted
Closed Nov to Mar
Proprietor Mazzoni family

La Pergola
Restaurant with rooms

La Pergola is relaxed and informal, and
very much a family affair. Don't come
here looking for up-to-the-minute decoration, or even for clues on how they did it
many years ago. But, set as it is on a little
bay to the south-west of Bellagio, this simple hotel is away from the tourist bustle
and there is a fishing village feel tothe area.
The hotel takes its name from the pergola
that shelters diners at its enchanting lakeside restaurant, the focal point of the
entire establishment. Really only a matter
of centimetres from the water, this proximity is not just romantic: it is also reflect-
ed in the restaurant's enticing menu which
features dishes based on fish from the
lake, alongside a selection of non-fishy
regional alternatives with wines to match.

A long passage, attractively flagged with
black stone and housing a love-seat and a
few pieces of furniture, connects the small
reception with the restaurant's terrace.
The bedrooms are reached by a large
staircase which rises from the passage.The
good sized room are simple and clean, and
most have large windows with glorious
views of the lake, and the best have balconies. There's no air conditioning, but
each room has a serious-looking ceiling
fan. It's only a few minutes walk to Bellagio.

Via San Vigilio 1, 24100
Bergamo

Tel 035 4373004
e-mail il.gourmet@tiscali.it
website www.gourmet-bg.it

Nearby Brescia (48 km); Milan
(50 km); Lakes Como, Lecco
and Iseo.
Location in Città Alta (High
Town); car parking
Food breakfast, lunch, dinner;
room service
Price €
Rooms 11; 2 double, 7 twin, 3
with bath, 6 with shower, 1
single with shower, 1 suite with
bath; all rooms have phone,
TV, air conditioning, minibar,
hairdrier
Facilities restaurant, bar,
garden
Credit cards AE, DC, MC, V
Disabled no special facilities
Pets not accepted
Closed late Dec to early Jan
Proprietor Aldo Battista
Beretta

Gourmet
Restaurant with rooms

Bergamo is quite a favourite with the foodies and, given the pretty stiff competition downtown, it must have taken a certain amount of confidence to hang out a shingle in the High Town with 'gourmet' on it. Although the emphasis here is obviously on food, the rooms are not to be sniffed at. They are modern and slightly bland, but are somewhat softened by their furniture and wooden fittings.

The entrance to Ristorante Gourmet is airy and spacious, with a pale tiled floor and a small seating area. This is not a seasonal business: there is as much dining space indoors as there is outside on the large (covered) but uncrowded terrace. The atmosphere is gently civilized and unforced, with pleasant staff taking their cue from the charming owner. The menu is a refined document, wide-ranging and creative with a broad selection of regional specialities, with an extensive wine list. The whole place is dotted with lush, well-cared-for plants, and guests have the use of a lovely private garden when they feel the need for some real peace and quiet. A reader tells us he enjoyed his stay, though he had reservations about his room. Dinner, on the other hand, was 'excellent, served by waiters who breathed the spirit of the *Commedia dell Arte*'.

Loc. San Gaudenzio, 27050
Cervesina, Pavia

Tel 0383 3331
e-mail info@castellosangauden-
zio.com
website www.castellosangau-
denzio.com

Nearby Voghera (6 km); Pavia
(25 km); Milan (56 km).
Location 6 km NW of
Voghera, exit Casei Gerola
from the 'Autostrada dei Fiori';
car parking
Food breakfast, lunch, dinner
Price €€€
Rooms 45; 35 double and twin,
7 single, 3 suites, all with bath
or shower; all have phone, TV,
minibar, safe, some have air
conditioning **Facilities** sitting
rooms, dining room, conference
rooms, bar, indoor pool, solarium, lift/elevator **Credit cards**
AE, MC, V **Disabled** 2 adapted
rooms **Pets** not accepted
Closed rest Tue **Manager**
Pierangelo Bergaglio

Cst. di S. Gaudenzio
Converted castle

Set in formal gardens less than 60 km
from Milan, the spacious and elegant
Castello di San Gaudenzio has been
owned over the years by a succession of
smart Italian families and has the ivy, walls,
towers, gateways, statuary and other
embellishments to prove it. Times have
changed: the horses are now gone from
the stables and have been replaced by an
indoor swimming pool and solarium, and a
spectacular barrel vault has been turned
into a conference room. Period furniture is
watched over by ancestral portraits, and
red and black marble fireplaces remind
you that wood-burning can be done in
considerable style.

Most of the bedrooms are brand new,
with handsome bathrooms to match, but
their pale striped wallpapers and hangings,
polished parquet or stone floors, panelled
and frescoed ceilings and light, elegant furniture have successfully integrated them
with the well-restored older portions of
the castle. Almost all look out over the
garden. There are three suites, the most
baronial (and expensive) of which occupies two stories of a tower.

The restaurant offers Italian and international dishes and the wines on their list
include some specially bottled for the
castello. The staff are extremely professional and helpful.

Valnontey, 11012 Cogne, Aosta
Valley

Tel 01657 49177
e-mail labarme@tiscali.it

Nearby Cogne (3 km); Aosta
(30 km); Turin (135 km).
Location in the heart of Gran
Paradiso National Park
Food breakfast, lunch, dinner
Price €€€
Rooms 15, all with bathroom,
TV and telephone
Facilities with sauna, Jacuzzi
and massages, a ski/mtb rental
and a garage.
Credit cards MC, V
Disabled 2 suitable rooms
Pets by arrangement
Closed Oct-Nov
Manager Stefano Herren

La Barme
Country hotel

La Barme is the only hotel in the village of Valnontey to stay open year round – something of a feat when in winter months you can hardly see it for all the snow, and proof, perhaps, of the hard-working attitude of the Herren family. This former dairy, converted into a hotel by Mr Herren and now run by his sons, is a small, family set up, with 15 bedrooms.

Valnontey lies at the foot of the *Parco Nazionale del Gran Paradiso*, Italy's foremost adventure playground. You won't find luxury here, but, in such a rugged and remote location we think that simplicity strikes a happier note. While the owners will do everything in their power to make your stay comfortable some may find it, well, simple. That said, La Barme's charm is its lack of sophistication. Whitewashed walls and pale pine furniture in the main rooms give the place a simple, Alpine feel. The bright red stove in the breakfast room is one of only a few hints of colour in the main rooms, but none feel remotely drab. Bedrooms are clean, all have a fresh feel, though none are particularly individual.

Mountain photos cover the walls (as if the stunning views from each room weren't enough) making you keen to rent one of the hotel's mountain bikes or a pair of cross country skis and venture out into the great outdoors.

Erbusco

Via Vittorio Emanuele 11, 25030
Erbusco, Brescia

Tel 030 7760550
e-mail info@albereta.it
website www.albereta.it

Nearby Brescia (20 km); Bergamo
(30 km).
Location 3 km N of A4 Milan-
Venice motorway (Rovato exit); car
parking
Food breakfast, lunch, dinner; room
service
Price €€€€–€€€€€€
Rooms 48; 25 double, 10 twin, 32
with bath, 3 with shower, 3 single
with shower, 9 suites with bath; all
rooms have phone, TV, air conditioning, minibar, hairdrier, safe
Facilities sitting rooms, billiard
room, restaurant, bars, meeting
rooms, health and fitness centre,
indoor swimming pool, garden, tennis, helipad
Credit Cards AE, DC, MC, V
Disabled not suitable
Pets not accepted **Closed** never
Proprietors Moretti family

L'Albereta
Country villa

In the middle of the famous vineyards of
Francioforta, L'Albereta is an ancient
manor which has had a very elegant and
upmarket new life breathed into it. Home
of the Moretti family, who still own it, this
(Relais & Châteaux) villa is so smart that,
unless they have met you at the station or
airport, you might just consider nipping
through a car-wash before driving up to
the front door. But you needn't bother,
because the staff here are very professional, though not in the least precious. You will
also find muted marble, arches, parquet,
wrought iron, chintz, beams, flowers and
vineyards as far as the eye can see. Virtually
everything has been put here to please
you and this includes Gualtiero Marchesi's
double-starred restaurant which is as
much of a draw as the stunning modern
bedrooms. His kitchen is a symphony of
stainless steel, copper and starched white
chefs' uniforms. If you feel an urgent need
to work off the effects of a particularly
good dinner, you can either play tennis or
get your exercise flitting between the
Jacuzzi, the sauna and the solarium. Last
but not least, just in case you are thinking
of arriving by helicopter, L'Albereta help-
fully publishes its GPS co-ordinates so that
your navigation system can deliver you
with pinpoint precision.

Gardone Riviera

Corso Zanardelli 132, 25083
Gardone Riviera, Brescia

Tel 0365 20158
e-mail info@villafiordaliso.it
website villafiordaliso.it

Nearby Brescia (40 km);
Sirmione (35 km).
Location on SS572, 3 km NE
of Salò; ample car parking
Food breakfast, lunch, dinner
Price €€€€–€€€€€
Rooms 7; 6 double, one suite,
all with bath or shower; all
rooms have phone, TV, air
conditioning, minibar
Facilities sitting room, dining
room, tower with bar, terraces,
garden
Credit cards AE, DC, MC, V
Disabled no special facilities
Pets not accepted
Closed Nov–Feb; restaurant
Mon lunch and dinner, Tues
lunch
Proprietors Tosetti family

Villa Fiordaliso
Restaurant with rooms

Michelin-starred Villa Fiordaliso has been well known as one of the best restaurants in Northern Italy for some years, but it is also a chic and romantic small hotel. Built in 1902, the pale pink and white lakeside villa was home to Gabriele d'Annunzio, and later to Claretta Petacci, Mussolini's mistress. Inside, the intricately carved wood and marble work on walls, floors and doorways and the splendid gold and frescoed ceilings are the perfectly pre-served remnants of another age. A magnif-icent Venetian-style marble staircase, with columns and delicate wrought ironwork leads from the reception hall at garden level to the intimate first-floor restaurant and up to the seven luxurious bedrooms. Three of these have been left with their original furniture and decoration. The Claretta suite, a room of impressive dimensions with terrace and lake view, has a stunning marble bathroom. Other rooms are decorated in a lighter style with fresh wallpapers and fabrics.

The shady garden, bordering the lake (and, unfortunately, the main road), is a wonderful setting for the elegant summer restaurant, immaculately decked out in a terracotta and white colour scheme.

Viale Rimembranza 20, 25084
Gargnano, Lago di Garda,
Brescia

Tel 0365 71022/71289
e-mail info@villagiulia.it
website www.villagiulia.it

Nearby ferry to Lake Garda.
Location 150 m from middle
of resort, with garden and terrace down to lake; parking
Food breakfast, lunch, dinner
Price €€€€
Rooms 22 double and twin,
one single, all with bath or
shower; all have phone, TV,
minibar, safe, hairdrier, air conditioning, internet connection
Facilities dining room, veranda taverna, sitting room, beach,
pool, sauna, Turkish bath,
Jacuzzi
Credit cards AE, DC, MC, V
Disabled access possible **Pets**
small dogs only (10 kg)
Closed mid-Oct to Apr
Proprietors Bombardelli
family

Villa Giulia
Lakeside hotel

Once a simple *pensione*, Villa Giulia is
a beautiful, spacious house, built
over a hundred years ago in Victorian
style with Gothic touches. The
Bombardelli family has been here for fifty
years, and have gradually upgraded their
hotel to become one of the most delightful places to stay on Lake Garda.

For a start, it has a wonderful location,
with gardens and terraces running practi-
cally on the water's edge. Inside, light and
airy rooms lead off handsome corridors –
a beautiful dining room with Murano chandeliers, gold walls and elegant seats; a civilized sitting room with Victorian armchairs; and bedrooms which range from
light and modern to large rooms with timbered ceilings, antiques and balconies
overlooking the garden and lake. The
rooms in the rear annexe are less appealing, lacking view and air conditioning; other
rooms are in three garden chalets. At garden level a second, simpler dining room
opens out on to a terrace with ample
space and gorgeous views. At any time of
day, it is a lovely spot to linger among the
palm trees and watch the boats plying the
blue waters of Garda. The beautiful swimming pool is an added bonus.

Via Silvio Bonomelli, 25049
Iseo, Brescia

Tel 030 9822977
e-mail relais@idueroccoli.com
website www.idueroccoli.com

Nearby Brescia (20 km); Lakes
Idro and Garda.
Location 4 km SE of Iseo up a
mountain road; car parking
Food breakfast, lunch, dinner
Price €€
Rooms 19; 15 double and
twin, one single, 3 suites, all
with bath; all rooms have
phone, TV, minibar, hairdrier,
safe
Facilities sitting room, bar,
dining room, garden,
swimming pool, tennis
Credit cards AE, DC, MC, V
Disabled access possible
Pets accepted
Closed Nov to mid-Mar
Proprietor Guido Anessi

I Due Roccoli
Mountain inn

Lake Iseo is in the misty, southernmost
foothills of the Alps. Sixty miles one
way would take you into Switzerland and
it is not much further in another to reach
Austria. The lake's principal island,
Monteisola, is the largest on any European
lake and home to about 2,000 people.
Between the southern tip of the lake and
the *autostrada* connecting Milan with
Venice lies the Franciacorta, a region highly respected for the quality of its wines. Up
a winding mountain road to the south-east
of the lake, elegant and tranquil in its carefully tended park, lies I Due Roccoli. Built
of stone, and beautifully decorated inside,
here is a place to rest and recharge bat-
teries. Simply to praise the views is selling
the place short because even the swimming pool has one, and from the moment
you spot the vases of fresh roses on each
of the tables on the fabulous terrace you
know you have come to the right place.

Fish from the lake, organically-grown
produce from their own gardens and
home-cured ham all feature on the menu.
The spacious and spotless rooms are decorated in modern style with fine prints
hanging on the walls. The staff are every bit
as charming as their hotel. Our readers
concur: 'maybe the best view anywhere I
have been'; 'amazing bargain'; 'great food'.

Via Regina 81, Lenno, 22019
Tremezzo Como

Tel 0344 40415
e-mail
sangiorgio.hotel@libero.it

Nearby Tremezzo,
Cadenabbia, Villa Carlotta (2-4
km); Bellagio.
Location on lakefront; car
parking and garage
Food breakfast, lunch, dinner
Price €€
Rooms 29; 26 double, 20 with
bath, 6 with shower, 3 single;
all rooms have phone,
hairdrier, safe
Facilities dining room, reading
room, table tennis, terrace,
tennis
Credit cards MC, V
Disabled access difficult
Pets not accepted
Closed Oct-Apr
Proprietor Margherita
Cappelletti

San Giorgio
Lakeside hotel

This large white 1920s villa on the shores of Lake Como stands out against a backdrop of wooded hills and immaculate gardens running right down to the shore. A path lined with potted plants leads down through neatly tended lawns to the lakeside terrace and the low-lying stone wall which is all that divides the gardens from the pebble beach and the lake. There are palm trees, arbours and stone urns where geraniums flourish. If you wish to take a trip on the lake the ferry landing-stage lies close by.

The interior is no disappointment. The public rooms are large and spacious, leading off handsome halls. There are antiques wherever you go, and attractive touches such as pretty ceramic pots and copper pots brimming with flowers. The restaurant is a lovely light room with breathtaking views and the salon is equally inviting, with its ornate mirrors, fireplace and slightly faded antiques. Even the ping-pong room has some interesting antique pieces. Bedrooms are large and pleasantly old-fashioned. Antiques and beautiful views are the main features, but there is nothing grand or luxurious about them – hence the reasonable prices. One of our reporters rates this his favourite hotel – 'sensational view, friendly reception, firm bed, great towels'.

Maleo

Via Trabattoni 22, 26847
Maleo, Milano

Tel 0377 58142
e-mail info@ilsolemaleo.it
website www.ilsolemaleo.it

Nearby Piacenza; Cremona
(22 km).
Location behind church, off
main piazza in village, 20 km
NE of Piacenza; car parking
Food breakfast, lunch, dinner
Price €€
Rooms 3; 2 double, one single
with bath; all rooms have
phone, TV, air conditioning,
minibar; one apartment
Facilities sitting room, 3 din-
ing rooms, garden
Credit cards MC, V
Disabled no special facilities
Pets accepted
Closed Jan, Aug, restaurant
Sun eve, Mon
Proprietors Mario and
Francesca Colombani

Sole
Restaurant with rooms

The exterior of this 15thC coaching
inn is marked solely by a gilt
wrought-iron sun. Inside, the walls are
whitewashed, the ceilings timbered and
the arched chambers carefully scattered
with antique furniture, copper pots and
ceramics. There are three dining areas:
the old kitchen, with its long table, open
fire and old gas hobs where on occasion
dishes are finished in front of the guests;
a smaller dining room, with individual
tables; and the stone-arched portico
which looks out on to the idyllic garden.

The late Franco Colombani had brought
his own distinctive personality to the
regional cuisine – dark, tasty stews, roast
meats and fish, accompanied by vegetables
from the kitchen garden and fine wines
from the unfathomable cellars. Now his
son and daughter are continuing with the
tradition that has helped rate the Sole as
among Italy's finest restaurants.

The three traditionally styled, air-conditioned bedrooms above the restaurant all
have individual high points, and good bathrooms, and make great places in which to
collapse after a delicious dinner.

Piazza Concordia 14, 46100
Mantova

Tel 0376 220500
e-mail hotel@hotelsanloren-zo.it
website www.hotelsanloren-zo.it

Nearby Piazza dell'Erbe;
Basilica di Sant'Andrea;
Palazzo Ducale.
Location in city centre; garage
Food breakfast
Price ⓔⓔⓔ
Rooms 32; 23 double and
twin, 9 suites, 25 with bath, 7
with shower; all rooms have
phone, TV, air conditioning,
minibar, hairdrier
Facilities sitting room, meet-
ing rooms, bar, terrace
Credit cards AE, DC, MC, V
Disabled 2 specially adapted
rooms **Pets** not accepted
Closed never
Proprietors Giuseppe and
Ottorino Tosi

San Lorenzo
Town hotel

San Lorenzo is smart, conservative, tech-
nologically up-to-date and as central as
it could possibly be. It is literally surrounded by pearls of Mantua's historic architecture. Even if you are only there for a satel-
lite-connected conference, skip past the
registration desk, go straight up to the
roof terrace, look around you, and marvel
at how easy it is to slip back a few centuries (some rooms have terraces overlooking the monuments).

Inside is a hotel where all the 'i's have
been dotted and the 't's crossed. It is the
sort of place where you just know, as you
step across the threshold, that there are
no spiders lurking behind the plentiful
antiques. The public rooms are quiet and
well dressed with fresh flowers, elegant
furnishings and furniture, some fine paintings, porcelain and a fascinating collection
of 16thC brass offertory plates.

The staff are friendly and can provide
you with a potted history of Mantua and a
suggested walking tour with helpful notes
on the places and buildings you will see
along the way. The bedrooms are spacious
and bright ('I hated the lighting in mine',
comments our inspector) each with its
own complement of things ancient and
modern; and the bathrooms were immaculate. Overall, a well-run, brilliantly located, if slightly characterless base.

Viale Regina Margherita 15,
20052 Monza, Milano

Tel 039 382581
e-mail
reservation@hoteldelaville.com
website
www.hoteldelaville.com

Nearby Villa Reale; *duomo*;
Milan (15 km).
Location in city centre, in
front of Villa Reale; car parking
Food breakfast, lunch, dinner
Price €€€€
Rooms 62; 21 double and
twin, 8 with bath, 13 with
shower, 39 single, 2 suites, all
with shower; all rooms have
phone, TV, air conditioning,
minibar, hairdrier, safe
Facilities restaurant, bar,
meeting rooms; billiards,
sauna, gym (for annexe only)
Credit cards AE, DC, MC, V
Disabled one specially adapted
room **Pets** not accepted
Closed Aug, Christmas
Proprietors Nardi family

Hotel de la Ville
Town hotel

When you arrive at the slightly dreary exterior of this hotel (facing Villa
Reale, the former summer house of
Savoy's royal family) your first thought may
be that you have made a ghastly mistake.
Actually you have done the opposite,
because you are in for a delightful surprise.
The atmosphere inside is one of opulent
but understated elegance: vases of fresh
flowers highlight the superb decoration,
and throughout the hotel there is a never-
ending succession of rare objects collected by Tany Nardi, the owner, for whom
perfection is obviously a passion. The corridors are dotted with things like silver
trays of little crystal glasses or pieces of
perfectly preserved antique luggage, as
well as collections of porcelain, glass,
clocks, walking sticks and more. Persian
rugs, antique furniture, pots, plants, gilt-
framed pictures and polished marble are
lit subtly, to persuade you to leave the
cares of the world at the front door.

Bedrooms are beautifully furnished,
bathrooms are pristine, and in the elegant,
cosy wood-panelled restaurant the food
earns very favourable reviews. Adjacent is
a turn-of-the-century villa restored to create 12 luxurious rooms and four suites,
decorated with antiques and gorgeous fabrics. Reports welcome.

Piazza Venezia 5, 21020 Ranco,
Varese

Tel 0331 976507
e-mail soleranco@relais-
chateaux.com
website www.ilsolediranco.it

Nearby Lakes Lugano and
Como; Milan (67 km).
Location on E side of Lake
Maggiore, N of Angera; car
parking
Food breakfast, lunch, dinner
Price €€€€–€€€€€
Rooms 15; 3 double, 4 junior
suites, 8 suites, one single, all
with bath; all rooms have
phone, TV, air-conditioning,
minibar, hairdrier, safe
Facilities restaurant, breakfast
room, garden, pool
Credit cards AE, DC, MC, V
Disabled one specially adapted
room **Pets** not accepted
Closed Jan to mid-Feb
Proprietors Brovelli family

Sole
Restaurant with rooms

As you enter the Sole's light and airy
foyer, you can't be sure whether you'll
be met by the fifth or the sixth generation
of the Brovelli family: Carlo and his son
Davide run the restaurant and Andrea,
Davide's younger brother, now looks after
the hotel in this long-lived family business
overlooking Lake Maggiore. Either way you
will instantly realize that they have avoided
the demon of self-importance which so
often follows in the trail of culinary hon-
ours (currently one Michelin star and
accolades for the superb wine cellar). This
is a friendly place where they have combined a superb restaurant, a splendid view
of the lake and truly delightful rooms.

To add to the expectations aroused by
the star (there used to be two, and may
well be again) you should know that,
despite the sophistication of their menu,
the Brovellis are loyal to their region and
feature many local delicacies. Except in
poor weather, when tables retreat into the
charming dining room, they are set on the
terrace. The bedrooms are a treat, decorated in sophisticated country style with
ankle-deep pile carpets and colour co-
ordinated curtains, bedspreads and paintwork. The bathrooms are sparkling white
with big tubs, bigger towels and stacked
with high-quality 'freebies'.

San Fedele d'Intelvi

22010 San Fedele d'Intelvi,
Como

Tel 031 831132
email info@villasimplicitas.it
website www.villasimplicitas.it

Nearby Lakes Como, Lugano
and Maggiore; Como 20 km.
Location 2 km up mountain
from San Fedele d'Intelvi; car
parking
Food breakfast, lunch, dinner
Price €€
Rooms 16 double and twin, all
with shower; all rooms have
phone
Facilities dining room, sitting
room, billiard room, garden,
table tennis
Credit cards AE, DC, MC, V
Disabled not suitable
Pets accepted
Closed mid-Oct to Mar
Proprietor Ulla Wagner

Villa Simplicitas
Country villa

As you get further from the A9 two
things happen: the roads get smaller
and a delicious sense of peace begins to
creep over you. The final 2 km to
Simplicitas are up a roughish mountain
road, but when you finally reach this utterly unpretentious 19thC villa, where wild
flowers grow up to the windows, just
switch off your engine, open the door and
listen to the glorious sound of absolutely
nothing at all. This is a much-loved, lived-in
house, oozing charm and character and
filled with 19thC antiques and objects (and
a magnificent billiard table) and an air of
rustic gentility. Meals, taken on the terrace
in fine weather, usually feature produce
from the surrounding 80-hectare farm.

The bedrooms (some small), most with
lovely views, are like comfortable guest
rooms in a private house, with a liberal
scattering of knick-knacks. A recent visitor reports that he could hear every word
from the next room, however. Overall,
with the exception of electric lights, the
20th century hasn't made much impression on the villa. Standards of housekeeping have been criticized by a couple of
readers. Once your energy levels are
restored, you can walk, ride, play tennis or
golf nearby. 'Gorgeous building in a wonderful setting and perfect for children' - so
ends the latest report.

Vicolo Bisse (Via Bocchio) 5,
25019 Sirmione, Brescia

Tel 030 916014

Nearby Lake Garda; Brescia
(39 km); Verona (35 km).
Location just inside city walls,
next to castle, on lake; car
parking (50 m)
Food breakfast, lunch, dinner
Price €
Rooms 16; 12 double, twin
and triple, 4 with bath, 8 with
shower, 4 single with shower
Facilities sitting room, dining
room, lift/elevator, terraces,
tiny beach
Credit cards not accepted
Disabled access difficult except
to restaurant
Pets not accepted
Closed Nov to Easter
Proprietors Marcolini family

Grifone
Restaurant with rooms

Although the Grifone is one of the cheapest and simplest hotels in this guide, it also has one of the loveliest locations, and makes a great place to stay for a night or two. Essentially it is a restaurant specializing in fish ('the waiter removed the bone with the air of a man cleaning his spectacles, a routine gesture, performed with aplomb' writes a correspondent) with a mouth-watering selection of antipasto to start. It has an enticing tree-filled terrace overlooking both Lake Garda and the ramparts of Sirmione's castle; also a tiny sandy beach.

The entrance is found off a narrow street just inside the city walls. A small sitting room equipped with television and cheerful bamboo furniture leads to a little patio where breakfast is served (though our reader was directed to the baker's shop to buy it himself) and on to the scrap of beach. Bedrooms are simple, furniture is basic, the fans noisy, but everything is spotless. Some rooms look right over the castle walls, and the five balconies are full of flowers. Those on the top floor enjoy the best views: rooftops, mountains, and of course the lake. There is no traffic noise in this pedestrian zone, but you may be woken by church bells. The younger generation of the Marcolini family who run the Grifone are friendly and helpful.

Via XX Settembre 35
23829 Varenna

Tel 0341 830 298
e-mail
hotelmilano@varenna.net
website www.varenna.net

Nearby Lake Como; Bellagio
and Menaggio (15 min boat
ride); Bergamo (50 km).
Location 100 feet above Lake
como
Food breakfast, lunch, dinner
Price €€
Rooms 11, all with balcony or
terrace; 1 apartment with
kitchen and living room
Facilities bar, internet,
laundry/dry cleaning
Credit cards V, MC, EC
Disabled not suitable
Pets not accepted
Closed restaurant closed Tues
and Sun
Proprietors Bettina & Egidio
Mallone

Albergo Milano
Town hotel

Varenna has a serious parking problem
and access to this hotel is by a narrow,
flagged-stoned lane from the tiny, picturesque square: about 200 yards of uneven
going that might trouble the very elderly
or disabled. It's just wide enough for a mini
Cinquecento, so most people walk.

About 30m above Lake Como, with a
fine wooded garden on one side and the
pantiled roofs of the old town on the
other, the Milano is perfectly placed. The
owners both worked in 'grand' hotels and
it shows. The Milano is not grand, but it is
immaculate and great stress is laid on
service and personal contact. There is no
mini bar in your room (just two bottles of
wine, water and some grappa) because
they like to be asked for ice. We noticed,
and appreciated, a warm welcome in good
English; a pretty peasant-made high-chair
in the dining room; lots of fresh flowers; a
flat-screen TV concealed behind a remov-
able painting; and English and German
books to amuse you if you grow tired of
the view from the terraces. This is a small
hotel but a very good one with a highly
regarded restaurant. If you want a room in
the spring or in September, make sure you
book well ahead.

Gargnano

Baia d'Oro
Lakeside hotel

Giambattista Terzi was born in one of a pair of neighbouring fishermen's cottages built on the edge of the lake in 1780, and his wife was the moving force behind turning them into a hotel in the 1960s. Since then the facilities have slowly been updated. To appreciate the fabulous setting, you should arrive by boat. You can almost dip your hand in the lake from the romantic dining terrace, a splendid vantage point from which to watch night succeed day. The Terzis have gradually redecorated the bedrooms in slightly dubious shades of pink and blue, with painted wooden furniture, shiny fabrics and mirrored glass bedheads. Not to everyone's taste, but comfortable.

Via Gamberera 13, 25084 Gargnano, Brescia

Tel 0365 71171
e-mail hotel-baiadoro@gardalake.it
website www.gardalake.it/hotel-baiadoro
Food breakfast, lunch, dinner
Price €€€
Closed mid-Nov to mid-Mar
Proprietors Terzi family

Milan

Dei Mercanti
City hotel

Centrally located in a small side street off Via Dante, the Antica Locanda dei Mercanti is a delightfully decorated hotel in a 17thC building, each room furnished in unique style, some with four-posters, some with wrought iron bedsteads, with beautiful duvet covers and curtains. Some of the rooms are relieved by stencilled borders, others have details (like climbing roses) painted over the base colour. Our inspector thoroughly enjoyed her most recent stay here, but we have received an angry complaint too: tiny, ill-equipped bathrooms, freezing rooms, problems with the booking and the bill, a missing breakfast-in-bed, and, worst of all, 'rude' service. Oh dear. We are investigating, and will report. Let us know your impressions.

Via San Tomaso 6, 20123 Milano

Tel 02 8054080
e-mail locanda@locanda.it
website www.locanda.it
Food breakfast, snacks
Price €€€
Closed never
Manager Alessandro Basta

Via Goldoni 31, 20129 Milano

Tel 02 701561
e-mail townhouse31@town-
house.it **website** www.design-
hotels.com
Food breakfast **Price** €€€
Closed 3 weeks around
Christmas and New Year, Aug
Proprietor Ornella Borsato

Milan Town House 31
City hotel

A Design Hotel that manages to be human as well as cool, the 17-room Town House opened in 2002 and occupies an elegant turn-of-the-century building house in a residential area near Porta Venezia. The style is a relaxed, contemporary take on an 'Out of Africa' idea (reflecting the owner's preferred travel destinations) with neutral colours effectively offsetting some fine antiques, beautiful ethnic pieces, Moroccan throws and artful flower arrangements. The cocktail bar on the back terrace plays host to a sleek crowd at night.

This is a useful (albeit pricey) address for anyone wanting discreet style combined with easy-going personal service.

Area introduction

The remarkable city of Venice, famed throughout the world for its incomparable beauty, artistic wealth and sheer originality is the focal point of this region. A feast of small hotels are described in the following pages, distilled from our in-depth regional guide, The Charming Small Hotel Guide to Venice and North-East Italy. Room prices in Venice are undeniably steep, but if you choose carefully, and secure a canal or lagoon view, you will discover some memorable places in which to stay.

An alternative to staying in Venice itself is to base yourself somewhere on the vast Veneto Plain that fans out from Venice to the foothills of the Dolomites. Here are the great cities of Padua, Treviso, Vicenza and Verona, the villas of Palladio and other attractions, such as the charming little hill towns of Asolo and Follina. You will find some excellent bases from which to explore Venice and the Veneto in these pages. In Vicenza a reader recommends the '50-room, family-run, value-for-money, simple and charming' **Albergo San Raffaele** (tel 0444 545767) with 'almost Tuscan' bedrooms, hidden away on the ascent to the Santuario on Monte Berico. For something smarter you could try **Villa Michelangelo** 7 km away (tel 0444 550300).

The province of Veneto takes in the eastern shores of Lake Garda, where we also have some recommendations. Other hotels on Lake Garda can be found in the Lombardia section of this book. To the east, the Venetian Plain edges into the province of Friuli-Venezia Giulia, where we recommend a couple of places in the south. The north of the province, where it rises to the Carnic Alps with meadows and pine forests, is empty of hotels of our sort, and indeed short on any hotels at all, being little visited by tourists.

Far more popular as a mountainous destination is the province of Trentino-Alto Adige, only a couple of hours' drive but a world away from Venice and its great plain. It feels like Austria, has a special autonomous statute and is largely German-speaking. Owners and staff of the Alpine hotels you will find in its mountains may not even speak Italian... you are more likely to be greeted in German. Place names are extremely confusing, as each town and village, mountain and valley has both an Italian and German name. We have given the Italian translation. Hotels are often Tyrolean chalets, with wooden furniture, ceramic stoves, traditional fabrics; the food too, is mainly Austrian, at least on the simpler menus, while the more sophisticated hotels serve creative variations on the theme. The scenery amongst the Dolomites is beautiful, and there are plenty of activities to pursue both in winter and summer. New to this edition is the **Rosa Alpina** (see page 79).

Via Collegio 33, 31011 Asolo,
Treviso

Tel 0423 951332
e-mail info@albergoalsole.com
website
www.albergoalsole.com

Nearby Palladian villas;
Possagno (10 km).
Location at the top of Piazza
Maggiore; private car park
Food breakfast, dinner
Price €€
Rooms 23; 14 double and
twin, 2 with bath, 12 with
shower, 8 single, 2 with bath, 6
with shower, 1 suite with bath;
all have phone, TV, air conditioning, minibar, hairdrier, safe
Facilities breakfast room, dining room, bar, fitness centre,
lift/elevator, terrace **Credit
cards** AE, MC, V **Disabled** 2
adapted rooms **Pets** accepted
Closed Christmas, New Year,
restaurant Nov-Mar, Wed
Proprietors Silvia and Elena
de Checchi

Al Sole
Town hotel

From a glorious position, perched above
the Piazza Maggiore on the steep hill up
to the massive fortress, the Rocca, this
16thcC villa has a splendid view of the
medieval town with its higgledy-piggledy
streets. Its deep pink and cream façade is
original and appealing, while the trendy, hi-
tech interior – hallmark of the dynamic
young sisters Silvia and Elena de Checchi –
makes a dramatic contrast.

Almost every room has white rough-cast
walls and mellow wood floors, enlivened by
daring colour combinations for fabrics and
furniture. Although the look is mainly cool
and modern, a few antiques and the occasional bowl and pitcher hark back to the
past. Recalling former stars in Asolo's firma-
ment, such as 'Eleanora Duse' and 'Gabriele
d'Annunzio', the bedrooms are all different;
the former has light painted furniture, the
latter, ornate church-style pieces. Some
rooms have huge claw-foot baths; some
have massage showers, just one of the many
four-star comforts. Perhaps the ultimate of
these are the state-of-the-art loos for the
ground floor, which electronically flush, lift
and then replace the seat, complete with
hygenic paper cover, at the appropriate
times. A panoramic restaurant, La Terrazza,
has now been opened, and the hotel also
has a small fitness centre.

Via Canova 298, 31011 Asolo, Treviso

Tel 0423 523411 **e-mail** villacipriani@sheraton.com **website** www.sheraton.com/villacipriani

Nearby Palladian villas; Possagno (10 km).
Location on NW side of village; with garage parking
Food breakfast, lunch, dinner; room service
Price €€€–€€€€€
Rooms 31; 29 double and twin, 2 single, all with bath; all rooms have phone, TV, air conditioning, minibar, hairdrier
Facilities sitting room, dining rooms, bar, meeting room, lift/elevator, terrace, garden, wellness area
Credit cards AE, DC, MC, V
Disabled access difficult
Pets accepted
Closed never
Manager Hermann Gatti

Villa Cipriani
Country villa

Asolo is a beautiful medieval hilltop village commanding panoramic views, a jewel of the Veneto. The Villa Cipriani, a jewel of the Sheraton Group, now part of the huge Starwood Group, is a mellow ochre-washed house on the fringes of the village, its deceptively plain entrance leading into a warm reception area which immediately imparts the feeling of a hotel with a heart (and a house with a past: it was once the home of Robert Browning). Today it is graced by the prettiest of rose- and flower-filled gardens, and meals are served on the terrace or in the restaurant overhanging the valley. As for the gracious and comfortable bedrooms, make sure you ask for one with a view, and try for an 'exclusive' rather than a 'superior' double. The latter are not particularly spacious, while the former include a sitting area; two rooms have terraces.

Villa Cipriani is a relaxing country hotel, whose views, comfort, peaceful garden and good food make it particularly alluring. However, some reports complain of prices that were hard to justify, also mentioning intrusive wedding parties and brash clientele. Others have been full of praise.

Via Mulino 45, 33080 Bannia
di Fiume Veneto, Pordenone

Tel 0434 957911
e-mail
info@ultimomulino.com **website** www.ultimomolino.com

Nearby Pordenone (10 km);
Venice (80 km); Trieste (80
km).
Location 10 km SE of
Pordenone, exit from A28 at
Azzano Decimo; in own garden
with parking
Food breakfast, lunch, dinner
Price €€ **Rooms** 8 double
and twin, 4 with bath, 4 with
shower; all rooms have phone,
TV, air conditioning, minibar
Facilities breakfast room, sit-
ting rooms, dining rooms, bar,
music/conference room, gar-
den, terrace **Credit cards** AE,
DC, MC, V **Disabled** no facil-
ities **Pets** accepted **Closed** 10
days Jan, Aug; restaurant closed
Sun eve, Mon **Proprietors**
Mattarello family

L'Ultimo Mulino
Converted mill

As the name suggests, this 17thC building is one of the very last functioning
mills in the area. In use until the 1970s, the
three old wooden wheels are still in working condition; indeed, they are set in
motion in the evenings for the benefit of
guests. The lovely stone house and garden
are set in gentle farmland and surrounded
by three rivers; the soothing sounds of
water are everywhere.

Opened as a hotel in 1994, restoration
work has been carried out with great taste
and flair, preserving as much as possible of
the original character of the house. The
long, open-plan sitting room and bar area
have even incorporated the hefty innards
of the mill machinery. Throughout, attractive fabrics are teamed with handsome
antique furniture, rustic stone and woodwork, and soft, elegant lighting. The comfortable and stylish bedrooms, while different in layout, are all along similar lines with
wooden fittings and pale green and cream
country fabrics. Those on the second floor
have attic ceilings and some have squashy
sofas. Bathrooms are in pale grey marble.
New owners have recently taken over, and
have opened the restaurant for lunch as
well as dinner, with fish a speciality.

Barbiano

San Giacomo 6, 39040
Barbiano, Bolzano

Tel 0471 650055 **e-mail**
info@baddreikirchen.it
website www.baddreikirchen.it

Nearby Bressanone (17 km);
Val Gardena (10 km).
Location 21 km NE of
Bolzano, exit from Brennero
Autostrada at Chiusa, head S
through Barbiano (6 km); hotel
car park on right (call and the
hotel will send a jeep to collect
you from car park)
Food breakfast, lunch, dinner
Price €
Rooms 26; 16 double and
twin, 2 family, 8 single, all with
bath or shower **Facilities** sitting rooms, bar, restaurant,
games room, library, garden,
terraces, swimming pool, table
tennis, tennis court (1 km)
Credit cards MC, V **Disabled**
access difficult **Pets** accepted
Closed Nov to May
Proprietors Wodenegg family

Bad Dreikirchen
Mountain hotel

The name of this idyllically situated hotel, a 14thC chalet owned by the Wodenegg family for 200 years, derives from its vicinity to three small churches which date back to the Middle Ages. The fact that you can only reach the hotel by four-wheel-drive taxi also makes for the perfect escape.

The large old building, with its shingled roof and dark wood balconies, has won-derful views and is surrounded by mead-ows, woods, mountains and quantities of fresh air. There's plenty of space for guests, both inside and out, and the atmosphere is comfortably rustic with an abundance of aromatic pine panelling and carved furni-ture. A cosy library provides a quiet cor-ner for reading, and simple but satisfying meals are served in the pleasant dining room or on the adjacent veranda, from which the views are superb. Bedrooms in the original part of the house are particu-larly charming, being entirely wood-panelled throughout.

To sum up, the words of a guest at Bad Dreikirchen in 1908 are still appropriate: 'I stayed for some days...the weather was continually fine, the position magnificent, and the food good.' Recent guests warmly agree. 'I fell in love with the place. Delightfully relaxed atmosphere, charming young owners.'

Campo di Lago 100, 39052
Caldaro, Bolzano

Tel 0471 960093/960048
e-mail
pensionleuchtenburg@iol.it
website
www.kalterersee.com/pension-
leuchtenburg

Nearby swimming and fishing
in lake.
Location 5 km SE of Caldaro,
on the edge of the lake; in
courtyard with car parking
Food breakfast, dinner
Price €
Rooms 19; 15 double and
twin, 3 with bath, 12 with
shower, 2 single, 2 triple, all
with shower; rooms have TV
(on request)
Facilities sitting area, dining
area, bar, terrace, beach
Credit cards MC, V **Disabled**
not suitable **Pets** accepted
Closed Nov to Easter
Proprietors Sparer family

Leuchtenburg
Country guesthouse

This solid stone-built 16thC hostel once housed the servants of Leuchtenburg castle, an arduous hour's trek up the steep wooded mountain behind. Today, guests in the *pension* are well cared for by the friendly owners, while the castle lies in ruins. The setting is enviably tranquil, right on Lago di Caldaro, better known (at least to wine buffs) as Kalterer See. Cross a road and you are at the water's edge, where a little private beach is dotted with umbrellas and sunloungers.

Back in the *pension*, the Sparers provide solid breakfasts and three-course dinners of regional cuisine in an unpretentious, homely atmosphere. White-painted low-arched dining rooms occupy the ground floor; above is the reception, with a large table littered with magazines and surrounded by armchairs. There is another sitting area on the first floor, leading to the bedrooms. These have pretty painted furniture and tiled floors (second floor rooms are plainer). Each one tells a story: for example, the 'old smoke room' was where food was smoked. All are large, and some share the views enjoyed from the terrace across vineyards to the lake. Prices could hardly be lower.

Follina

Via Martiri della Libertà,
31051 Follina, Treviso

Tel 0438 971277
e-mail info@hotelabbazia.it
website www.hotelabbazia.it

Nearby 11thC abbey;
Palladian villas; Asolo (20 km).
Location in town centre, fac-
ing the abbey; car parking
Food breakfast, lunch, dinner;
room service
Price €€€€–€€€€€€
Rooms 18; 12 double and
twin, 6 suites, all with shower,
bath or Jacuzzi; all rooms have
phone, TV, safe, hairdrier; 12
have air conditioning
Facilities breakfast room, sit-
ting room, dining room, tea
room, terrace, garden; garage,
hot tub
Credit cards AE, DC, MC, V
Disabled not suitable
Pets accepted
Closed Jan
Proprietors Giovanni and
Ivana Zanon

Villa Abbazia
Town hotel

The hotel consists of two buildings: a
17thC *palazzo* and, adjacent, an
enchanting little art nouveau villa.
Standards of decoration and comfort in
both are exceptionally high – rarely have
we met hoteliers (brother and sister)
more keen to please their guests – and the
Abbazia is now a Relais et Châteaux hotel.
If you find the lobby and balconied breakfast area a bit much – a sugary pink confection of candy-striped walls strewn with
roses, draped tables and floral china – you
will not be disappointed by the bedrooms.
Each one is individually decorated, and all
are delightful: sophisticated and very feminine in English style, full of thoughtful
touches. Three rooms have private balconies, at no extra cost. Best of all is the
villa with its pillared portico, carved flour-
ishes on its four façades and sweeping
staircase. The Abbazia's restaurant, La
Corte, is beautifully decorated with stone
walls and pillars and an enchanting mural
depicting the highlights of the region as
seen from a balcony. If you want to eat
out, try Da Gigetto in Miane (where you
should be sure to visit the wine cellars).

The Zanon's have prepared a helpful list
of local information, including routes you
can follow on the hotel's bicycles. And they
have now opened a second hotel across
the street, dei Chiostri (see p110).

37020 Gargagnago di
Valpolicella, Verona

Tel 045 7703622 **e-mail**
serego@seregoalighieri.it
website www.seregoalighieri.it

Nearby Verona (18 km); Lake
Garda (14 km).
Location signposted off the
road from Pedemonte to San
Ambrogio, 18 km NE of
Verona; in own extensive
grounds with ample parking
Food breakfast
Price apartment sleeping 2-4
people €€€–€ per night;
weekly rates available
Rooms 8 apartments for 2, 3
or 4 people, each with kitchen,
bathroom with shower, phone,
TV, air conditioning **Facilities**
reception, breakfast room, ter-
race meeting room, estate pro-
duce shop **Credit cards** AE,
DC, MC, V **Disabled** not suitable **Pets** not accepted **Closed**
Jan **Proprietor** Conte
Pieralvise Serego Alighieri

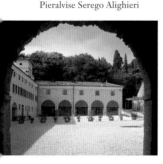

Foresteria Serego Alighieri **Villa apartments**

In 1353, the son of Dante, who had been exiled in Verona, bought Casal dei Ronchi, and there his direct descendants have lived ever since. Today, overseen by Count Pieralvise Serego Alighieri, the estate is a prosperous producer of Valpolicella wines (much improved in recent years and shaking off their 'cheap and nasty' reputation) as well as olive oil, balsamic vinegar, honey, jams and rice. The family home is a lovely yellow ochre build-ing fronted by formal gardens which over-look the vineyards. Beyond are the former stables, now beautifully converted to make eight apartments, simple yet sophisticated, sleeping two to four people. In each one you find a gleaming chrome kitchen, coun-try furniture, soothing green cotton fab-rics, white walls, marble bathrooms. No. 8 spirals up a slim tower: minute sitting room, stairs to a minute kitchen, more stairs to the bedroom. Open a door in the bedhead and there's a tiny window behind. No. 1 is the most spacious, with dining table and elegant chairs. Breakfast is served in a room decorated with old fam-ily photographs on the ground floor. Wine tasting can be arranged for eight people or more. There are good restaurants nearby.

Via Steinach 25, 39022
Lagundo, Bolzano

Tel 0473 448553 **e-mail**
info@puenthof.com **website**
www.puenthof.com

Nearby Bolzano (28 km);
Brennero (70 km); the
Dolomites.
Location 3 km NW of
Merano, outside village; in own
grounds with ample car
parking
Food breakfast
Price €
Rooms 12 double and twin, 2
with bath, 10 with shower; all
rooms have phone, TV, mini-
bar, safe **Facilities** 2 breakfast
rooms, sitting room, bar,
restaurant, sauna, solarium,
garden, tennis courts, swim-
ming pool
Credit cards AE, DC, MC, V
Disabled one room on ground
floor **Pets** accepted
Closed Nov to mid-Mar
Proprietors Wolf family

Der Punthof
Country hotel

Via Claudio Augusto, a Roman road to
Germany, passed what is now the
entrance to Der Pünthof, and the watchtower built to guard the road forms an
integral part of the hotel. The main building was a medieval farmhouse and has
been in the Wolf family since the 17th century. They opened it as a hotel 40 years
ago, housing guests in the barn, but over
the decades other buildings have been
added. Although Lagundo is a rather dreary suburb of Merano, once inside the
hotel's electronic barrier you could be
miles from anywhere with only orchards,
vineyards and stunning scenery in view.

The public rooms are in the old building: breakfast is served in a pale green *stube*
with wooden floor, low ceiling, ceramic
stove and traces of the original decoration
on the panelled walls. Bedrooms in the
barn are modern and comfortable, but uniform, though some have private terraces
on to the garden. The most appealing are
the rooms in the square tower. One has
polished floorboards, a wood ceiling and
antique bed. There are five well-equipped
self-catering chalets, and six simpler
cheaper rooms in another annexe.

Levada

Via Marco Polo 2, Levada di
Piombino Dese, Padova

Tel 049 9350308
e-mail gargan@gargan.it
website www.gargan.it

Nearby Palladian villas; Venice
(20 km); Padua (26 km).
Location 20 km N of Venice,
in Levada take Via G. Carducci
opposite the church and turn
left into Via Marco Polo; in
own garden with car parking
Food breakfast, lunch, dinner
Price €
Rooms 6; 4 double and twin, 2
family rooms, all with shower;
all rooms have TV
Facilities dining rooms, sitting
area, garden
Credit cards not accepted
Disabled access difficult
Pets not accepted
Closed Jan, Aug
Proprietors Calzavara family

Gargan
Country guesthouse

The setting is rural, on a working farm, and the farmhouse is typical – attractive enough, but not especially prepossessing. A donkey brays in the garden. We walked in quite unprepared for the level of sophistication of this *agriturismo;* it's in a league of its own. The ground floor comprises a hallway with cool white walls and beams painted pale green, plus five interconnecting dining rooms. Furnished only with antiques, these rooms have delicate lace curtains, timbered ceilings, and an array of pictures on their white walls. Our visit coincided with Sunday lunch, and every table was immaculately laid with a white cloth, fine china and gleaming silver; an open fire crackled in the hearth.

The ingredients used in the delicious dinners are mainly produced on the farm. Signora Calzavara is in charge of the cooking and provides a full American breakfast and other meals when required.

The six bedrooms are enchanting. Floors are strewn with rugs; most have wrought-iron bedheads and fine walnut furniture. It's best to book by fax unless you speak Italian.

Merano

Via Fragsburg 3, 39012
Merano, Bolzano

Tel 0473 244071
e-mail info@fragsburg.com
website www.fragsburg.com

Nearby Promenades along the
Passirio river in Merano;
Passirio valley, Schloss Rametz;
Dolomites.
Location 6 km NE of Merano,
in own gardens with ample
parking
Food breakfast, lunch, dinner
Price €–€€€€
Rooms 20; 6 double and twin,
12 suites, 2 single, all with
bath; all rooms have phone,
TV, safe, hairdrier
Facilities sitting rooms,
library, smoking room, dining
rooms, terrace, lift, sauna, gym,
wellness spa, garden
Credit cards MC, V
Disabled one specially adapted
room **Pets** accepted
Closed Nov to Easter
Proprietors Ortner family

Castel Fragsburg
Converted castle

A lovely drive along a narrow country lane, through mixed woodland and past Alpine pastures brings you to the east of Merano where Castel Frangsburg – 300 years old and a hotel for more than 100 years – commands splendid views of the Texel massif.

Externally, Fragsburg still looks very much the hunting lodge, with carved wooden shutters and balconies. A terrace along the front of the house, covered with wistaria, is a wonderful place to eat or drink: you seem to be suspended over the mountainside. The adjoining dining room can be opened up in warm weather, and the food – a seven course dinner – is 'very good and carefully served' according to a recent visitor, with a huge breakfast buffet accompanied by Prosecco. In cooler weather you can choose from various Tyrolean-style sitting rooms and a congenial little library. Bathrooms, recently renovated, are modern and spotless and bedrooms all have balconies, carved pine furniture and colourful country fabrics. A wellness centre has now been added to the sauna and gym.

The wooded gardens provide plenty of space for lazing – as well as a wooden shelter reserved for all-over suntanning. Delightful owners. The hotel has recently undergone extensive restoration, so reports would be welcome.

Merano

Via Verde 72, 39012 Merano, Bolzano

Tel 0473 446282
e-mail info@villativoli.it
website www.villativoli.it

Nearby Passirio river promenades; Passirio valley; the Dolomites.
Location on edge of town; in own grounds with ample car parking
Food breakfast, lunch, dinner
Price €€
Rooms 21; 16 double and twin, all with bath or shower, 5 suites with bath; all rooms have phone, TV, hairdrier
Facilities sitting room, dining room, bar, library, indoor swimming pool, sauna, lift, terrace, garden
Credit cards AE, DC, MC, V
Disabled access difficult **Pets** accepted
Closed mid-Dec to mid-Mar
Proprietors Defranceschi family

Villa Tivoli
Edge-of-town hotel

Almost in countryside, yet close to the town centre, standing in apple orchards, the pale yellow villa is surrounded by an 'exquisite' terraced garden filled with over 2,000 different plants. Inside all is cool and chic, spacious and light, yet not intimidating. The ground floor is open-plan, with a glass-walled dining room; over the bar an extraordinary contemporary fresco of many-breasted Artemis, a recurring theme in the hotel. Another corner holds a sitting area, elegantly furnished with antiques and there is a traditional wood-panelled Tyrolean *stube*. Outside, a terrace with tables shaded by yellow umbrellas – as well as a new rock-lagoon surrounded by cypress and stone – and in the basement, a pool room with gaily painted walls. Bedrooms, named after Mediterranean flowers, are all different, all comfortable, with south-facing balconies. Some are huge, with separate sitting areas; some are furnished with antiques, others are very contemporary. Bathrooms are large, with double basins. Our reporter was hooked: 'Smart but relaxed; staff warm and welcoming, owners genuinely friendly, aiming to please; mountainous breakfast buffet, designed to see you through till evening, and a delicious dinner (half board includes five courses) with excellent local wines.'

Mogliano Veneto

Via Preganziol 1, 31020
Mogliano Veneto, Treviso

Tel 0415 9727
e-mail info@hotelvillacondul-
mer.com **website**
www.hotelvillacondulmer.com

Nearby Palladian villas, Venice
(18 km).
Location 12 km S of Treviso,
N of road to Mogliano Veneto;
in own grounds with ample
parking.
Food breakfast, dinner
Price €€€
Rooms 43 double, twin, single,
junior suites, 8 apartments, all
with bath or shower; all rooms
have phone, TV, air conditioning, minibar, hairdrier
Facilities breakfast room, bar,
sitting rooms, TV room, dining rooms, garden, swimming
pool, tennis courts, 9- and 18-
hole golf **Credit cards** AE,
DC, MC, V **Disabled** access
difficult **Pets** accepted **Closed**
never **Proprietor** Davide Zuin

Villa Condulmer
Country villa

For the price of a three-star hotel in
Venice you can stay in this impressive
18thC villa 20 minutes away. One very satisfied couple wrote to say that they will do
just that whenever they visit the city again.

Flanked by annexes, Villa Condulmer
stands four-square in a miniature park
designed by Sebatoni. From the moment
you walk in you will, like our correspon-
dants, be struck by the sheer scale, not
only of the rooms but of the furnishings.
The vast central hall is decorated with
baroque stucco in subtle colours, inset
with murals. Two extravagantly large
Murano chandeliers hang from the high
ceiling, but comfortable armchairs make it
a room to relax in, not just admire. A pair
of grand pianos bear witness to Verdi's visits here. The more dilapidated is his; the
other, a copy. The dining room ('delicious
food') is in restful pale green and white,
and there is an intimate stuccoed bar. The
most exotic, and expensive, bedrooms are
the upstairs suites The double rooms in
the main villa are decorated in bright silk
damasks, but we prefer the more
restrained annexe rooms, where the peace
and quiet, the comfortable beds and the
heavy linen sheets should guarantee a
good night's sleep.

Bulla, 39046 Ortisei, Bolzano

Tel 0471 797335
e-mail info@uhrerhof.com
website www.uhrerhof.com

Nearby Val Gardena;
Castelrotto (13 km); Bolzano
(26 km).
Location in mountainside
hamlet, 13 km F. of
Castelrotto, off Castelrotto-
Ortisei road; garage parking
Food breakfast, dinner
Price €€
Rooms 11; 8 double and twin,
4 with bath, 4 with shower, 3
single with shower; 2 apart-
ments for 2-5 with kitchen; all
rooms have phone, TV, hair-
drier, safe
Facilities dining room, bar, sit-
ting room; lift, garden, health
centre
Credit cards MC, V
Disabled suitable **Pets** not
accepted **Closed** Nov to mid-
Dec, 2 weeks after Easter
Proprietors Zemmer family

Uhrerhof Deur
Mountain chalet

The name means 'House of the Clocks',
and their ticking and chiming, along
with birdsong, are very often the only
sounds which break the silence at this traditional chalet set in a tucked-away hamlet
1,600 metres above sea level. Indeed, noise
levels hardly rise above a whisper, and
Signora Zemmer is at pains to point out
that this is a place only for those seeking
total peace and quiet. Outside, there is a
grassy garden from which to enjoy the
wide and wonderful view. Inside, all the
rooms, including the balconied bedrooms,
are bright, simple and beautifully kept, with
plenty of homely details. The core of the
chalet is 400 years old, and includes the all-
wood *stube* with working stove. The three
adjoining dining rooms have wooden
benches round the walls, Tyrolean fabrics
for curtains and cushions, bright rugs on
terracotta floors and pewter plates displayed in wall racks. Signor Zemmer is the
chef, and his simple yet delicious food is
elegantly presented on pewter plates.

Underneath the house is a surprisingly
smart health complex, with huge picture
windows so that you can relax in the
open-plan Turkish bath and soak up the
view. The hotel is strictly non-smoking.

38057 Pergine, Valsugana,
Trento

Tel 0461 531158
e-mail verena@castelpergine.it
website www.castelpergine.it

Nearby Trento (11 km); Lake
Caldonazzo (3 km);
Segonzano.
Location off the SS47 Padua
road, 2 km SE of Pergine; in
own grounds with ample car
parking
Food breakfast, dinner
Price €
Rooms 21; 13 double and
twin, 8 with shower, 4 single, 3
with shower, 4 triple, 3 with
shower; all rooms have phone
Facilities sitting room, dining
rooms, bar, garden
Credit cards MC, V
Disabled access difficult
Pets accepted
Closed Nov to Easter
Proprietors Verena Neff and
Theo Schneider

Castel Pergine
Converted castle

This medieval hilltop fortress is managed with enthusiasm by an energetic
and cultured Swiss couple, Verena and
Theo. Past and present coexist happily in a
rather alternative atmosphere, and the
castle has a truly lived-in feel despite its
grand dimensions and impressive history. A
recent visit confirmed that this is one of
the most affordable and distinctive hotels
in the region. Though it must be said that
it's an aquired taste: one reader comments
on the 'daunting approach, strange modern
art, refectory-style dining room and
Spartan comfort'.

The route from the car park to the
hotel leads you under stone arches, up
age-worn steps and through vaulted chambers to the airy, round reception hall
where breakfast is also served. The two
spacious dining rooms have wonderful
views, and the cooking is light and innova-
tive. As you would expect from their price,
bedrooms are by no means luxurious, and
some are very small, but all are furnished
in simple good taste; the best have splendid, heavy, carved wooden furniture and
wall panelling.

One of the most enchanting features of
the castle is the walled garden. Spend an
hour reading a book, or simply watching
the mountains through the crumbling ramparts, and you may never want to leave.

Via Dolada 21, Plois, 32010
Pieve d'Alpago, Belluno

Tel 0437 479141
e-mail info@dolada.it
website www.dolada.it

Nearby Belluno (20 km);
Nevegàl ski area (18 km).
Location in the hamlet of
Plois, signposted from Pieve
d'Alpago; ample parking
Food breakfast, lunch, dinner
Price €
Rooms 7 double and twin, all
with shower; all rooms have
phone, TV
Facilities restaurant, terrace,
garden
Credit cards AE, DC, MC, V
Disabled no special facilities
Pets accepted
Closed never
Proprietors De Prà family

Dolada
Restaurant with rooms

A twisting road leads from the Alpago valley to Pieve, and then corkscrews on up to the little hamlet of Plois. Albergo Dolada turns out to be a handsome building with faded apricot walls and green-shuttered windows with a little garden which looks out over snow-capped mountains and the Santa Croce lake and valley far below (there are wonderful walks straight from the door).

Built in 1923, Dolada has been owned and run as an inn by four generations of the De Prà family. The much vaunted kitchen (one Michelin star, with another in the offing) is overseen by Enzo De Prà, aided by his son Riccardo, while his wife Rossana, a professional *sommelier*, and daughter Benedetta are a cheeful and friendly presence front of house. 'The food' our reporter comments, 'was divine, and the welcome could not have been more friendly. I would recommend the white bedroom, for its spaciousness, if you can get it, but don't worry if not'. The modern bedrooms are named for their colour schemes; the pink one can come as a bit of a shock the morning after an evening of serious over-indulgence in the elegant restaurant, but a long walk in the hills, with wonderful views all around, should sort things out.

Redagno di Sopea

39040 Redagno, Bolzano

Tel 0471 887215
e-mail info@zirmerhof.com
website www.zirmerhof.com

Nearby Cavalese (15 km).
Location 5 km N of
Fontanefredde, off the SS48; in
garden with ample car parking
Food breakfast, lunch, dinner
Price €–€€
Rooms 32; 22 double and
twin, 4 with bath, 18 with
shower, 6 single with shower, 4
suites, 1 with bath and 3 with
shower; rooms have TV on
request
Facilities dining room, sitting
room, bar, library, sauna, and
steam room, spa, pool, garden,
vineyard
Credit cards MC, V
Disabled ground floor bedrooms available
Pets accepted
Closed mid Nov to 25th Dec,
7th Jan to 1st May
Proprietor Sepp Perwanger

Zimerhoff
Mountain hotel

Situated just outside the tiny hamlet of Redagno di Sopra, this 12thC *mas* has been in the Perwanger family since 1890. Views are of mountains, green pastures and forests with few signs of civilization to mar the landscape. 'Idyllic', a contented guest tells us. The interior has been carefully restored. The dim, low-ceilinged hall with its intricate wood carving, ticking grandfather clock and old fireplace, immediately plunges you into the atmosphere of an old family home. There is a tiny cosy library, a sitting-cum-breakfast room with an open fire for winter days, and a rustic bar with a grassy terrace, from which to enjoy the superb views. The large wood-panelled dining room houses two elaborate ceramic stoves, and makes a fine setting in which to enjoy the local dishes and sophisticated wines on offer.

The comfortable bedrooms vary enormously in size, but all are attractive with traditional carved furniture (much of it made on the premises) and pretty fabrics; the largest rooms are on the top floor. For the energetic, there's plenty to do, particularly in winter, from skating and curling on the lake to cross-country and downhill skiing.

San Cassiano in Badia

Strada Micura de Ru 20, 1-
39030 San Cassiano in Badia

Tel 0471 849500
e-mail info@rosalpina.it
website www.rosalpina.it

Nearby Blozano (80 km); golf
course.
Location in centre of town, 50
metres from church
Food breakfast, lunch, dinner
Price €€€–€€€€
Rooms 51; all rooms have
hairdrier, minibar, TV, phone,
internet
Facilities indoor swimming
pool, sauna, spa, bar, free use of
mountain bikes
Credit cards MC, V, EC
Disabled not suitable
Pets accepted
Closed late Sept-Dec, late
April-June
Proprietor Paolo Pizzinini

Rosa Alpina
Country villa

We tend to shy away from Relais and Chateaux branding, but this hotel has been in the Pizzinini family for three generations and they run it as if it were a small hotel – catering to their guests' every whim. There are more than 50 bedrooms, but care has been taken to furnish each in an individual style. Exposed wooden beams complement warm curtains; many rooms have fireplaces, some even have tiled stoves. Decoration throughout is rustic but chic, and furniture has been lovingly collected over the years – each room feels as though care has been taken over its decoration.

Breakfast is renowned, and delicious home-made jams, fresh coffee and Tyrolean produce more than set you up for the day. Simple food using fresh, local ingredients is served in three restaurants, each offering something different: choose from the Fondue Stube, the Wine Bar & Grill or the gourmet starred Michelin restaurant (to avoid disappointment book well ahead for the latter). A range of facilities including a luxurious spa make this hotel worth a detour. It's good for the adventurous, keen to explore the surrounding mountains, but ideal too for the sybarite, who simply wants to soak up the glorious setting.

San Floriano del Collio

Via Oslavia 2, 34070 San
Floriano del Collio, Gorizia

Tel 0481 884051
e-mail isabellaformentini@tis-
calinet.it **website**
www.golfhotelformentini.com

Nearby Gorizia (5 km); Trieste
(43 km); Udine (40 km).
Location in town, just outside
castle walls; private grounds;
car parking
Food breakfast, self-service
afternoon cold buffet
Price €€€–€€€
Rooms 15; 12 double and
twin, 2 single, 1 suite in tower,
all with bath or shower; all
rooms have TV, minibar; 12
rooms have phone; 3 rooms
have no phone but air conditioning **Facilities** sitting room,
breakfast room, garden, pool,
tennis court **Credit cards** AE,
DC, MC, V **Disabled** not suitable **Pets** accepted **Closed**
15th Dec–March **Proprietor**
Contessa Isabella Formentini

Golf hotel Castello Formentino **Converted castle**

We asked for feedback on this hotel recently, and had plenty. Most speak very positively, praising the 'lovely' rooms ('we lit the little candles in our big modern bathroom'), the 'lavish' breakfast and the 'very reasonable' prices.

The hotel's name, referring to its nine-hole golf course (now relocated about 14 km away), gives the impression of something modern, but it is in fact two ancient renovated houses just outside the walls of Castello Formentini, which has belonged to the Formentini family since the 16th century. The present owner, Contessa Isabella Formentini, has filled the rooms of the tiny hotel with family furniture and pictures. Each beautifully decorated and spacious bedroom is named after a prestigious wine, emphasizing the vinous interest of the Formentini family. Three of them are within the castle walls, but all guests are at liberty to use the grounds and swimming pool. The family's restaurant, called Castello Formentini, is open only for groups (minimum 8-10 people) but guests are directed to another excellent restaurant nearby. This is a charming spot, with wooded countryside spread out around the hilltop castle.

San Osvaldo

San Osvaldo 19, 39040 Siusi,
Bolzano

Tel 0471 706013
e-mail
info@tschoetscherhof.com
website www.tschoetscher-hof.com

Nearby Castelrotto (5 km);
Bolzano (17 km); Sciliar
Natural Park (10 km).
Location in hamlet, 5 km W
of Castelrotto; with parking
Food breakfast, lunch, dinner
Price €
Rooms 8; 7 double and twin, 1
single, all with shower
Facilities dining rooms,
terrace
Credit cards MC, V
Disabled access difficult
Pets accepted
Closed Dec to Mar
Proprietors Jaider family

Gasthof Tschotsch-erhof **Country guesthouse**

Don't be put off by the unpronounce-able name; for lovers of simple, farm-house accommodation in an unspoiled rural setting, this hostelry could be ideal.

The narrow road from Siusi winds through apple orchards, vineyards and open meadows, eventually arriving at the tiny hamlet of San Osvaldo and this typi-cal 500-year-old farmhouse with its adja-cent dark wood barn. The name, painted on the outside of the building, is almost hidden by the clambering vines, and the old wooden balconies are a colourful riot of cascading geraniums. The sun-drenched terrace is a perfect spot for relaxing, as well as for eating.

Inside, we were beguiled by smells from the kitchen at the end of the hall, and were drawn to the warmth of the low-ceilinged old *stube* with gently ticking clock, rough wood floor and simple white ceramic stove.

A rustic stone stairway leads up to the modest but tidy bedrooms, some of which have balconies. They have no frills, but after a long day in glorious countryside, we were too tired to notice.

San Vigilio

San Vigilio, 37016 Garda,
Verona

Tel 045 7256688
e-mail info@punta-sanvigilio.it
website www.locanda-sanvig-
ilio.it

Nearby Garda (2 km); Verona
(45 km); ferry services (4 km).
Location 2 km W of Garda,
on promontory; parking avail-
able 150 m away
Food breakfast, lunch, dinner
Price €€€€€
Rooms 14; 11 double and
twin, 3 suites, all with bath or
shower; all rooms have phone,
TV, air conditioning, minibar,
hairdrier; most rooms have safe
Facilities sitting room, dining
room, bar, terrace, walled
garden
Credit cards AE, MC, V
Disabled not suitable
Pets accepted
Closed Nov to before Easter
Proprietor Conte Agostino
Guarienti

Locanda San Vigilio
Lakeside hotel

In general the east side of Lake Garda is less upmarket than the west but this hotel's idyllic setting, on a lush peninsula, Punta San Vigilio, dotted with olive trees and cypresses, is a conspicuous exception. The property is owned by Conte Agostino Guarienti, who lives in the 16thC villa that dominates the headland. An air of discreet exclusivity pervades the *locanda* (royalty are among regular guests) yet the atmosphere is far from stuffy. Of the public rooms, our favourite is the elegant dining room, right on the lake, with a comfortingly creaky wooden floor. A ceramic stove occupies one corner and sideboards display plates and bottles. You can eat in here, on a little arched veranda or under huge white umbrellas on the terrace where terracotta pots overflow with flowers.

The seven bedrooms in the main house are all different, though they have beautiful antiques and fabrics in common. Only one has no view. Other bedrooms are in separate buildings and more rustic in style. In the evening the place comes into its own: with the day trippers gone, guests can wander the peninsula or sit with a drink at one of the Taverna's vine-shaded tables. Whether you arrive by car through an avenue of cypress trees, or, even more magically, by boat, you will find this a gem of a hotel.

Siusi allo Sciliar

Bagnidi Razzes, 39040 Siusi
allo Sciliar, Bolzano

Tel 0471 706131
e-mail info@badratzes.it
website www.badratzes.it

Nearby Bolzano (22 km); Siusi
National Park; skiing (10 km).
Location 22 km NE of
Bolzano, 3 km SE of Siusi; in
own grounds with ample car
parking
Food breakfast, lunch, dinner
Price €
Rooms 48; 22 double, 8 single,
3 suites, 15 family rooms, all
with bath; all rooms have
phone, hairdrier; 18 rooms
have TV and safe
Facilities dining rooms, sitting
rooms, bar, playroom, indoor
swimming pool, sauna, garden,
garage
Credit cards EC, MC, V
Disabled suitable **Pets** accepted **Closed** Sunday after Easter
to mid-May
Proprietors Scherlin family

Bad Ratzes
Mountain hotel

Leaving the small town of Siusi in search
of Bad Ratzes, the road winds uphill
past green meadows and into a dense forest where Hansel and Gretel would have
felt at home. When at last you reach it in a
clearing, the hotel, large and modern, looks
disconcertingly grim, but the warmth and
enthusiasm of the Scherlin sisters will put
you immediately at ease. Inside, the decoration is dull 1960s and 1970s, but comfortable. Public areas — including a formal
sitting room with open fireplace, a children's playroom and two dining rooms —
are extensive. All but four of the spotless
bedrooms have balconies.

Food is important at Bad Ratzes: local
dishes are carefully prepared and pasta is
home made. One of the sisters bakes reg-
ularly, and her recipes are recorded in a little booklet. This is one of a group of family hotels in the area and there are many
thoughtful child-orientated extras: pots of
crayons and paper on the dining tables, a
booklet of local bedtime stories, walks for
children, a special menu and so on. Adults
are not neglected; there is wonderful and
varied walking in the neighbourhood and a
free ski bus runs to the slopes in winter. A
recent visitor could not praise this 'superb,
family-friendly hotel' highly enough, and
was thoroughly charmed by the Scherlins.

Torri del Benaco

Piazza Calderini 20, 37010
Torri del Benaco, Verona

Tel 045 7225411 **e-mail**
info@hotel-gardesana.com
website www.hotel-garde-
sana.com

Nearby Bardolino (11 km);
Malcesine (21 km); Gardaland.
Location in town centre, on
waterfront, in pedestrian zone;
unload at hotel, private parking
150 m away
Food breakfast, dinner
Price €
Rooms 34; 31 double, 3 single,
all with shower; all rooms have
phone, TV, air conditioning
(Jul and Aug)
Facilities dining room, bar,
lift, terrace
Credit cards AE, DC, MC, V
Disabled no special facilities
Pets not accepted
Closed Nov and Dec
Proprietor Giuseppe
Lorenzini

Gardesana
Lakeside hotel

Torri del Benaco is one of the showpiece fishing villages which are dotted
along the shore of Lake Garda, and
Gardesana, the former harbourmaster's
office, is in a plum position. It is a treat to
tuck into the chef's speciality fish soup on
the delightful first floor dining terrace
which overlooks the central *piazza*, 14thC
castle and bustling port. The wrought-iron
balustrade is decked with cascading geraniums, the tables are elegant, the waiters
smartly uniformed, and the food, particularly the fish, fresh and delicious. It makes
a perfect vantage point for watching the
boats come and go, and the changing
colours of the lake. Drinks can also be
taken on the ground floor terrace, which
extends out on to the *piazza*.

The building has a long history, as its
exterior would suggest, with its stone
arches and mellow stucco walls; but the
entire interior has been smartly modernized in recent years to produce an essentially modern and very comfortable, if simple, hotel. The green and white bedrooms
are almost all identical: wooden floors,
wooden furnishings, soft fabrics, plenty of
little extras. If you can, try to book one of
the corner rooms; these have the advantage of facing both the lake and the *piazza*;
otherwise choose a third floor room,
overlooking the lake with balcony.

Fondamenta Bollani,
Dorsoduro 1058, 30123
Venezia

Tel 041 5210188
e-mail info@pensioneaccademia.it **website** www.pensioneaccademia.it

Nearby Accademia gallery;
Scuola Grande dei Carmini.
Location where the Toletta
and Trovaso canals meet the
Grand Canal; vaporetto
Accademia or water taxi
Food breakfast
Price €€€€–€€€€€
Rooms 29; 22 double and
twin, 9 with bath, 13 with
shower, 7 single, 6 with shower; all rooms have phone, TV,
air conditioning, hairdrier, safe
Facilities breakfast room, bar,
sitting room, garden
Credit cards AE, DC, MC, V
Disabled not suitable **Pets** not
accepted **Closed** never
Proprietor Giovanna Salmaso

Accademia
Town hotel

Still one of the best loved hotels in
Venice, the Accademia continues to
exert its considerable charm on a stream
of contented guests. Despite recent modernisations such as sliding front doors and
air conditioning, both the hotel and its staff
have the knack of making guests feel like
travellers from another, more genteel, age
rather than modern-day tourists.

The Accademia's privileged canalside
location is both convenient and calm, but
what really distinguishes the *pensione* is its
gardens – the large canal-side patio, where
tables are scattered among plants in classical urns, and the grassy rear garden where
roses and fruit trees flourish. Built in the
17th century as a private mansion, Villa
Maravege retains touches of grandeur, and
most of the furnishings are classically
Venetian (the Murano chandeliers for
once tasteful and harmonious). Perfect for
sitting and relaxing is the finely furnished
first floor landing, while the bedrooms
have inlaid wooden floors and antiqued
mirrors. The airy breakfast room has crisp
white tablecloths and a beamed ceiling;
but, weather permitting, guests will
inevitably opt to start their day in the
hotel's beautiful gardens.

Rio Terrà Foscarini,
Dorsoduro 884, 30123 Venezia

Tel 041 5230058
e-mail info@aglialboretti.com
website www.aglialboretti.com

Nearby Accademia gallery;
Zattere; Gesuati.
Location alongside the
Accademia gallery; vaporetto
Accademia
Food breakfast, lunch, dinner
Price €€
Rooms 23; 13 double and
twin, 5 single, 5 family rooms,
all with bath or shower; all
rooms have phone, modem
point, TV, air conditioning,
minibar, hairdrier
Facilities sitting rooms, dining
room, bar, lift, terrace
Credit cards AE, MC, V
Disabled no special facilities
Pets accepted
Closed Jan occasionally;
restaurant Wed, Thurs lunch
Proprietor Anna Linguerri

Agli Alboretti
Town guesthouse

The Alboretti is distinguished by its warm welcome, and genuine family atmosphere. Reception is a cosy wood-panelled room with paintings of Venice on the walls and a model of a 17thC galleon in its window; the ground floor sitting room is small, but a second sitting room on the firstfloor makes a comfortable retreat (the TV is rarely used); the terrace behind the hotel, entirely covered by a pergola and set simply with tables and chairs, is a delight, especially for a leisurely breakfast in summer. The building's fourth floor is now part of the hotel, and includes another terrace for guests.

The style of the bedrooms is predominantly simple, some with a nautical theme, and most with an antique or two. Like the rest of the hotel, they are well cared for and spotlessly clean, but the bathrooms, though totally renovated, are tiny, as are some of the rooms. None are large, but three are recommended for their garden views, and one also has a balcony on which you can have breakfast.

A recent reporter (who ended up staying for longer than planned) praises the friendly atmosphere and charming proprietor, but was somewhat taken aback by his tiny bedroom.

Rio di San Vio, Dorsoduro
628, 30123 Venezia

Tel 041 5204733
e-mail alberto@hotelameri-can.com **website** www.hote-lamerican.com

Nearby Accademia gallery;
Zattere; Santa Maria della
Salute.
Location midway along canal,
which runs between Grand
Canal and Giudecca Canal;
vaporetto Accademia or water
taxi
Food breakfast
Price €€€
Rooms 28; double and twin
and single, all with bath or
shower, phone, TV, air condi-
tioning, minibar **Facilities** sit-
ting area, breakfast room,
terrace
Credit cards AE, MC, V
Disabled not suitable
Closed never
Proprietor Salvatore Sardo

American
Town hotel

Set in a peaceful backwater of Dorso-duro, yet close to the Accademia and the Grand Canal, this is a quiet, dignified hotel with spacious reception rooms and a tiny terrace where you can take break-fast under a pergola in summer. The pub-lic areas have a sombre Edwardian air, with wood panelling and silk damask on the walls, tapestry or velvet upholstered chairs, oriental rugs on Venetian mosaic floors, frilly white curtains and potted plants. Corridors are also panelled in wood, with little tables and chairs placed here and there. Bedrooms – all newly renovated – vary in size, as do the bath-rooms, and though unexceptional they have pretty Venetian painted furniture (with minibars mercifully disguised as free-standing cupboards), ornate gilt mir-rors and pretty Paisley-print bedspreads.

If you choose the American, you should do what you can to secure one of the nine bedrooms that overlook the canal. Nos 301 and 201 are particularly recommend-ed, with three canal-facing French win-dows on two sides, and narrow balconies from where you can watch the water traf-fic drift by.

Calle della Frescada,
Dorsoduro 3888-3887/b,
30123 Venezia

Tel 041 710401/710817
e-mail
info@locandacafoscari.com
website www.locandacafos-
cari.com

Nearby Scuola Grande di San
Rocco; Frari; Accademia
gallery.
Location between Campo San
Tomà and Palazzi Foscari;
vaporetto San Tomà
Food breakfast
Price €
Rooms 11; 6 double and twin,
3 with shower, 3 with basin
only; 1 single with shower, 2
triples without shower, 2 family
rooms without shower
Facilities breakfast room
Credit cards MC, V **Disabled**
not suitable **Pets** not accepted
Closed 15 Nov–20 Jan, late Jul
Proprietor Valter Scarpa

Ca' Foscari
Town guesthouse

You will need help finding Calle Frescada, a little lane tucked almost out of sight and unmarked on most maps: take Calle Larga Foscari towards the Frari, and at the junction with Crosera, turn right. Calle Frescada runs across the end, and the hotel faces down Crosera. Happily our inspector's maddening search for this little one-star hotel was worth the effort – Ca' Foscari is a cut above. Somehow its charming, modest exterior – smart front door and bell pull, little lantern displaying its name – tells the story, and the interior does not disappoint, nor the welcome from Valter and Giuliana Scarpa.

On the ground floor is a little breakfast room. A couple of flights of stairs, and you are in a fresh, white corridor with white-painted doors leading to the bedrooms. These are modest, as you would expect, but pristine, with lacy curtains and pretty bedspreads and white-tiled minute bathrooms, or, in rooms without bathrooms, decent basins. Note that the communal bathroom only has a shower, not a bath. The metal-framed beds are much more comfortable than they look. An excellent budget hotel in a bustling residential neighbourhood. As we went to press the owners had just sold the hotel to new proprietors, who plan to make changes. Reports would be welcome.

Fondamenta Zattere ai
Gesuati, Dorsoduro 780,
30123 Venezia

Tel 041 5206466
e-mail la.calcina@libero.it
website www.lacalcina.com

Nearby Gesuati church;
Accademia gallery.
Location on W side of San Vio
canal; vaporetto Zattere or
water taxi
Food breakfast, light snacks,
lunch, dinner
Price €–€€
Rooms 29; 3 suites; 19 double
and twin, 2 with bath, 20 with
shower, 7 single, 1 with bath, 3
with shower, 3 with washbasin;
all rooms have phone, air conditioning, hairdrier, safe; apartments also available with space
for 2 **Facilities** breakfast room,
terrace **Credit cards** AE, DC,
MC, V **Disabled** not suitable
Pets not accepted **Closed**
never **Proprietors** Alessandro
and Debora Szemere

La Calcina
Town hotel

The house where Ruskin lived is hard to resist, both for its historical connec-tion and for its location facing the sunny straits of the Giudecca canal. The simple *pensione*, inherited by a go-ahead young couple, is nowadays a stylish small hotel whose calm, uncluttered rooms provide a welcome antidote to an excess of Venetian rococo. The pretty ground floor reception rooms now including a bar and a cosy, informal bar/restaurant/café, La Piscina.

Unlike many hotels in the city there is a marked difference in price between the rooms at the front, with views across the glittering water, and the darkish back rooms, which have no view, but are equal-ly comfortable. Most expensive are the corner rooms, where the sun streams in from two directions. None of the rooms is large, but all compensate with cool cream walls, warm parquet floors, antiques and gleaming bathrooms with heated towel rails. Meals are served in summer on the terrace in front of the hotel, or the lovely, sunny deck that juts out into the canal (or you can book the romantic roof garden for two), and in winter in the marble-floored restaurant/bar with a picture win-dow, so that even if you opt for a bedroom at the back you can still enjoy the vista.

Venice

Dorsoduro 979/a, 30123
Venezia

Tel 041 2401411
e-mail info@capisanihotel.it
website www.capisanihotel.it

Nearby Accademia gallery;
Guggenheim museum.
Location between the
Accademia and Zattere;
vaporetto Accademia, Zattere
Food breakfast, lunch, dinner
Price €€€€–€€€€€
Rooms 29; 23 double and
twin, 4 junior suites 2 studios,
all with bath; all rooms have
phone, TV, air conditioning,
minibar, hairdrier
Facilities sitting room, inter-
net point, restaurant, bar,
Turkish bath, solarium, terrace
Credit cards AE, DC, MC, V
Disabled 2 specially adapted
rooms
Pets accepted
Closed never
Proprietors Serandrei family

Ca' Pisani
Town hotel

Blatantly flying in the face of Venetian hotel tradition, the Ca' Pisani, built in the shell of a deep-pink 16thC *palazzo*, is cool, hip and undeniably chic.

Inside, the overall style is designer mini-malist, but the odd original feature (brick arches, roof beams, painted coffered ceil-ings, marble floors), and the collection of fine '30s and '40s beds, mirrors and wardrobes softens this to a certain extent. Decorative themes are consistent throughout both public areas and bed-rooms. Silver (above the reception area, in bedroom furniture, in mirror frames, on light fittings, in steel chair frames) is a sta-ple and lightens dark ebony, pale acid-green and pale violet paintwork, and black and orange leather chairs. Warm, hard-wood floors and wood doors are all given a contemporary twist. Bathrooms, in either deep mauve or palest grey marble specked with silver, are straight from the pages of a design magazine. The bedrooms have Bang&Olufsen phones and TVs and electrically-operated window blinds. Biscuit-coloured bedcovers and cushions look smart against crisp white linen sheets. Breakfast is served in the base-ment restaurant where you can also enjoy a light meal.

Corte Grimani, S.Marco, 4402
30124 Venice, Italy

Tel 041 2410719
e-mail info@cortegrimani.com
website
www.cortegrimani.com

Nearby St Mark's Square,
Rialto bridge and associated
sights, Ca'Pesaro four *vaporetto*
stops, Gallerie dell'Accademia
15 mins walk. Shopping nearby
Location off canal in private
courtyard. Ask for directions
Food none, but shopping and
breakfast on request
Price €€€ per two people per
day (children under 8 stay free)
Rooms 15 apartments sleeping
2-5/6; all have phone, satellite
TV, air conditioning, safe,
refrigerator, bath or shower,
hairdrier **Facilities** each has
own seating area and sitting
room **Credit cards** MC, V,
DC **Disabled** not suitable **Pets**
not accepted **Closed** never
Proprietors Bianchi family

Corte Grimani
Town self-catering

An interesting new venture, opened in
2006 by Donatella and Guido Bianchi,
who for many years ran the Bucintoro – a
star among our Venice hotels (see below).
Donatella promises that the Corte
Grimani will have many of the Bucintoro's
qualities, even though it is apartments, not
a hotel. Fifteen units have been created in
a 17th century *palazzo,* two minutes' on
foot from St Mark's Square. A water gate
on the nearby canal allows water taxis to
take guests and their luggage right up to
the entrance. We understand that the
Bianchi's have tried to give the self-catering formula a new twist, appropriate to
Venice: the apartments are highly serviced,
spacious and very comfortable.

Decoration of the three different
grades of apartment range from the
sophisticated to the charming; many have
views. Some sleep up to six people, most
sleep five, but if only two occupy, rates are
fairly adjusted. Corte Grimani is central
for the main sites, and for shopping – see
to the left under 'nearby'.

The Bucintoro closed in 2006 and its
future remains uncertain.

Calle Larga XXII Marzo, San
Marco 2283/a, 30124 Venezia

Tel 041 5205844
e-mail info@hotelflora.it
website www.hotelflora.it

Nearby Piazza San Marco.
Location 300 m from Piazza
San Marco in cul-de-sac off
Calle Larga XXII Marzo;
vaporetto San Marco
Food breakfast
Price €€€€
Rooms 44; 32 double and
twin, 6 single, 6 family, all with
bath or shower; all rooms have
phone, TV, air conditioning,
hairdrier, safe
Facilities reading room, break-
fast room, bar, lift, garden
Credit cards AE, DC, MC, V
Disabled 2 rooms on ground
floor **Pets** accepted
Closed never
Proprietors Roger and Joel
Romanelli

Flora
Town hotel

Such is the popularity of this small hotel,
tucked away down a cul-de-sac close to
San Marco, that to get a room here you
have to book weeks, even months in
advance. You only need to glimpse the garden to know why it is sought after.
Creepers, fountains and flowering shrubs
cascading from stone urns create an
enchanting setting for breakfast, tea or an
evening drink in summer.

The lobby is small and inviting, enhanced
by the views of the garden through a glass
arch; the atmosphere is one of friendly efficiency. There are some charming double
bedrooms with painted carved antiques
and other typically Venetian furnishings,
but beware of other comparatively spartan rooms, some of which are barely big
enough for one, let alone two. Coveted
rooms include two on the ground floor
facing the garden and the three spacious
corner rooms, the topmost of which has a
marvellous view of Santa Maria della
Salute. The venerable Flora has been run
by the charming Romanelli family, father,
son and grandson, for over 40 years
(young Gioele now runs his own place, the
excellent Locanda Novecento; see p99).
Praise continues to flow in, though one
visitor mentions that the breakfast room
felt crowded in the morning.

Venice

Strada Nova, Cannaregio 4391,
30131 Venezia

Tel 041 5212612
e-mail aisantia@tin.it **website**
www.locandasantiapostoli.com

Nearby Ca' d'Oro; Santi
Apostoli; Miracoli.
Location just E of Campo
Santi Apostoli; vaporetto Ca'
d'Oro
Food breakfast
Price €–€€€; apartment
prices on request
Rooms 11 double and twin, 6
with bath, 4 with shower; all
rooms have phone, TV, air
conditioning, minibar,
hairdrier
Facilities breakfast room, sit-
ting room, lift
Credit cards AE, DC, MC, V
Disabled not suitable
Pets accepted **Closed** Jan to
mid-Feb, 2-3 weeks in Aug,
sometimes 2 weeks in Dec
Proprietor Ludovica Bianchi
Michiel

Loc. Ai Santi Apostoli
Town hotel

Be on the lookout for a pair of handsome dark green doors which herald
the discreet entrance of this converted
palazzo. Beyond is a scruffy courtyard and
a quirky lift that takes you up to the third
floor. What lies in store for you here is
totally unexpected: a lovely apartment that
has been transformed by the Bianchi
Michiel family into an elegant, if pricey,
B&B, one of the first, and still one of the
best *locandas* to open in recent years in
the city. The sitting room is the epitome of
style: oil paintings hang on glossy apricot
walls; heavy lamps rest on antique tables;
sofas and chairs are covered in quiet
chintz or swathed in calico. At the far end,
a triptych of wood-framed windows overlooks the Grand Canal. Ornaments and
books left casually around make it feel
more like a home than a hotel.

Large and individually decorated, the
bedrooms have been done out in glazed
chintzes and stunning strong colours. Like
the sitting room, they are dotted with
antiques and pretty china knick-knacks.
The two on the Grand Canal are considerably dearer than the rest. Stefano also
owns a one-bedroom apartment on the
second floor, with a vibrant green colour
scheme, no view of the canal, but a sunny
roof terrace.

Campo SS Apostoli,
Cannaregio 5043, 30131
Venezia

Tel 041 2411570
e-mail info@anticodoge.com
website www.anticodoge.com

Nearby Santi Apostoli;
Miracoli; Rialto.
Location across little bridge
on W side of Campo Santi
Apostoli; vaporetto Ca'd'Oro
Food breakfast
Price €–€€€€
Rooms 20, all double or twin,
10 with shower, 10 with bath
(some with Jacuzzi), some for
up to 5 people; all rooms have
phone, TV, air conditioning,
minibar, safe, hairdrier
Facilities bar, breakfast room
Credit cards MC, V
Disabled access possible; stair-
lift **Pets** not accepted
Closed never
Proprietor Mariella Bazzetta

Loc. Antico Doge
Town guesthouse

Don't be put off by first impressions at
the Antico Doge. Its entrance may
not be to your taste, but the long, wide
peach-coloured hallway, decorated with
glitzy white Murano glass lights and garish
paintings of Venice, gives little hint of the
charm and splendour that lies one floor
up. Keep going, pausing at the small reception desk (where you will find a friendly
and professional welcome) and, mounting
the stairs, you will soon arrive on the *piano
nobile* of this privately owned *palazzo* with
a long history. The central *salone*, which
doubles as a breakfast room and bar, is
resplendent in gold, with vases of fresh
flowers. Bedrooms drip with silk, brocade
and damask on walls, windows and beds.
Huge chandeliers, gilt mirrors, antique furniture and fine rugs on parquet floors
complete the picture. In one suite hangs a
picture of a startled looking Doge Marin
Falier, whose mansion this once was.

Close to the Rialto, in a delightfully
domestic and watery area of Cannaregio,
just round the corner from both the
Locanda Ai Santi Apostoli (p 93) and the
Locanda Leon Bianco (p 97), the Antico
Doge is, like them, a cut above many similar bed and breakfast establishments.

Venice (Torcello)

Torcello, 30012 Burano,
Venezia

Tel 041 730150
e-mail
info@locandacipriani.com
website
www.locandacipriani.com

Nearby Venice (40 mins);
lagoon islands.
Location in centre of island,
overlooking the cathedral;
vaporetto Torcello (line LN
from Fondamente Nove)
Food breakfast, lunch, dinner
Price €€€
Rooms 6; 3 double with sitting
rooms, 3 single, all with bath;
all rooms have phone, air conditioning
Facilities sitting room, dining
room, bar, terrace, garden
Credit cards AE, MC, V
Disabled not suitable **Pets**
accepted
Closed Jan to mid-Feb
Proprietor Bonifacio Brass

Locanda Cipriani
Restaurant-with-rooms

The tiny lagoon island of Torcello is the
cradle of the Venetian civilization, yet
all that remains are two serenely beautiful
religious buildings, the church of Santa
Fosca, and the Byzantine cathedral. The latter has a haunting mosaic of the Madonna,
and from its campanile, there is a wonderful view of the lagoon. When the tourists
drift home at the end of the day, Torcello's
magic takes hold, and only the half dozen
or so residents, and the handful of guests
at the Locanda Cipriani are there to share
the privilege. In the past, these have included Hemingway, Chaplin and Paul Newman;
and the entire British royal family have
lunched here. The inn, opened in 1934 by
Giuseppe Cipriani and still in the family,
has six bedrooms: simple and homely yet
sophisticated, with polished wood floors,
attractive pictures on white walls, writing
desks, *objets d'art,* comfortable sofas and
armchairs. Air conditioning has been
installed, but mercifully not televisions.

The Locanda's *raison d'être* has always
been its restaurant. Though it is a memorable experience to eat here, prices are
steep, reflecting not so much the quality of
the food, but its long-standing fame.
Romance, however, is guaranteed. In fact,
we can think of nowhere more romantic
to stay in all of northern Italy.

Campo del Ghetto Nuovo,
Cannaregio 2892, 30131
Venezia

Tel 041 2759292
e-mail
ghetto@veneziahotels.com
website
www.veneziahotels.com

Nearby Train station;
Madonna del Orto; Jewish
museum.
Location in Campo del Ghetto
Nuovo, ten minutes walk from
the train station. vaporetto
Ponte Guglie, San Marcuola
Food breakfast
Price €€€
Rooms 9 double and twin, all
with bath; all have phone, TV,
air conditioning, minibar, safe
Facilities breakfast room
Credit cards AE, MC, V
Disabled one ground floor
room **Pets** not accepted
Closed never **Proprietor**
Alessandra Mascharo

Locanda del Ghetto
Town guesthouse

Surrounded on all sides by water, the Campo del Ghetto Nuovo is the evocative, rather melancholy heart of what was the world's first Jewish ghetto. Quiet and contemplative, it lies only five minutes walk from heaving Lista di Spagna yet within easy reach of the peaceful Cannaregio backwaters. This stylish, nine-room locanda opened in early 2002, in a building which dates from the 15thC. Several of the rooms still have the original decorated wooden ceilings.

Seen from the Campo, the reception area glows invitingly from behind big windows under a little portico. On the ground floor is a small breakfast room overlooking the canal while upstairs, the light and airy bedrooms, though varying in shape and size, are all done out in the same elegant, understated style; pale cream walls, honey-coloured parquet floors, pale gold bedcovers and curtains, smart reproduction furniture, brass fittings and soft lighting. Two have small terraces on the Campo while another, (the smallest), has two original Gothic windows and an ancient fireplace serving as a bed head. Bathrooms are super-smart and even equipped with their own phones.

Corte Leon Bianco,
Cannaregio 5629, 30131
Venezia

Tel 041 5233572
e-mail info@leonbianco.it
website www.leonbianco.it

Nearby Santi Apostoli;
Miracoli; Rialto.
Location in courtyard between
Santi Apostoli and Santa
Giovanni Crisostomo canals;
vaporetto Ca' d'Oro, Rialto
Food breakfast
Price €€
Rooms 7; 6 double and twin
with shower, one family with
bath; all rooms have phone
Facilities none
Credit cards AE, DC, MC, V
Disabled not suitable
Pets not accepted
Closed never
Proprietors Stefano Doria and
Massimo Bernardi

Locanda Leon Bianco
Town guesthouse

If windows on to the Grand Canal are your heart's desire, but you are on a budget, then here is the answer. The Leon Bianco is hidden away in an enclosed courtyard, behind a sturdy door in the wall, and approached by stone steps rising up a cavernous brick-walled stairwell. The spacious, simple rooms have carved mahogany beds, big old cupboards, undulating floors and immense tilted wooden doors. Three look over the Grand Canal, with wonderful views of the Rialto market and the *traghetto* that plies back and forth across the canal, while a fourth, though it lacks a view, is equally romantic, with a dramatic fresco of Moors and camels taken from a painting by Veronese emblazoned across one wall. The locanda, only a few years old, but old-fashioned in feel, occupies one floor of an old *palazzo* and has a reception area and seven large, attractive bedrooms with small, modern bathrooms. Although it doesn't offer the services or address of the ritzy San Marco hotels, the modest prices are irresistible by comparison. A word of warning, however: a reader wrote to us to complain that her booking was cancelled in a preremptory fashion, with little help given to finding alternative accommodation. More reports, please.

Riva degli Schiavoni, Castello
4149, 30122 Venezia

Tel 041 5205044
e-mail venice@hotelmetro-
pole.com **website** www.hotel-
metropole.com

Nearby San Marco;
Accademia; Rialto.
Location midway along the
Riva, next to the church of La
Pièta; vaporetto San Zaccaria,
Arsenale or water taxi
Food breakfast, lunch, dinner;
room service
Price €€€
Rooms 72; 56 double and
twin, 3 single, 10 junior suites,
3 family; all rooms have phone,
TV, air conditioning, minibar,
safe, hairdrier
Facilities breakfast room, sit-
ting room, dining room, lift,
garden **Credit cards** AE, DC,
MC, V **Disabled** access
possible **Pets** accepted
Closed never
Proprietors Beggiato family

Metropole
Town hotel

Of the half dozen or more hotels along
the Riva degli Schiavoni, with its
matchless views of the lagoon, this is our
favourite. Still in private hands, it has
endearing touches (the owner, Signor
Beggiato, is a collector: everywhere you
look are carved angels, lecterns, church
pews, corkscrews, crucifixes, cigarette
cases, fans) and a core of twinkle-eyed staff
who have been there forever. It's a canny
choice in winter, when the velvet-hung
salone, its table heaped with cakes at tea-
time, and the intimate wood-panelled and
muralled restaurant (a former chapel
where Vivaldi taught singing to orphan
girls), are most inviting. Run by chef
Corrado Fasolato, it now has a Michelin
star. Reports would be welcome.

In the morning, the generous buffet
breakfast is served in a pretty room, a
vision in candy pink and white, decorated
with antique fans. Bedrooms vary from
traditional (such as cosy no. 350 with private *altana*) to wildly kitsch (complete
with flying cherubs in no. 251). It's a busy
tourist hotel in a bustling location, but it
has character, atmosphere, and a genuinely
warm heart.

Campo San Maurizio, San
Marco 2683/84, 30124 Venezia

Tel 041 2413765
e-mail info@novecento.biz
website www.novecento.biz

Nearby San Marco;
Accademia; Rialto.
Location off Campo San
Maurizio on Calle del Dose;
vaporetto Santa Maria del
Giglio
Food breakfast
Price €€€
Rooms 9 double, 8 with bath,
one with shower; all rooms
have phone, TV, air condition-
ing, music, minibar, safe,
hairdrier
Facilities honesty bar, sitting
room, breakfast room,
courtyard
Credit cards AE, DC, MC, V
Disabled not suitable
Pets accepted
Closed never
Proprietors Gioele and Heiby
Romanelli

Novecento
Town hotel

Off Campo San Maurizio, just around the corner from the Gritti Palace, the recently opened Locanda Novecento is a wonderful addition to the Venice hotel scene. It's attractive, enveloping, refreshingly different and run with touching commitment by young Gioele Romanelli, and his wife, Heiby. Gioele knows what he is doing: his father owns and runs the excellent Hotel Flora (p92).

It's a bit like walking into a Marrakech *riad*, with furniture, beds and fabrics imported from Morocco, Thailand and Pakistan, and a whiff of incense in the air. There are beamed ceilings, plaster walls, stained bottle glass windows, big cushions on the sitting room floor, amusing beds, superb bathrooms. Music plays in your room at the touch of a button. The old beamed Venetian house, just off the main route between San Marco and the Rialto, lends itself beautifully to its new makeover, which, the Romanellis tell us, is inspired by the great Fortuny, who was himself inspired by the Orient. With just nine bedrooms and a little courtyard garden, the atmosphere is cosy and intimate. We think this new hotel deliciously different compared with the Venice norm.

Casaifrani, San Polo, 2542-30125
Venezia

Tel 041 2750015
e-mail info@oltreilgiardino-
venezia.com

Nearby 20 mins walk from San
Marco square, 10 mins from
train station, Rialto
Location just around the corner
from the Church of the Santa
Maria Gloriosa dei Frari, on San
Polo
Food breakfast, lunch, dinner
Price €€€
Rooms 6, all rooms have
phone, TV, fireplace, air condi-
tioning, fridge, minibar,
internet
Facilities garden, complimen-
tary bar
Credit cards DC, MC, V
Disabled not suitable
Pets by arrangement
Closed never
Proprietor Lorenzo Muner

Oltre il Giardino
Country villa

If a twenty minute walk to the Rialto
from your door is too much for you,
then avoid Oltre il Giardino. This minor
inconvenience aside – one which many
would consider an advantage – this country house hotel is a real find.

Arriving here (either by canal or road)
you feel as though you have stepped into
an aristocratic friend's house, and, inter-
estingly, Alma Mahler (the composer's
widow) lived here in the 1920s. The six
bedrooms (soon to be eight) are all beautifully decorated in different colours: one
dove grey, another turquoise, another
ivory and so on. They are all spacious, full
of family heirlooms, yet touches such as
brightly coloured rugs give them a contemporary feel. Real care is taken over
each visitor's comfort: towelling robes and
slippers are provided in the bedroom,
fresh flowers by the bed.

The private walled garden is a highlight:
to be able to relax, eat breakfast, enjoy a
siesta or an evening aperitif in such a tranquil setting is all too rare in this heaving
city. One guest describes the hotel as a
'beautiful sanctuary', but adds that if you're
looking for action then you'll be disappointed, as without a restaurant or bar the
atmosphere can be subdued.

Fondamenta Soranzo,
Dorsoduro 316/b, 30123
Venezia

Tel 041 5237937
e-mail avenezia@palazzetto-
daschio.it **website**
www.palazzettodaschio.it

Nearby Santa Maria della
Salute; Accademia; Zattere.
Location on canal between
Grand and Guidecca Canals;
vaporetto Salute
or water taxi
Food none
Price €€
Rooms 4 apartments, 2 with
one bedroom, 2 with 2 bed-
rooms; all with phone, kitchen
and bathroom; phone; maid
service
Credit cards not accepted
Disabled not suitable
Pets not accepted
Closed never
Proprietor Contessa Anna da
Schio

Palazzetto da Schio
Apartments in private house

Fondamenta Soranzo is a tranquil backwater lined with attractive houses,
including this red-painted *palazzetto*, home
of the da Schio family for the past 300
years. The present incumbent, Contessa da
Schio, lives on the ground floor and *piano
nobile* while other parts of the house have
been converted into four charming and
comfortable apartments, available from
any period of time from two days to three
months. Note, though, that the apartments
are considerably less expensive when
taken per week or per month, rather than
per night. They are largely furnished with
family antiques, including pictures and mirrors, with modern bits and pieces to fill
the gaps. The topmost apartments (not for
those who don't like stairs) has wide views
and large sitting rooms, while the apartments on the mezzzanine floor have views
on the canal and the garden and cosy,
antique-filled living rooms.

The entrance hall of the *palazzetto*, lit by
precious Venetian torch lamps and opening
on to the garden, is splendid. This, and the
fine three-bedroom *piano nobile* apartment, can be hired for parties at any time
of the year and is available to stay in for
one month in the summer.

Via Quattro Fontane 16, 30126
Lido, Venezia

Tel 041 5260227 **e-mail**
ILAQuattrofontane@ila-
chateau.com **website**
www.ilachateau.com/quattrof/

Nearby Venice; lagoon islands.
Location set back from
seafront on S side of Lido, near
Casino; vaporetto Santa Maria
Elisabetta
Food breakfast, lunch, dinner
Price €€€
Rooms 58; 54 double, 4 single,
35 with bath, 23 with shower;
all rooms have phone, TV, air
conditioning, hairdrier, safe
Facilities sitting room, writing
room, dining room, bar; tennis
court and beach cabins
available
Credit cards AE, DC, MC, V
Disabled access difficult
Pets accepted
Closed Nov to April
Proprietors Friborg-
Bevilacqua family

Quattro Fontane
Seaside hotel

The longer we lingered at the Quattro Fontane, the more it grew on us. At first the 150-year-old mock Tyrolean building struck us as rather gloomy and suburban, but we soon warmed to the charmingly decorated reception rooms, particularly the *salone* and the little writing room. Mementos of the owners' travels are dotted around the hotel on walls and shelves – carved wooden figures, painted shells, model ships, porcelain, stamps. In the baronial dining room, with its cavernous hearth and bold red chairs, service was directed with courtesy by the long-serving head waiter. In warm weather you can eat out on the wide tree-filled terrace that encircles the hotel.

The bedrooms in the main building have plenty of character and are individually decorated with an assortment of furniture, pictures and fabrics, comfortable if not luxurious. Those in the 1960s annexe are more streamlined, but here too each is different, attractive and cosy, with gaily tiled bathrooms. A dignified hotel, elderly now, but still spruce, and in our opinion the best on the Lido.

Campo Bandiera e Moro,
Castello 3608, 30122 Venezia

Tel 041 5285315
e-mail info@venicelaresiden-
za.com
website www.venicelaresiden-
za.com

Nearby San Giorgio degli
Schiavoni; Arsenale.
Location on small square 100
m behind Riva degli Schiavoni;
vaporetto Arsenale, San
Zaccaria
Food breakfast
Price €
Rooms 14; 12 double and
twin, 2 single, all with bath or
shower; all rooms have phone,
TV, air conditioning, minibar,
safe, hairdrier
Facilities sitting room, break-
fast area
Credit cards MC, V
Disabled not suitable **Pets**
accepted **Closed** never
Proprietor Giovanni Ballestra

La Residenza
Town hotel

La Residenza appeals to true lovers of Venice who appreciate the chance to stay in the grand Gothic *palazzo* which dominates this dusty and enigmatic square, whose little church, San Giovanni in Bragora is one of the city's most appealing.

Just to enter is an experience: huge doors swing open to reveal an ancient covered courtyard and stone steps leading up to a vast baroque hall with beautifully coloured, lavishly carved plaster walls. Taking breakfast here in the early morning light is a rare treat, though the hushed atmosphere can be a little oppressive.

This, however, is not a grand hotel, but a modest two-star in immodest surround-ings. Those devotees – and these were many – who appreciated the combination of grotty, kitsch and antique in the bed-rooms under the hotel's former owner-ship mourn the fact that they have all now been renovated (calm and pretty, but stan-dard); other, more recent guests, appreci-ate the modernisations and feel that as long as the central hall remains unchanged, La Residenza retains it special appeal.

By the way, the famous smell – of cats? or is it boiled cabbage? – seems to have retreated to the hallway; some say it has gone altogether.

Calle della Rosa, Santa Croce
2232, 30135 Venezia

Tel 041 5241768
e-mail cassiano@sancassiano.it
website www.sancassiano.it

Nearby Ca' d'Oro; Rialto
markets; Rialto Bridge.
Location on Grand Canal,
opposite Ca' d'Oro; vaporetto
San Stae or water taxi
Food breakfast
Price €€€€
Rooms 36; 20 double and
twin, 12 triple and family, 4
single, all with bath or shower;
all rooms have phone, TV, air
conditioning, minibar, hairdri-
er, safe
Facilities sitting room,
breakfast room, bar
Credit cards AE, MC, V
Disabled 2 rooms specially
adapted
Pets accepted
Closed never
Proprietor Franco Maschietto

Ca'Favretto San Cassiano **Town hotel**

Arriving by boat at San Cassiano's private jetty on the Grand Canal is considerably easier than finding your way by
foot through a maze of tortuous, narrow
alleyways from the nearest *vaporetto* or
traghetto point (ask for a brochure to be
sent so that you can follow its map). It also
means that you can appreciate the 14thC
palazzo's best feature: its deep red Gothic
façade which faces the Grand Canal's
greatest glory, the Ca' d'Oro. Inside, the
hotel has a rather fusty feel to it, with
heavy Venetian furnishings and a fairly lack-
adaisical staff – characteristics we also
found in its sister hotel, the Marconi. What
it does have, however, is some endearingly
grandiose rooms, and the six facing the
canal are splendid, with capacious reproduction antique wardrobes, matching
desks and carved bedheads, floating white
curtains bordered by velvet or brocade
pelmets, and oriental carpets. Sadly, they
are no longer the same price as rooms
without a view, but you should do all you
can to secure one. The light, elegant breakfast room with huge windows and waterfront views is a delight. In recognition of
its historic status as the house of the
18thC Venetian painter, Favretto, the hotel
is now officially a 'Residenza d'Epoca', and
proud of it.

Salizzada San Samuele, San
Maro 3358, 30124 Venezia

Tel 041 5205165
e-mail info@allber-
gosansamuele.it **website**
www.albergosansamuele.it

Nearby Accademia gallery;
Frari; Campo Santo Stefano.
Location in quiet area of San
Marco, between Campo Santo
Stefano and Grand Canal;
vaporetto San Samuele.
Food breakfast
Price €€
Rooms 10; 8 double, 2 single,
7 with shower; all rooms have
phone
Facilities sitting room, break-
fast room, bar
Credit cards not accepted
Disabled not suitable
Pets not accepted
Closed never
Proprietor Domenico,
Roberto and Bruno

San Samuele
Town guesthouse

A budget establishment with young managers, a fresh lick of paint, 300-year old
Venetian marble floors and a pleasant, airy
feel to the bedrooms.

The *pensione* is installed on the upper
floors of a pretty house in a wide street
leading to the San Samuele *vaporetto* and
traghetto landing stage. Ring the bell for
admission, enter a pleasant little courtyard
and start climbing the stairs, of which
there are quite a few – this hotel is for the
young and fit.

On our last visit, all the bedrooms had
recently been redecorated, their main decorative feature being a square of pink
colour on the wall behind each low,
skimpy-looking bed (an inspector informs
us that they are adequately comfortable).
Bathrooms are modern, each enlivened by
a jolly shower curtain. What gives these
rooms the edge over others in the same
price range, however, is the presence of
not one but two large windows with views
over the street. The two rooms at the
back make up in quiet what they lack in
light. Breakfast, if you want it, is served in
the rooms.

We have had good reader feedback
about this modest, two-star establishment.
Run by three friends, it's the sort of places
that is much appreciated but hard to find:
an affordable hotel that doesn't disappoint.

Venice

Zattere ai Gesuati, Dorsoduro
779, 30123 Venezia

Tel 041 5222340/5286858
e-mail pensioneseguso@tis-
cali.it **website** www.pensione-
seguso.it

Nearby Accademia gallery;
Gesuati church.
Location 5 mins' walk S of
Accademia, overlooking
Giudecca canal; vaporetto
Zattere or water taxi
Food breakfast, lunch, dinner
Price €–€€€
Rooms 36; 31 double and
twin, 5 single, 9 with bath, 9
with shower; all rooms have
phone
Facilities dining room, sitting
room, lift, terrace
Credit cards AE, MC, V
Disabled access possible **Pets**
accepted
Closed mid-Dec to mid-Feb
Proprietors Seguso family

Seguso
Town guesthouse

Sitting on the sunny promenade of the Zattere, lapped by the choppy waters of the wide Giudecca canal, gives you the distinct feeling of being by the seaside. This open setting, with a grand panorama across the lagoon, is just one of the charms of the Seguso. A *pensione* in the old tradition, it is family-run, friendly and solidly old-fashioned. And (unlike most hotels in Venice) prices are modest; the Seguso is not noted for its food, but half board here costs no more than bed-and-breakfast alone in hotels of similar comfort closer to San Marco.

The best bedrooms are the large ones at the front of the house, overlooking the canal – though for the privilege of the views and space you may have to forfeit the luxury of a private bathroom (only half the rooms have their own facilities). The main public rooms are the dining room, prettily furnished in traditional style, and the modest sitting room where you can sink into large leather chairs and peruse ancient editions of travel writing and guidebooks. Breakfast is taken on the front terrace – delightful. Fellow guests are often friendly, interesting and great Venice enthusiasts. Group bookings (maximum 30 people) are accepted, though not in September and May.

Corso Portoni Borsari 4a,
37121 Verona

Tel 045 8003060
e-mail
info@hotelgabbiadoro.it
website www.hotelgabbi-
adoro.it

Nearby Piazza delle Erbe;
Loggia del Consiglio; Arena.
Location in medieval centre of
the city, S of Porta Borsari;
garage parking available
Food breakfast
Price €€€€
Rooms 27; 8 double and twin,
19 suites, all with bath or
shower; all rooms have phone,
TV, air conditioning, minibar,
hairdrier, safe
Facilities breakfast room, sit-
ting room, orangery, bar, meet-
ing room, lift, terrace **Credit
cards** AE, DC, MC, V
Disabled access difficult
Pets accepted **Closed** never
Proprietor Camilla Balzarro

Gabbia d'Oro
Town hotel

This stylish hotel in a 17thC *palazzo*,
luxurious but never ostentatious,
boasts an attention to detail rarely
encountered nowadays. A small, beautifully wrapped gift awaits your arrival, and the
staff are as charming and polished as the
hotel itself. The public rooms, entered
through massive wood doors with gilt
decoration, are comfortable as well as elegant: there are plenty of places in which to
sit and relax, and sofas are large
and deep. Wooden floors, beams and
brickwork are much in evidence; the sitting room shares one wall with the
Gardello Tower. Furnishings, chandeliers,
silver-framed photographs, ornaments and
antiques are always in keeping. Little lamps
lend a glow to the panelled bar, and the
new orangery is restful, with its green-and-
white colour scheme and view out over
the terrace.

Frescoes, restored or reproduced from
the originals, recur as friezes both downstairs and in the bedrooms. Suites out-
number doubles. In almost all, beds are
shrouded in a canopy of antique lace. No.
404, dark red with sloping walls, rafters,
and nooks and crannies, is so romantic
that it's normally chosen for honeymoon-
ers. Prices are rather high, but we felt justifiably so.

Vicolo Listone 3, 37121
Verona

Tel 045 8007512
e-mail hoteltorcolo@virgilio.it
website www.hoteltorcolo.it

Nearby Arena; Via Mazzini,
Piazza delle Erbe.
Location just off Piazza Brà;
garage parking
Food breakfast
Price €€
Rooms 19; 13 double and
twin, 4 single, 2 family, one
with bath and 18 with shower;
all rooms have phone, TV, air
conditioning, minibar, safe,
hairdrier; 10 rooms have mini-
bar and safe
Facilities sitting area, breakfast
room, courtyard, lift
Credit cards AE, DC, MC, V
Disabled access difficult
Pets accepted
Closed mid-Jan
Proprietors Silvia Pomari and
Diana Castellani

Torcolo
Town hotel

The Torcolo is an inexpensive hotel in
an excellent location at the heart of
lively Verona. 'Its most outstanding quality,'
writes one recent guest, 'was the warmth
and friendliness of our welcome and the
consistent helpfulness of the staff.' Other
positive comments continue to filter
through. Every room is individually decorated in varying styles – Italian 18thC, art
nouveau, modern – and all are fresher and
have more charm than one normally finds
at this price. Ours contained a complete
set of Liberty-style bedroom furniture
which had belonged to owner Silvia
Pommari's parents when they first mar-
ried. It was set off by white linen curtains
and a colourful patchwork bedspread.
Ceramic tiled bathrooms are somewhat
cramped; the best have separate shower
cubicles, and many have been renewed
recently. Rooms are double-glazed against
the considerable street sounds (people,
not cars) but, despite air conditioning, they
can get fuggy, especially in warm weather.
Breakfast, including a jug of fresh orange
juice, a good assortment of bread and
croissants and yoghurt, can be taken in
your room, which might be preferable to
the rather cramped little breakfast room.
In summer, it is served buffet-style in the
small off-street courtyard.

Barbarano Vicentino

Via Castello 6, 36021
Barbarano, Vicenza

Tel 0444 886055
e-mail
info@castellomarinoni.it
website www.castellomari-
noni.it
Food none
Price €
Closed never
Proprietors Marinoni family

Il Castello
Country villa apartments

Il Castello refers to a handsome villa built in the 17thC on the ruins of an ancient castle which looks down over the medieval village of Barbarano Vicentino. Occupied for more than 100 years by the Marinoni family, it retains the original perimeter walls of the castle, and its cellars. There is a formal Renaissance garden. You can choose from three separate apartments, each with one or two bedrooms, and fully equipped kitchens and bathrooms; or you can take the whole house. Rooms, white-painted and airy, with Venetian marble floors, are somewhat spartan in feel, despite the use of old family furniture throughout.

Cortina d'Ampezzo

Via Majon 110, 32043 Cortina
d'Ampezzo, Belluno

Tel 0436 2400
e-mail info@hotelmenardi.it
website www.hotelmenardi.it
Food breakfast, lunch, dinner
Price € €
Closed Oct to mid-Dec, Apr
to mid-May
Proprietors Menardi family

Menardi
Town hotel

This family-run hotel evolved from a coaching inn when its owners, the Menardi family, began hiring out horses. During the First World War, Luigi Menardi began to transform the rustic inn into a proper hotel. Today the long white building has proliferated carved green wood balconies and tumbling geraniums, plus extra rooms and a separate annexe behind, but the Menardi family can still justifiably proclaim: 'same house, same family, same relaxed atmosphere'. Inside, antique pieces, painted religious statues and old work tools are mixed with local custom-made furnishings which look somewhat dated, but which are nonetheless comfortable. The atmosphere is one of traditional warmth and service is polished.

Follina

Hotel dei Chiostri
Town hotel

The owners of Follina's Villa Abbazia (see p68), which we have admired ever since it opened a few years ago, have now created a simpler, more modern but no less stylish place to stay right across the street. The Hotel dei Chiostri, built on the ruins of an old monastery, and right beside the lovely cloister of the 11thC abbey, has 15 sophisticated rooms decorated in cool colours with pretty floaty curtains and well-designed contemporary furniture. As at the Abbazia, attention to detail is admirable. Only breakfast is served here; the hotel shares the Abbazia's lovely restaurant, Il Corte.

Piazza IV Novembre 20, 31051 Follina, Treviso

Tel 0438 971805
e-mail info@hoteldeichiostri.com
website www.hoteldeichiostri.com
Food breakfast
Price €€
Closed mid-Jan to mid-Feb
Proprietors Zanon family

Madonna di Campiglio

Bio-Hotel Hermitage
Mountain hotel

We were alerted to this modern 'bio' hotel (it was refurbished in 1999 using only natural materials such as solid wood floors and pure wool carpets, ecological water and electricity supply and so on) by an enthusiastic guest who praised everything, but most of all the relaxed 'at home' family atmosphere and the 'superb' food (home-made pumpkin pasta with black truffle, wild rabbit *alla cacciatore*, sweet chestnut mousse). Also: well equipped rooms ('fantastic mattresses'); a parkland setting; shuttle to the town centre and ski slopes; sun terrace; indoor pool; sauna. 'I'm going back', says our correspondent, 'this time for the alpine flowers'.

Via Castelletto Inferiore 63, 38084 Madonna di Campiglio, Trentino

Tel 0465 441558
e-mail info@biohotelhermitage.it
web www.biohotelhermitage.it
Food breakfast, lunch, dinner
Price €€
Closed Sep to Dec
Proprietors Maffei family

Marlengo

Vicolo San Felice 2, Marlengo,
39020 Merano, Bolzano

Tel 0473 222020
e-mail info@oberwirt.com
website www.oberwirt.com
Food breakfast, lunch, dinner
Price €€€
Closed mid-Nov to mid-Mar
Proprietors Waldner family

Oberwirt
Mountain resort hotel

Originally a simple inn, Oberwirt has been run by the Waldner family since 1749. Today, three generations currently work in the hotel: Signor Waldner's beaming mother, dressed in a *dirndl*, is at reception, while his daughter runs the restaurant. The hotel is often full, and, though it has plenty to recommend it, character and intimacy are not strong features.

The *raison d'être* is the food, which features local produce – highlights include fried duck liver, lamb cutlets in a herb crust and *marscapone* and compote of bitter cherries between layers of strudel pastry.

Merano

Via Labers 25, 39012 Merano,
Bolzano

Tel 0473 234484
e-mail
schlosslabers@rolmail.net
website www.castellolabers.it
Food breakfast, lunch, dinner
Price €€€
Closed Nov to Apr
Proprietors Stapf-Neubert
family

Castello Labers
Converted castle

On a hillside to the east of Merano, Castello (or Schloss) Labers is immersed in its own lush orchards and vineyards, with direct access to mountain walks through Alpine pastures. The hotel has been in the Neubert family since 1885.

On a bad day, the Castel wouldn't look out of place in an Addams family film, but it has its charm, and the interior is welcoming. Bedrooms vary enormously in size and standard: some elegantly proportioned with antique furniture, others rather too drab and basically furnished.

The ambience? 'Elderly', writes a guest. 'Very pleasant, very quiet, but rather elderly.'

Missiano

Missiano, 39050 San Paolo,
Bolzano

Tel 0471 636000
e-mail info@schloss-hotel-korb.com
website www.schloss-hotel-korb.com
Food breakfast, lunch, dinner
Price €€
Closed Nov to Mar
Proprietors Dellago family

Schloss Korb
Converted castle

Rising up from the fertile vineyards and orchards that surround the outskirts of Bolzano is the 11thC tower which forms the centrepience of Schloss Korb. The hotel's entrance is a riot of colour – flowering plants set against walls of golden stone and whitewash – and a terrace, awash with plants, hangs out over the valley. The interior is traditional; reception is a cool, dark tiled hall set about with a most eccentric collection of objects, while bedrooms are large, with lovely views over the vineyards. The best are in the tower, as well as the apartment with its carved furniture. There are two pools, indoor and outdoor. The feel of the place is relaxed, though not intimate.

Pinzolo

San Antonio di Mavignola 72,
38086 Pinzolo, Trento

Tel 0465 502758
e-mail info@masodoss.com
website www.masodoss.com
Food breakfast, dinner; lunch on request
Price €€; weekly rates available
Closed never
Proprietors Caola family

Chalet Maso Doss
Mountain chalet

Here's the real thing: a simple, heart-warming 17thC chalet in the Brenta Valley, set amidst the spectacular landscape of the Adamello-Dolomiti di Brenta National Park. In winter you can explore on cross-country skis, in summer on mountain bikes provided by the chalet, taking a packed lunch if you wish. On your return: wood panelling and simple furniture, check tablecloths and lace curtains, a warm fire, an excellent dinner, a Finnish sauna, and one of six cosy bedrooms with warm duvets and hand-embroidered sheets. Guests gather for a drink before dinner, and the atmosphere is very much that of a welcoming private house.

San Valburga d'Ultimo

39016 San Valburga d'Ultimo, Bolzano

Tel 0473 795319
e-mail eggwirt@rolmail.net
website www.eggwirt.it
Food breakfast, lunch, dinner
Price €
Closed mid-Nov to mid-Dec
Proprietors Schwienbacher family

Eggwirt
Mountain guesthouse

The quiet and unspoiled Val d'Ultima lies 30 kilometres south-west of Merano. In this ideal setting for both summer and winter sports, the Gasthof Eggwirt has existed as a hostelry since the 14th century, and today the Schwienbacher family welcome guests as if to their own home. The hotel is on the edge of the village with a large terrace at the front and superb views all around.

The bright bedrooms have lots of wood and cheerful duvet covers. An inexpensive, relaxed and friendly family hotel offering some excellent ski deals for children.

Venice

Campiello Nuovo, Santo Stefano, San Marco 3457, 30124 Venezia

Tel 041 523 4754
e-mail info@locandafiorita.com **website** www.locandafiorita.com
Food breakfast **Price** €–€€
Closed never
Proprietor Renato Colombera

Locanda Fiorita
Town guesthouse

If you are looking for budget prices and a quiet yet central location, look no further than this bargain hotel, a red-painted villa tucked away in a quiet, little visited square off Campo Santo Stefano. Rooms are small and functional, with modern white furniture which include desks, bedside tables, even beds. You will find a comfortable bed, but skimpy towels and a lack of shelves, though there is plenty of cupboard space. 'With its beamed ceiling, mint green walls and large windows my room was a perfectly pleasant one in which to wake up,' comments one guest 'especially when one reflects on what it cost'. Breakfast is taken at wooden tables along the wall in the reception area, or, more comfortably, in your room.

Venice

Corte Zorzi, San Marco 1083,
30124 Venezia

Tel 041 5204827
e-mail info@locandaorseolo
website www.locandaorseolo
Food breakfast
Price €€€
Closed never
Proprietors Perruch family

Locanda Orseolo
Town hotel

It's the really exceptional warmth of the young owners of Locanda Orseolo that really makes it stand out. The hotel, just a few paces from Piazza San Marco, was opened in 2002, one of the new breed of sophisticated places to stay in former private homes, and it was purchased only in 2003 by Matteo, Barbara, Bruno and Francesco, whose genuine warmth and helpfulness towards their guests is a real boon in the hard-nosed world of Venetian hospitality. The hotel itself is smart and spotless; the 15 rooms (which have temperature controls) vary in size, some large, some with bathrooms that are a little cramped. The breakfasts-'eggs any way, excellent coffee'-are praised, but not so much as that wonderful welcome.

Venice

Riva del Vin, San Polo 729,
30125 Venezia

Tel 041 5222068
e-mail info@hotelmarconi.it
website www.hotelmarconi.it
Food breakfast
Price €€€
Closed never
Proprietor Franco Maschietto

Marconi
Town hotel

The Marconi is a typical Venice hotel, encapsulating both what is right and what is wrong about many of them. As so often, the location is enviable (right by Rialto Bridge). The building is a 16thC *palazzo* with a 19thC entrance hall, marbled pillars, velvet hangings, and green and gold embossed ceiling. Best of all are the two sought-after rooms with balconies which overlook the Grand Canal, more expensive, but worth it. Bedrooms are fairly simple, but mahogany furniture and damask curtains make them seem old-fashioned. The hotel was renovated not that long ago, but its dark wood fittings and dated fabrics give it a rather gloomy air.

Venice

Calle della Madonna, San
Marco 3614, 30124 Venezia

Tel 041 5204909
e-mail piccolafenice@fenice-
hotels.it **website** www.fenice-
hotels.it
Food breakfast
Price €€-€€€; weekly
rates available
Closed Jan
Proprietor Michele Facchini

Piccola Fenice
Town hotel

The Teatro La Fenice has at last risen
from the ashes after the disastrous fire
which rendered it a stark shell. The famous
adjacent hotel, Fenice et des Artistes,
where performers used to put up, has
looked too gloomy and faded for us to
include in our guide for some years, but we
have always been impressed by its sister
hotel, the Piccola Fenice. It consists of
seven suites sleeping between two and six
people. On the wide first floor landing
there is a sitting area with desk and armchairs. The topmost apartment, with little
balcony overlooking the rooftops, would
be perfect for a family.

Venice

Calle Goldoni, San Marco
4486, 30124 Venezia

Tel 041 5200011
e-mail
info@hotelserenissima.it
website
www.hotelserenissima.it
Food breakfast
Price €€
Closed never
Proprietor Roberto dal Borgo

Serenissima
Town hotel

Readers' reports confirm that this is one
of the most endearing and best-kept
two-star hotels in town. Our inspector
told us that she found it much pleasanter
to stay here than in many a more expensive
three-star, and, given its central location
just a few paces from the Doge's Palace,
she deemed it value for money – a rare
experience in Venice. Bedrooms are admit-
tedly small (a triple will give two people
more room), but neat and pretty, some
with purpose-made wooden fittings, others
with more attractive Venetian painted
headboards, cupboards and bedside tables.
There's a charming first floor breakfast
room, and corridors are hung with colourful modern paintings.

Area introduction

The Via Emilia, the Roman road (now a motorway) stretching along the foothills of the Apeninne mountains from Piacenza to Rimini, gives this region its name. Bounded by the River Po to the north and the wooded slopes of the Apennines to the south, Emilia-Romagna is fertile and prosperous, its countryside a patchwork of fields, hills and plains, with most of its cities strung out along the Via Emilia, with Bologna in the centre.

Bologna, the regional capital, famed for its food, is primarily a business centre with business-style hotels to match; but it is also a city of learning (it has the oldest university in Europe) and of art (including beautiful Renaissance buildings) so there is much to attract the tourist, and we can recommend the four hotels owned by the Orsi family. See pages 117 and 128 for descriptions of the **Corona d'Oro** and the **Commercianti**, and make a note of the **Orologio** (tel 051 231 253) and the **Novecento** (tel 051 7457311).

In Modena, Bologna's long-time rival with a stunning Romanesque cathedral, we recommend the **Canalgrande** (tel 059 217160). With 78 bedrooms, it is somewhat large for a full entry in this guide, but it is nevertheless a stylish, peaceful and comfortable villa set in beautiful gardens in the middle of the city.

Finding a satisfactory hotel in Parma is also tricky. Our best recommendation is the very central **Torino** (tel 0521 281046). In Ferrara we can thoroughly recommend a homely B&B, **Locanda Borgonuovo** (see page 123) but for something grander, try the luxurious **Duchessa Isabella** (tel 0532 202121). In Reggio Emilia, noted for its Parmigiano Reggiano and its balsamic vinegar, we can recommend the **Hotel Posta** (page 129).

The Adriatic coast of this region is not notable for small hotels, but we have finally found a lovely one in Ravenna for this edition – the **Albergo Cappello** (page 126). Or you could try the **Bisanzio** (tel 0544 217111), or the simple but central **Centrale Byron** (tel 0544 212225).

Dotted about the region, in small towns or villages and in the countryside, we can recommend a clutch of other hotels, some of which are old favourites, others new discoveries. In addition, a reader writes to thoroughly recommend **Agriturismo Cavaione** (tel 051 589006), a country inn about 15 minutes drive (or bus ride) outside Bologna. 'The room was sunny and comfortable, the views from the balcony gorgeous, and the staff friendly and helpful.' Just what our guide is all about.

Via Oberdan 12, 40126
Bologna

Tel 051 236456
e-mail corona@inbo.it
website www.bolognahotel.net

Nearby Piazza Maggiore;
Piazza del Nettuno.
Location in city centre, close
to the two leaning towers in
Piazza di Porta Ravegnan; with
garage parking
Food breakfast
Price €€€
Rooms 35; 27 double, 8 single,
all with shower; all rooms have
phone, TV, air conditioning,
minibar, safe
Facilities breakfast room, sit-
ting area, bar, TV room
Credit cards AE, DC, MC, V
Disabled not suitable
Pets accepted
Closed Aug
Proprietor Mauro Orsi

Corona d'Oro
Town hotel

The Corona d'Oro lies in the historic
old city, close to the two famous leaning towers, in a cobbled street which for
most of the time is closed to traffic.
Enticing food shops (including a wonderful
delicatessen) give you some idea of why
the city came to be nicknamed Bologna La
Grassa (the Fat).

The Corona d'Oro became a hotel in
1890, though the original building dates
back to 1300. It is here that Italy's first
printing press was established and there
are still a few features surviving from the
original *palazzo*. In the early 1980s the
hotel was bought by a packaging magnate,
who elevated it from a simple hotel to
four-star status, successfully combining the
old features with the stylish new. The
14thC portico and Renaissance ceilings
were preserved, while the plush bedrooms
were provided with all modern conveni-
ences. The showpiece was the hallway, with
its fine art nouveau frieze supported on
columns. Light streaming from above, fresh
flowers and lush feathery plants create a
cheerful, inviting entrance.

If you are arriving by car, be sure to get
the hotel's route-map; without it, you
will never find your way through the
Bologna maze.

Piazza Carducci 5, 48013
Brisighella, Ravenna

Tel 0546 81209
e-mail info@gigiole.it
website www.gigiole.it

Nearby Bologna (50 km);
Ravenna (42 km); Faenza (17
km).
Location in centre of town;
with public car parking in front
Food breakfast, lunch, dinner
Price €€
Rooms 10; 7 double, 2 single,
1 suite, all with shower; all
rooms have phone, TV, air
conditioning, minibar,
hairdrier
Facilities restaurant, bar, sit-
ting room, lift, terrace
Credit Cards AE, DC, MC, V
Disabled no special facilities
Pets accepted
Closed hotel closed one
month Jan-Feb, restaurant
closed Mon
Proprietor Tarcisio Raccagni

Gigiolè
Restaurant-with-rooms

B risighella is a picturesque small town
and thermal spa 13 km south-west of
Faenza in an area famous for its production of clay and ceramics. The town is also
known for its excellent olive oil. The
Gigiolè stands across from the main
church, a vaguely French-looking shuttered
building with a shaded terrace in front.

The French style extends to the food:
Tarcisio Raccagni, the chef, has been put on
a par with the famous Paul Bocuse. Like
Bocuse, he places great stress on using
local seasonal ingredients of top quality
and the results are superb: succulent
meats, delicious soups and imaginative use
of vegetables and herbs – all that is best in
contemporary Italian cooking, and at
affordable prices. The restaurant is a mixture of rustic and elegant; stone arches
and walls are hung with copper pots and
local ceramics while tables are laid with
crisp, white linen and glasses gleam. Our
inspectors' only complaint was the loud
piped music.

The once sub-standard bedrooms and
bathrooms are now thoroughly comfortable and the spacious rooms incorporate a
sitting area (one suite has a kitchen).
Floors are parquet and the furniture
throughout is modern.

Brisighella

Borgo Rontana 34, 148013
Brisighella, Ravenna

Tel 0546 85493
e-mail info@varnello.it
website www.varnello.it

Nearby Ravenna, Faenza (14
km).
Location about 14 km W of
Faenza, in own grounds with
private car parking; ask for
directions
Food breakfast; lunch and din-
ner by arrangement
Price €€
Rooms 6, 4 double and 2 suites
for 2-5, all with bath and show-
er; all rooms have phone, TV,
air-conditioning, hairdryer,
fridge **Facilities** sitting room,
dining room, garden, pool
Credit cards AE, DC, MC, V
Disabled no special facilities
Pets accepted **Closed** Jan and
Feb **Proprietors** Giovanni and
Liana Liverzani

Relais Varnello
Country guesthouse

A newly converted farmhouse in the
extraordinary, barren-but-beautiful
Rontana hills, where you will get (even by
the best Italian standards) a great welcome
and personal attention. Some Dutch readers discovered it for us and were 'deeply
impressed' by the hospitality of the
Liverzanis. More accolades have flowed:
'we were flabberghasted, by the hotel's
position, the comfort of our rooms and,
not least, by the hospitality of the owners'
reads one. It really seems that the
Liverzanis are natural hosts with a great
love for their locality, which is full of historical interest.

Everything is in superb new condition
and artfully restored. A pleasantly home-
like sitting room is furnished with
antiques, some from Liverzani family
homes. The same private-house feel continues in the four bedrooms, each decorated and equipped differently, with attractive, unobtrusive fabrics, handsome iron
bedsteads; one suite has a four-poster with
hangings. Two apartments, one with Finnish
sauna, are available in an annexe. The
grounds are extensive, and it's good walking country. By the way, the Liverzani family have lived in this corner of Italy for
1,000 years and Giovanni was an Olympic
rapid-fire pistol shooter.

Brisighella

Via Cavina 11, 48013
Brisighella, Ravenna

Tel 0546 84545
e-mail info@torrepratesi.it
website www.torrepratesi.it

Nearby Faenza (25 km);
Ravenna (50 km).
Location 8 km SW of
Brisighella: take the SS302 for
Florence, turn off to Valetta
just after Fognano and follow
signs; car parking
Food breakfast, dinner; light
lunch on request
Price €€€
Rooms 9; 3 doubles and 6
suites, 8 with bath, 1 with
shower; 3 rooms in annexe; all
have phone, TV, air conditioning, minibar **Facilities** sitting
rooms, dining room, garden,
pool **Credit cards** AE, DC,
MC, V **Disabled** 2 suites **Pets**
accepted **Closed** never
Proprietors Nerio and Letizia
Raccagni

Torre Pratesi
Country hotel

The solid, square tower that forms part
of this unusual hotel dates from 1510,
while the adjacent farmhouse was added
much later. Lovingly restored in 1993, it
enjoys a remote and spectacular position
on a hill with superb views over vineyards,
olive groves and woods. As many of the
original features of the building as possible
have been preserved, and modernization
has been carried out using traditional
materials; wood, stone, wrought iron and
marble. Modern equipment in the bedrooms is discreetly hidden in drawers and
cupboards. Furnishings and colour
schemes have been kept simple throughout – terracotta floors, warm, honey-
coloured walls, leather armchairs and
imaginative contemporary lighting.
Bedrooms and bathrooms are surprisingly
stylish; those housed in the tower itself
enjoy 360° views.

We've always been confident that the
Raccagnis are warm and charming hosts.
However, we did receive one negative
report from a recent visitor, who thought
the place overpriced. Dinner is made
largely with produce from the estate, and
this visitor comments that there was great
pressure to buy their homegrown prod-
ucts, too. Reports would be welcome.

Via Gaidello 18, 41013
Castelfranco Emilia , Roma

Tel 059 926806
e-mail info@gaidello.com
website www.gaidello.com

Nearby Modena (10 km);
Bologna (25 km).
Location on outskirts of
Castelfranco Emilia near the
Via Emilia (State Highway 9),
between Modena and Bologna;
ample car parking
Food breakfast, lunch, dinner
on request
Price €-€€
Rooms 7 apartments sleeping
2-6 people, 2 double rooms
with bath; all rooms have TV,
fridge, hairdrier
Facilities sitting room, dining
room, terrace, garden, lake,
solarium **Credit cards** MC, V
Pets not accepted
Disabled access difficult
Closed Aug; restaurant closed
Sun eve, Mon **Proprietor**
Paola Giovanna Bini

Villa Gaidello
Country hotel

Villa Gaidello Club is the creation of
three sisters, one an architect, who
took on the long neglected land and farm
buildings of the old family home, situated
in green, peaceful surroundings with a lake
full of wildfowl. Today it is still run by one
sister, Paola Giovanna Bini (another went
to live in the United States, where she
runs a similar operation in Middleburg,
Virginia). Recent renovation and restoration has resulted in a total of seven apartments, each with kitchen and bathroom, of
varying sizes, as well as two double bedrooms. Three of the apartments are in the
casa padronale, one, for example, occupies
the old beamed stable, using the manger
for a bedroom. Other apartments are
elsewhere on the estate, a couple of minutes' drive away. All apartments display a
simple, rustic elegance.

Emphasis at Il Gaidello is on the rural,
simple and fresh. The restaurant is in
another converted stable, where the food
is prepared by *rezdore* (skilled country
women) and overseen by Paola. The
regional speciality, *tortellini in brodo*, is
always on the menu, as well as wonderful
antipasto and excellent dishes of chicken,
rabbit and guineau hen. The food is usually
served at long wooden tables. Don't miss
Paola's walnut liqueur.

Castel Guelfo

Via Santa Croce 5, 40023
Castel Guelfo, Bologna

Tel 0542 670102
e-mail solarola@fastamail.it
website
www.locandasolarola.com

Nearby Bologna (25 km);
Ravenna (45 km); Faenza (30
km).
Location 4 km SE of Medicina;
A14 motorway exit Castel San
Pietro Terme; parking
Food breakfast, lunch, dinner
Price €€-€€€
Rooms 15; 14 double and twin,
1 suite, 2 with bath, 13 with
shower; all have TV, minibar,
hairdrier; 10 have air condition-
ing **Facilities** breakfast room,
restaurant, bar, sitting rooms,
billiard room, garden, pool
Credit Cards AE, DC, MC, V
Disabled ground floor rooms
Pets accepted **Closed** restau-
rant closed Mon, Tues lunch,
hotel never **Proprietor**
Antonella Scardovi

Locanda Solarola
Restaurant-with-rooms

The Solarola (situated in the middle of
very flat, unvisited part of rural Emilia
Romagna) started life in the 1989 as a
modest 'agriturismo' with a few rooms
above a rustic eatery. Nowadays its restaurant has a Michelin star for the cooking of
owner Antonella Scardovi, who began, after
a career as a publicist in Bologna, with no
more than her 'natural talent'.

The hotel has now expanded into
another building in the farm complex. The
decoration might be too 'pretty-pretty' for
some tastes; flowers dominate throughout, starting with the reception area. Each
bedroom is named after a different flower
and has the appropriate floral wallpaper,
quantities of lace, painted bedheads,
embroidered linens and framed floral
prints. Antonella's passion for collecting
'priceless bric-a-brac' results in each room
being very individual and full of her per-
sonally chosen objects. The comfortable
public rooms are crammed with prints and
old photos, tiffany lamps, lace cloths, pot
plants, books and magazines. Jazz plays
softly in the relaxed and cosy restaurant
with its sloping, beamed ceilings and low
lighting; a fire crackles in the grate in winter. Food is served under a pergola looking
on to open fields in summer.

Via Cairoli 29, 44100 Ferrara

Tel 0532 211100 **e-mail**
info@borgonuovo.com
website www.borgonuovo.com

Nearby Castello d'Estense;
Palazzo del Comune; cathedral
Location in pedestrian zone in
the centre of Ferrara; with car
parking (cars may be brought
to the hotel)
Food breakfast
Price €
Rooms 4 single, double and
twin, 2 apartments for 2-5, all
with bath, one with kitchenette; all rooms have phone,
TV, air conditioning, minibar,
safe, hairdrier
Facilities sitting room, breakfast room, patio garden **Credit
cards** AE, MC, V
Disabled not suitable **Pets**
accepted **Closed** never
Proprietor Filippo Orlandini

Locanda Borgonuovo
Town bed-and-breakfast

A surprising find right in the heart of
this old walled city, on which the
noble d'Este family (which held sway from
the late 13th century until 1598) has left a
lasting impression, this is a most welcome
place to stay, and makes a pleasant change
from normally characterless city-centre
accommodation. It's a genuine, family-run
private bed-and-breakfast, with four simple rooms available in the house – built
inside the walls of a 15thC monastery – of
its friendly owners, the Orlandinis.

The four bedrooms are soberly furnished with antiques; one has a kitchenette. In fine weather generous, home-
made breakfasts are served on the outdoor patio; in cooler weather you eat at a
table in the Orlandinis' own living room.
Advice is on hand about how to spend
your time in Ferarra, and bicycles are provided free of charge. The Locanda
Borgonuovo has a superb location, a few
yards from the Castello Estense and the
cathedral. Your hosts can also recommend
the best places to eat – restaurants, *trattorie* and *osterie*, and they have discount
agreements with some restaurants and
shops, as well as with the local golf course.
'Signora Orlandini is charming, full of fascinating information about Ferrara...and
she serves a brilliant breakfast', runs a
recent accolade.

Vicolo del Voltino 11, 44100 Ferrara

Tel 0532 20 69 81
e-mail info@locandadelladuchessi-na.it
website www.locandadelladuchessi-na.it

Nearby Mantova, Bologna
Ravenna
Location in town centre; parking
Food breakfast
Price €€-€€€
Rooms 5, all with bath/shower
Facilities garden, fitness centre, bicycles, kitchen for guests' use, restaurant
Credit cards AE, DC, MC, V
Disabled no special facilities
Closed August
Manager Evelina Bonzagni

Loc. della Duchessina
Town hotel

Pink. Blue. Pretty pastel shades. Lacey curtains. We don't often see such an effusion of feminine taste. Some of the bedrooms could almost have been decorated for a new baby, so sweetly co-ordinated and perfect it all is. Tiles in the gleaming bathrooms pick up the colour schemes of the bedrooms. Beware of bringing a boyfriend or husband here if he's in a bad mood: the dominant femininity might make it worse.

Seriously though, this relatively new address (opened in 2000) in Ferrara is definitely worth trying. It is in a charming little alley off Via Palestro, there's a pleasant small garden, and considering the standards of decoration and service, prices are pretty fair. It is the latest in Evelina Bonzagni's collection of character hotels in Ferrara, certainly the most intimate and home-like. Reports welcome.

Via Roma 38, 47837
Montegridolfo, Rimini

Tel 0541 855350
e-mail
montegridolfo@mobygest.it
website
www.montegridolfo.com

Nearby Pesaro (18 km);
Urbino (25 km); Rimini (28
km); beaches (15 km).
Location 30 km SW of Pesaro;
take the Urbino road from
Montecchio; in centre of village with parking outside walls
Food breakfast, lunch, dinner
Price €€-€€€€€
Rooms 23; 8 suites in castle, 7
doubles in annexe, 8 apartment
for 2-6; all have bath or shower, phone, air conditioning,
minibar **Facilities** restaurants,
bar, sitting rooms, garden, pool
Credit cards AE, DC, MC, V
Disabled not suitable **Pets**
accepted **Closed** never
Manager Giuliano Tassinari

Palazzo Viviani
Converted castle

Montegridolfo is a beautifully renovated hilltop hamlet dating from the
13th century, only 20 kms from the mad-
ness of the Adriatic coast, but light years
away in terms of atmosphere. Fashion
designer Alberta Ferretti took six years to
painstakingly restore the characteristic
pale stone buildings and cobbled streets,
opening the hotel in 1994.

At the centre is the castle, Palazzo
Viviani, housing eight luxurious suites, all
furnished with fine antiques; the grandest
is frescoed and has a canopied four poster.
The decoration fully respects the *palazzo's*
origins, while evocative lighting enhances
the beauty of the building. The adjacent
Casa del Pittore contains seven more
modest rooms, while some of the village
houses have been converted into self-
catering apartments. Breakfast is served in
the old *limonaia* of the castle or, in warm
weather, on the panoramic ramparts. For
other meals, there are four eateries (some
closed in winter) within the ancient walls
which offer anything from pizza or bread
and cheese to the more sophisticated
dishes based on regional specialities
served in the wine cellars of the castle.
Concerts and other events are pro-
grammed throughout the year.

Via IV Novembre 41, 48100
Ravenna

Tel 0544 219813
e-mail info@albergocappello.it
website www.albergocappello.it

Nearby Bologna, Rimini, Ferrara
Location in city centre, parking 150
m from hotel E13.00
Food breakfast, dinner, lunch
Price €€€
Rooms 7; 2 standard doubles, 3 jun-
ior suites and 2 suites, all with pri-
vate bathroom with shower or tub,
mini bar, air conditioning, tele-
phone, TV.
Facilities wine bar, sitting room,
restaurant, lift/elevator
Credit cards AE, DC, MC, V
Disabled access difficult
Pets small dogs accepted
Closed never
Proprietors Cappello Srl

Albergo Cappello
Town hotel

This unique place – a 14thC *palazzo* –
was restored, no expense spared,
some years ago by a wealthy Italian indus-
trialist. When he died, two imaginative
entrepreneurs turned it into a mixture of
cultutral centre, art gallery, restaurant and
hotel. It has only 7 rooms and suites situated on the top floors off a frescoed hall. 'I
stayed one night and found the decoration
so sophisticated' reports a Japanese visitor, responding to the large reception
area, the ornate wood panelled ceilings
and the individually designed bedrooms in
minimalist style (muted colours, in order
not to clash with the original architectural
features). Another (American) visitor
responded very differently, calling it a
'gloomy palazzo'. Of course, not everyone
likes historic buildings, but we think it's
atmospheric, rather than gloomy. 'My husband and I enjoyed our stay' says another
more balanced report, 'but our expectations were not over the top.' It's clean, and
the service is helpful, and you can have dinner in the courtyard. We've included it for
the first time in this new edition of the
guide not least because it's not a hotel in
the conventional sense of running a 24-
hour front desk – you let yourself back in
after dinner with the key provided.

Soragna

Via Roma 7, 47010 Portico di
Romagna, Forlì

Tel 0543 967053
e-mail
info@vecchioconvento.it
website www.vecchioconven-
to.it

Nearby Faenza (46 km);
Ravenna (70 km); Florence (80
km).
Location 30 km SE of Forlì, in
village; with limited garage
parking
Food breakfast, lunch, dinner
Price €
Rooms 15; 12 double and
twin, 9 with shower, 3 single, 2
with shower; all rooms have
phone
Facilities sitting room, dining
room, breakfast room, bar, terrace **Credit cards** AE, DC, V
Disabled access difficult **Pets**
accepted **Closed** never
Proprietors Marisa Raggi and
Giovanni Cameli

Al Vecchio Convento
Converted monastery

Portico di Romagna is a sleepy medieval
village centred on a single paved street
– the location of the Vecchio Convento.
The house was built in 1840 and converted in the mid-1980s into a hotel – with
panache that comes as a surprise in this
quiet backwater.

The dining room, at the back of the
house, is the main focus. With its beamed,
pitched ceiling, tiled floor and open fireplace, it has a stylishly rustic air. There is
also a stone-flagged family sitting room,
with piano, card table, books and games,
but in practice your sitting is more likely
to be done on the small terrace outside
the front door; the bar, just inside the
door, offers standing room only.

A severe stone staircase leads up to the
bedrooms. Here, the decoration is
again plain and classy – but set against that
is some glorious antique furniture. The
beds are particularly notable – we've
rarely seen such a collection of elaborate
pieces. Most rooms are adequately spacious, though some bathrooms at the top
of the house have outrageously low ceilings. Signor Cameli cooks traditional dishes with flair – even his chips are a herby
delight – while Marisa leads diners through
the day's choices with great good humour.
Sumptuous breakfasts, served with home-
made preserves.

Bologna

Art Hotel Commercianti
Town hotel

As its name suggests, Art Hotel Commercianti caters primarily for the business market, but in a city with few tourist hotels it is a useful place to know about, and several recent visitors have been impressed. It has an excellent position – right in the heart of things, just off Bologna's main square, next to a smart pedestrian shopping street. The hotel exudes an air of efficiency rather than notable character ('rooms aren't particularly memorable but they are very comfortable', says one reporter). The hotel makes a good central base. There is no restaurant – just a café-like breakfast room. Although the hotel is situated in a traffic-free zone, guests can gain access by car in order to park in the hotel's garage.

Via Pignattari 11, 40124 Bologna

Tel 051 7457511
e-mail commercianti@inbo.it
website www.bolognarthotels.it
Food breakfast
Price €€€
Closed never
Proprietor Serena Orsi

Busseto

I Due Foscari
Town hotel

It is hard to believe that this Gothic building is in fact only a few decades old, so convincing are its beamed ceilings, heavy antiques and iron candelabras. The hotel is situated on a fine *piazza* in the gentle city of Busseto, home town of Guiseppe Verdi, and also of the illustrious tenor, Carlo Bergonzi, who opened the hotel in 1965. Today it is run by his son, Marco, along with Roberto Morsia, with chef Enrico Piazzi in charge of the kitchen. The *raison d' être* of the place is its traditional restaurant (with terrace). As for wine, the restaurant boasts one of those amazing cellars which you can visit, stocked with more than 750 wines, from humble country bottles to the finest vintages. Bedrooms have been refurbished.

Piazza Carlo Rossi 15, 43011 Busseto, Parma

Tel 0524 930031
e-mail info@iduefoscari.it
website www.iduefoscari.it
Food breakfast, lunch, dinner
Price €
Closed restaurant closed Mon, 3rd week Aug
Proprietors Marco Bergonzi and Roberto Morsia

Reggio'Emilia

Piazza del Monte 2, 42100
Reggio Emilia

Tel 0522 432944
e-mail info@hotelposta.re.it
website www.hotelposta.re.it
Food breakfast
Price €€€
Closed 2 weeks Aug, 1 week
Christmas **Proprietor** Mr
Umberto Sidoli

Posta
Town hotel

Although on the large side for this guide, we draw attention to this city centre hotel for its splendid rococo interior. Built in 1280, the *palazzo* has an austere façade decorated with frescoed coats of arms, but the interior is altogether a different story. Best is the bar, whose fittings and furniture were transferred here from a famous 19thC *pasticceria* in nearby Via Emilia more than 30 years ago. Surprisingly for the hotel's size, there is no restaurant; breakfast is taken in a little stucco-decorated hall under a skylight on the first floor. Bedrooms, all different, are prettily decorated, and are well equipped, with comfortable bathrooms. The hotel has undergone extensive restoration recently – more reports please.

Soragno

Via Garibaldi 64, 43019
Soragna, Parma

Tel 0524 597100
e-mail
info@locandadellupo.com
website
www.locandadellupo.com
Food breakfast, lunch, dinner
Price €€
Closed Christmas
Proprietor Signor Dioni

Locanda del Lupo
Town hotel

Built by the princely Meli Lupi family whose fortress-castle dominates this quiet little Po Valley town, the 18thC Locanda del Lupo has a timeless air, especially in the series of dining rooms which makes up its noted restaurant. Like the rest of the hotel, they are simply decorated, yet remain rather grand, with beamed ceilings, terracotta floors, antiques, old fireplaces and pans hanging on whitewashed walls.

The air of quiet refinement is continued through the formal sitting room and the handsome bedrooms. These are mostly spacious, with heavily beamed ceilings and tiled floors, and furnished with antiques. We've received several negative comments about the staff, who speak very little English and are not 'especially friendly.' Another visitor, however, commented that the waiter was kind and very helpful with the menu.

Area introduction

No other region of Italy is as rich in good small hotels as Tuscany. Florence itself is brimming with fine places to stay. We have at last found entries in Pisa and Lucca (towns that have hitherto lacked the sort of accomodation that appeals to us). However, it is in the countryside that the greatest number of new places have opened (many of them 'agriturismi' - properties which earn a certain percentage of their income from the land - or 'B & Bs'); it seems that round every bend in the Tuscan countryside there is a notice indicating a place to lay your head. The problem is that many of these are mediocre to say the least, but we have tried to seek out some of the best and have come up with such gems as **Villa Il Poggiale** near San Casciano Val di Pesa and **Relais San Pietro a Polvano** near Castiglion Fiorentino. Of course, there is not room to give all the worthy place full entries, but we also liked the look of the following; **Podere Casato**, Castelnuovo Berardenga (tel 0577 352002), **Palazzo di Luglio**, Sansepolcro (tel 0575 750026) and the **Corte dei papi**, near Cortona (tel 0575 614109).

Along the coast itself, finding welcoming places to stay is more difficult although we have recommendations in Pietrasanta and Pugnano. Another possibility, if you want to sample up-market Italian beach culture in chic Forte dei Marmi is the friendly **Franceschi** (tel 0584 787114) which has a good restaurant. A little further south, in Livorno, you might consider the **Villa Godilonda** (tel 0564 835133), a spotless, modest seaside hotel near two sandy beaches. Right down south, on Monte Argentario, is the smart, spectacularly positioned **Torre di Cala Piccola** (tel 0586 670266) with its own beach while, in pretty Orbetello is the elegant **Relais San Biagio** (tel 0564 860543). Go inland a bit, and there is more choice, especially in the lovely Maremma area. We can recommend the **Podere Le Mezzelune** at Bibbonna (0586 670266) and the **Tenuta La Bandita** at Sassetta (page 207). There is also the **Pereti Country House** (0564 569671), a delightful renovated farmhouse (serving excellent food) immersed in spectacular countryside near Roccatederighi, down towards Grosseto.

The Tuscan island of Elba is big enough to absorb the many summer visitors it attracts without being swamped, although there are few charming small hotels here. There is one hotel which we do not feature in the guide but can recommend: **Capo Sud** (tel 0565 964021) is a complex of small modern villas, scattered among the trees at Lacona, a rather remote part of the island. There is a pool and a private beach. Or get away from it all at the lovely new addition **Pardini's Hermitage** (page 204) on the island of Giglio where a simple, house party atmosphere prevails (meals all together at a big table) and which can only be reached by boat from the main port.

Albinia

Località Parrina
Km 146 Via Aurelia
58010 Albinia, Grosseto

Tel 0564 865586
e-mail info@parrina.it
website www.parrina.it

Nearby Grosseto (35km), beaches, Parco dell' Uccellina nature reserve.
Location Off the SS Aurelia, 35 kms south of Grosseto
Food breakfast; lunch and dinner on request
Price €€
Rooms 3 suites, 9 doubles and 4 apartments sleeping 4 people each all with bath. All have hairdrier, rooms have air conditioning.
Facilities sitting room, restaurant, terrace, garden, pool, mountain bikes, horse riding (nearby)
Credit Cards DC, EC, MC, V
Disabled not suitable
Pets accepted willingly!
Closed never
Proprietors Marchesa Franca Spinola

La Parrina
Country villa

L a Parrina is a large farm and *agriturismo* estate which lies on the wide plain between the Argentario peninsula and the undulating farmland of the southern Maremma. Haunt of chic Italian yachties and very crowded in high summer, 'L'Argentario' boasts what is arguably Tuscany's most beautiful coastline and cleanest sea and yet it is close to one of the remotest areas of the region where ancient towns like Pitigliano sit dramatically on tufa outcrops.

The farm shop at La Parrina is popular with both locals and visitors who flock there to buy organic fruit and veg, olive oil, cheeses and excellent wines. It is approached up a long, dusty road lined with lofty eucalyptus trees; at the end is a sprawling old villa and farm complex which has gradually been built up to become a thriving business.

Guest accommodation is by no means luxurious, but rooms are comfortable and done out in pretty country style; you can choose between a B&B arrangement or a self-catering apartment.

The villa backs on to a lovely garden via a long, shady veranda which makes a tempting spot from which to while away hot summer afternoons if you don't want to battle with the crowds at the beach.

Viale Papa Giovanni XXIII,
59015 Artimino, Firenze

Tel 055 875141
e-mail hotel@artimino.com
website www.artimino.com

Nearby Prato (15 km);
Florence (24 km); Etruscan
museum.
Location 24 km NW of
Florence; car parking
Food breakfast, lunch, dinner
Price €€
Rooms 36 double and twin
with bath or shower, 1 single
with shower; all rooms have
phone, TV, air conditioning,
minibar; 44 apartments in
village with own pool
Facilities sitting room, break-
fast room, TV room, restau-
rant, garden, swimming pool,
tennis
Credit cards AE, DC, MC, V
Disabled ground floor rooms
Pets accepted **Closed** 10 days
Christmas-New Year **Manager**
Alessandro Gualtieri

Paggeria Medicea
Country hotel

Artimino is a village of some distinction, drawing visitors to see its museum and nearby Etruscan tombs. It also has
a number of imposing buildings, one being
a grand villa built by Ferdinand I of Medici
in the 16th century, who was struck by the
beauty of the surroundings. Now the outbuildings and servants' quarters of this
villa have been converted into an elegant
and peaceful hotel.

As befits its aristocratic pedigree, the
atmosphere is classy, but unshowy.
Furnishings are a stylish, unpretentious
mix of new and old, and original features
such as sloping rafters, chimneys and ceilings have, where possible, been retained
both in bedrooms and in public areas.

A short walk across manicured lawns
brings you to the restaurant Biagio
Pignatta (named after a celebrated Medici
chef). Its specialities are Tuscan dishes 'with
a Renaissance flavour' (*pappardelle sul
coniglio*, for instance – broad noodles with
rabbit sauce), served on a terrace overlooking hillsides of vines and olives. The
estate produces its own wine, which is
reverently decanted at your table.

Castellina in Chianti

Via Chiantigiana 29, 53011
Castellina in Chianti, Siena

Tel 0577 740444
e-mail info@albergoilcolom-
baio.it
website www.albergoilcolom-
baio.it

Nearby Siena (20 km);
Florence (40 km); San
Gimignano (30 km).
Location just N of Castellina
in Chianti; car parking
Food breakfast
Price €
Rooms 15 double with bath or
shower; all rooms have phone,
TV, hairdrier
Facilities sitting room, break-
fast room, garden, swimming
pool
Credit cards AE, DC, MC, V
Disabled access possible
Pets not accepted
Closed never
Manager Roberta Baldini

Il Colombaio
Country hotel

A new addition to the typically Tuscan farmhouse hotels that cluster around Castellina in Chianti, Il Colombaio is a successful example of a proven formula, and prices are still very reasonable. As you come from Greve in Chianti on the busy Chiantigiana road (SS 222), you will notice Il Colombaio on the right sur-rounded by lawns, shrubs and trees. Stone-built and capped with the tiled roofs at odd angles to one another so characteristic of Tuscany, the house has a pleasing aspect. It is, however, rather close to the road.

The restoration has been carried out with attention to detail, using country fur-niture to complement the rustic style of the building. The sitting room, which used to be the farm kitchen, is spacious and light with beamed ceilings, a traditional open fireplace and, in the corner, the old stone sink now filled with house plants. Breakfast is served in a small stone-vault-ed room on the terrace.

The bedrooms have all been furnished with wrought-iron beds and old-fashioned dressing tables; all have modern bath-rooms.

The lack of restaurant is not a problem as there are plenty of good eateries in the surrounding area.

Castellina in Chianti

Loc. Le Piazze, 53011
Castellina in Chianti, Siena

Tel 0577 743190
e-mail lepiazze@bonini.it
website
www.locandalepiazze.it

Nearby Siena (27 km);
Florence (50 km).
Location 6 km W of
Castellina in Chianti; car park-
ing
Food breakfast; lunch and din-
ner on request
Price €€€
Rooms 20 double and twin
with bath or shower; all rooms
have phone
Facilities sitting room, break-
fast room, bar, terraces, garden,
swimming pool **Credit cards**
AE, DC, MC, V
Disabled one specially adapted
room
Pets quiet dogs accepted by
arrangement
Closed Nov-April **Proprietor**
Maureen Skelly Bonini

Le Piazze
Country hotel

A welcome addition to the booming
hotel scene in the area around
Castellina in Chianti which, we feel, has the
edge on many of its competitors. Although
only 6 km from the bustling town, the
hotel is in completely secluded countryside reached by a long unsurfaced road
which seems to go on forever.

The hotel is, needless to say, a converted 17thC farmhouse, but in this case the
owners have deployed more imagination
and a greater sense of elegance than
usual. The buffet breakfast, for instance, is
served on tiled sideboards in a room
adjacent to the kitchen and separated
from it by a glass partition. Or you can
remove yourself to any of the numerous
terraces that surround the house for
uninterrupted views of classical Chianti
countryside.

Rustic antiques have, of course, been
used in the furnishing with the usual terracotta, exposed beams and white plaster,
but here and there the pattern is broken
by pieces from Indonesia. Bedrooms are
individually furnished with lavish use of
striped fabrics (avoid those in the roof
space – they can become unbearably hot);
bathrooms are large, with Jacuzzis or
walk-in showers big enough for a party.

Castellina in Chianti

Via Fiorentina, 53011
Castellina in Chianti, Siena

Tel 0577 740484
e-mail info@hotelsalivolpi.com
website
www.hotelsalivolpi.com

Nearby Siena (21 km); San
Gimignano (31 km); Florence
(45 km).
Location 500 m outside town,
on road to San Donato in
Poggio; car parking
Food breakfast
Price €
Rooms 19 double and twin
with bath or shower; all rooms
have phone
Facilities sitting room, break-
fast room, garden, swimming
pool
Credit cards MC, V
Disabled no special facilities
Pets not accepted
Closed never
Proprietor Angela Orlandi

Salivolpi
Country guesthouse

For no immediately obvious reason, the
unremarkable Chianti village of
Castellina contains a cluster of Tuscany's
most appealing hotels. This welcome addition to the catalogue, open since 1983,
offers a much cheaper alternative to its
two illustrious neighbours – Tenuta de
Ricavo (page 136) and Villa Casalecchi. It
occupies two well-restored farm buildings
and one new bungalow in a peaceful open
position on the edge of the village – sup-
posedly the location of the ancient
Etruscan Castellina – affording broad
views across the countryside.

There is a Spanish feel to the older of
the houses – iron fittings, exposed beams,
white walls, ochre tiles – and the spacious
rooms are both neat and stylish, with
some splendid old beds and other
antiques. The whole place is well cared for,
and has a calm, relaxed atmosphere.

The garden is impeccably tended, with
plenty of space, some furniture and a fair-
sized swimming pool. Breakfast ('*molto
abbondante*', claims the boss) is served in a
crisp little room in the smaller of the
houses, and although it is the only meal
provided, there is no shortage of restaurants nearby.

Castellina in Chianti

Loc. Ricavo 4, 53011
Castellina in Chianti, Siena

Tel 0577 740221
e-mail ricavo@ricavo.com
website www.ricavo.com

Nearby Siena (22 km);
Florence (45 km).
Location 4 km N of Castellina
in Chianti; car parking
Food breakfast, lunch (in summer); dinner
Prices €€€ 3-day minimum stay in high season
Rooms 23; 13 double and
twin, 2 single, 8 suites, all with
bath or shower; all rooms have
phone, TV, minibar, safe
Facilities sitting rooms, bar,
restaurant, terrace, gym, garden, 2 swimming pools, table
tennis **Credit cards** MC, V
Disabled ground floor rooms
available **Pets** not accepted
Closed Nov to Easter; restaurant closed Sun **Proprietors**
Christina Lobrano-Scotoni and
Alessandro Lobrano

Tenuta di Ricavo
Country hotel

If away from it all is where you want to
get – while retaining the possibility of
doing some serious sightseeing – Ricavo is
hard to beat. The hotel occupies an entire
hamlet, which was deserted in the 1950s
when people left the land for the cities in
search of work.

The grouping of houses along a wooded
ridge in the depth of the countryside
might have been conceived as a film-set
replica of a medieval hamlet. The main
house, facing a little square of other mellow stone cottages, contains some of the
bedrooms, and the several sitting rooms,
which are comfortably furnished with a
pleasant jumble of antique chairs and sofas
(one of them with a small library of
English, Italian, French and German books).
The hotel's restaurant, La Pecora Nera
('The Black Sheep'), is open to non-resi-
dents so advance booking is essential.

Breakfast can be taken out-of-doors, on
a little piazzetta at the front. At the right
time of the year the gardens are bright
with flowers, and there are plenty of
secluded corners, which make the place
seem calm and quiet even when the hotel
is full. The small garden pool is ideal for
quiet cooling off.

A visitor pronounces the hotel 'expensive, but professional and worth it', and the
food 'very satisfactory'.

Castelnuovo Berardenga

Loc. Borgo San Felice, 53019
Castelnuovo Berardenga, Siena

Tel 0577 359260/396561
e-mail info@borgosanfelice.it
website
www.borgosanfelice.com

Nearby Siena (17 km).
Location 17 km NE of Siena
in former estate village; car
parking
Food breakfast, lunch, dinner
Prices €€€€
Rooms 43; 24 double and
twin, 4 single, 15 suites, all
with bath or shower; all rooms
have phone, TV, minibar, air
conditioning, hairdrier, safe
Facilities sitting rooms, conference rooms, billiards room,
restaurant, beauty centre, gym,
swimming pool, tennis, bowls,
putting and pitching green
Credit cards AE, DC, MC, V
Disabled access difficult
Pets not accepted
Closed Nov-Apr
Manager Birgit Fleig

Relais Borgo S. Felice
Hilltop hotel

Borgo San Felice is larger than most of
the entries in this guide, but we include
it in the guide without hesitation. It is a
carefully renovated hilltop hamlet – like a
collection of charming small hotels.
Surrounded by cypresses and the vineyards of the renowned San Felice estate,
the peaceful village feels as if it has been
suspended in time: no intrusive neon signs,
no lines of cars, just the original Tuscan
qualities of perfectly proportioned space
setting off simple buildings of brick and
stone, and topped by a jumble of terracotta roofs. Even the swimming pool (which in
these parts all too often resembles a gap-
ing, blue gunshot wound) has been discreetly tucked away. Gravel paths, carved
well heads, pergolas, lemon trees in gigan-
tic terracotta pots, a church, a bell tower
and a chapel – this is the real Tuscany.

All the original features of the various
buildings have been retained: vaulted brick
ceilings, imposing fireplaces, old tiled
floors. The furniture is a stylish mixture of
old and modern and the sitting rooms are
full of intimate alcoves. An elegant restaurant completes the picture. Top of the
range – with prices to match.

Castiglion Fiorentino

Loc.Polvano 3, 52043
Castiglion Fiorentino, Arezzo

Tel 0575 650100 **e-mail**
polvano@technet.it
website www.polvano.com

Nearby Cortona (20 km);
Arezzo (25 km); Lake
Trasimeno (20 km).
Location 10 km east of
Castiglion Fiorentino in own
grounds with parking
Food breakfast, dinner
Prices €€€
Rooms 10; 4 doubles, 1 single,
5 suites, all with bath or show-
er; all rooms have phone, air
conditioning (suites and 2 dou-
bles), hairdrier
Facilities sitting rooms,
restaurant, breakfast room, ter-
race, garden, swimming pool
Credit cards AE, MC, V
Disabled no special facilities
Pets not accepted
Closed Nov-end Mar
Proprietor Luigi Protti

S. Pietro in Polvano
Country hotel

Situated in the hills above Castiglion
Fiorentino, Polvano is a tiny hamlet
comprising a clutch of buildings including
this solid stone farmhouse, purchased and
restored by the Prottis on retirement and
opened as a small hotel in 1998 which they
run with their family.

The house has been renovated with
good taste and a modern, clean touch
which does not in any way detract from
the inherent rustic charateristics of the
building (beamed ceilings, bricked archways, terracotta floors and so on). Solid
country furniture goes well with sofas
upholstered in pale cream fabric, wicker
arm chairs and bright, oriental rugs; two
comfortble sitting rooms have open fireplaces. The bedrooms, with their wrought-
iron bed heads and white covers, have a
similarly uncluttered feel. In cool weather,
food is served in the cosy former stables,
but in summer you can eat on the wide,
partially covered terrace that runs along
one side of the building from which views
of the open, unspoiled countryside, are
stunning. Antonietta and her daughter in
law are in charge of the food which, we
have heard, is excellent.

This is a delightful place where the
emphasis really is on peace and tranquility;
there are no TV's and children under 12
are discouraged.

Convento di San Francesco,
53040 Cetona, Siena

Tel 0578 238015
e-mail frateria@fbcc.it
website www.mondox.it

Nearby Pienza (40 km);
Montepulciano (26 km);
Montalcino (64 km).
Location 26 km S of
Montepulciano; car parking
Food breakfast, lunch, dinner
Price €€€
Rooms 7; 5 double, 2 suites, all
with bath or shower; all rooms
have phone, air conditioning,
minibar, hairdrier
Facilities sitting rooms,
restaurant, terrace, garden
Credit cards AE, MC, V
Disabled no special facilities
Pets not accepted
Closed Jan; restaurant Tue in
winter
Manager Maria Grazia Daolio

La Frateria
Converted convent

One of the more unusual entries in this guide and not a hotel in the strict sense but a place of hospitality run by a community that has withdrawn from the world. The buildings, grouped around a hillside church founded in 1212 by St Francis, built of light, golden stone, form a rambling complex. Only seven rooms and suites are available, so, even when it is fully booked, one never has the sensation of being in a busy hotel. There is no swimming pool and none of the rooms has a television.

This may sound monastic, but the setting and furnishings are of the same standard as a top-class hotel: antiques, paintings and colourful wooden carvings (generally religious in theme) and spacious rooms with stone and beige stucco walls. The restaurant is unexpectedly sophisticated (and expensive), serving a mixture of refined and hearty food using fresh produce from the gardens.

A quiet stroll around the monastery with its church and chapel, cloisters and courtyards, and hushed, peaceful atmosphere will help you realize why the young people of this community want to share their peace.

Chianciano Terme

Strada della Vittoria 63, 53042
Chianciano Terme, Siena

Tel 0578 69101
e-mail info@lafoce.com
website www.lafoce.com

Nearby Pienza (20 km);
Montepulciano (10 km).
Location 5 km SW of
Chianciano Terme (follow
signs for Monte Amiata and
Cassia); car parking.
Food dinner on request
Price appartment sleeping 2
people € weekly rates from
£700; minimum rent 1 week
Rooms 9 self-catering apart-
ments/houses sleeping 2-14, all
with bath and shower; all
apartments/houses have phone,
TV on request
Facilities terraces, garden,
pools, tennis, children's play-
ground **Credit cards** MC, V
Disabled 2 specially adapted
rooms **Pets** not accepted
Closed never **Proprietors**
Benedetta and Donata Origo

La Foce
Country apartments

Anyone who is familiar with the writing of Iris Origo will be particularly inter-ested in La Foce, the estate whose history during the Second World War is so vividly described in her book, *War in the Val d'Orcia*. Iris died in 1988, but her family still lives on the property in this remote but strangely beautiful corner of Tuscany, run-ning it as a working farm.

Several of the buildings on the large estate have been converted into superior self-catering accommodation, ranging from the delightful two-person Bersagliere to superb and quite grand Montauto which sleeps ten; the latter stands in its own extensive garden with lavender borders and a small pool.

Furnishings throughout the comfortable apartments are in sophisticated and taste-ful country style, predominantly antique, but with a few well-chosen modern pieces. There is plenty of colour, provided by bright rugs, cushions and cheerful fabrics. Each has its own piece of private garden and the use of a pool. Music lovers will appreciate the excellent chamber music festival which takes place on the estate each July.

Loc. San Martino, 52044
Cortona, Arezzo

Tel 0575 612 679
e-mail info@ilfalconiere.it
website www.ilfalconiere.com

Nearby Cortona (3 km);
Arezzo (29 km); Lake
Trasimeno (10 km).
Location just outside Cortona
overlooking Valdichiana; car
parking
Food breakfast, lunch, dinner
Price €€€€ **Rooms** 19;
13 double, 6 suites, all with
bath or shower; all rooms have
phone, TV, air conditioning,
minibar, hairdrier, safe
Facilities restaurant, garden,
swimming pools (May-Sep)
Credit cards AE, DC, V
Disabled no special facilities
Pets accepted
Closed early Jan to mid-Feb
Proprietors Riccardo Baracchi
and Silvia Regi

Il Falconiere
Country villa

The plain surrounding Lake Trasimeno,
over which Il Falconiere looks, was
once the scene of some of Hannibal's
fiercest battles against the Romans.
Nowadays, however, Il Falconiere is a
haven of civilized living. Reached through
quiet country lanes, bordered by vineyards
the main villa (built in the 17th century
around an earlier fortified tower) is set in
landscaped grounds of olives, rosemary
hedges, fruit trees and roses, which also
contain the old lemon house (now a
Michelin-starred restaurant) and the still-
functioning chapel with an adjoining suite.
Meticulous attention has been given to
every aspect of decoration, from *trompe-
l'oeil* number scrolls outside each room to
the hand-embroidered window-hangings
and finest bed linen. Persian rugs and handsome antiques rest easily on uneven, original terracotta floors. In the pigeon-loft of
the old tower, reached by a narrow, stone
spiral staircase, is a small bedroom with an
unsurpassed view of the Valdichiana. A villa
nearby has recently been converted to
create eight new bedrooms with their
own breakfast room and pool. The estate
produces its own excellent wine and olive
oil and cooking courses are organised too.
A recent report praises the hotel unequiv-
ocally: 'Everything combines to make this
one of the most stylish hotels in Italy.'

Via Guelfa 15, 52044 Cortona, Arezzo

Tel 0575 604348
e-mail info@hotelsanmichele.net
website www.hotelsan-michele.net

Nearby Diocesan Museum, Arezzo (29 km); Perugia (51 km).
Location in middle of town; garage nearby
Food breakfast
Price €€
Rooms 43; 40 double and twin and 3 suites, all with bath or shower; all rooms have phone, TV, minibar, air conditioning, hairdrier
Facilities sitting room, breakfast room, conference room
Credit cards AE, DC, MC, V
Disabled access possible
Pets small dogs accepted
Closed mid-Jan to early Mar
Proprietor Paolo Alunno

San Michele
Town hotel

It might sound like an easy matter to turn a fine 16thC Renaissance palace into a hotel of character, but we have seen too many examples of good buildings that have been brutalized by excessive and unwanted luxury, over-modernization and an almost wilful blindness to the original style, not to be delighted when the job has been properly done.

The Hotel San Michele has steered a precise course between the twin dangers of unwarranted adventurousness and lame timidity. White plaster and stark beams are complemented with rich modern fabrics; sofas of the finest leather stand on terracotta floors that seem glazed with a rich wax. Carefully-placed lights emphasize the gracefully interlocking curves of the cortile. The common rooms are full of such stylish features as frescoed friezes and immense carved stone fireplaces.

The bedrooms are more modest in style, with wrought-iron beds and rustic antiques; one report states that they are in need of refurbishment while another says that hers was decidedly cramped. Some of the more spacious ones have an extra mezzanine to provide separate sleeping and sitting areas. A recent guest felt that the welcome was somewhat impersonal and that there was 'a faint shadow of the corporate feel' to this hotel.

Via Faentina – Loc. Feriolo,
50030 Polcanto, Firenze

Tel 055 8409749
e-mail info@casapalmira.it
website www.casapalmira.it

Nearby Florence (16 km);
Fiesole (9 km).
Location halfway between
Florence and Borgo San
Lorenzo just off the SS302, Via
Faentina (from Florence turn
right to Feriolo just past
Olmo); car parking
Food breakfast, dinner on
request **Price** € **Rooms** 6; 4
double and twins, 1 single, 1
triple, 5 with shower, 1 with
bath; rooms have hairdrier on
request **Facilities** sitting room,
breakfast/dining room, terraces, garden with barbecue,
hot tub **Credit cards** not
accepted **Disabled** access difficult **Pets** not accepted **Closed**
Jan-Feb **Proprietors** Assunta
Fiorini and Stefano Mattioli

Casa Palmira
Country guesthouse

Leaving Florence, the old Faenza road
winds through olive groves and
cypresses before reaching the beautiful
and relatively unknown area of the
Mugello, and continuing up and over the
Apennines. Casa Palmira is set just off this
road in an oasis of green, a converted barn
attached to a stone farmhouse with
medieval origins.

Stefano and Assunta, the warm and
charming hosts, have done a beautiful job
of converting the barn into a relaxed and
comfortable guesthouse. The ground floor
sitting room is spacious and welcoming,
with a huge fireplace, squashy sofas and
chairs, an open kitchen area where breakfast is prepared, and a dining area. Upstairs,
the bedrooms all lead off a lovely sunny
landing, and while the public areas have
terracotta flagstones, the bedrooms all
have beautiful chestnut wood floors made
by Stefano (who also made the doors and
some of the furniture). Pretty fabrics and
patchwork quilts complement warm-
coloured walls and dusty green paintwork.
There are mountain bikes and a Smart for
guests to hire and wonderful walking nearby. There is even a hot tub in the garden,
and plans are underway for a Turkish bath
and swimming pool. Who needs Florence?

Via B. da Maiano 4, 50014 Fiesole,
Firenze

Tel 055 59163
e-mail pensionebencista@iol.it

Nearby Roman amphitheatre;
cathedral; Florence.
Location 2.5 km S of Fiesole on
Florence road; in own grounds with
garage and car park
Food breakfast, light lunch, dinner
Price €€€
Rooms 40; 26 double and twin, 11
single, 3 suite, all with bath or show-
er; all rooms have phone, hairdrier
Facilities sitting rooms, dining
room, terrace, garden
Credit cards MC, V
Disabled one adapted room
Pets accepted
Closed sometimes Dec-Jan
Proprietor Simone Simoni

Bencistà
Country guesthouse

This quintessential family-run *pensione* has provoked both ecstatic and disappointed reports from readers who have either fallen for its slightly faded charms or found it too reminiscent of a boarding house. We love it. Once a monastery, it stands on a hillside overlooking Florence and the surrounding countryside; views from the flower-decked terrace (where breakfast is served in summer) and many of the bedrooms are unforgettable. Added to this are the delights of the building itself, a handsome hall, three salons almost entirely furnished with antiques (including a little reading room with shelves of books and a cosy fire), plus plenty of fascinating nooks and crannies.

No two bedrooms are alike, and each has some captivating feature – a beautiful view, a fine piece of furniture, a huge bathroom or a private terrace. They are nearly all old-fashioned, with plain whitewashed walls and solid antiques; the accent is on character rather than luxury.

The dining room is simple, light and spacious (somewhat reminiscent of a refectory), overlooking the beautiful gardens. The food is totally unpretentious and there is no choice; you will be served with the sort of meal that a Florentine family would eat. One reader complained strongly about dinner while another thought it 'delicious'.

Via Gramsci 52-56, 50014 Fiesole, Firenze

Tel 055 5978336
e-mail info@lecannelle.com
website www.lecannelle.com

Nearby Roman Amphitheatre; Florence (8 km).
Location on main street N of the main square; public car parking
Food breakfast
Price €€
Rooms 2 double, 1 single, 1 triple, 1 family, all with bath or shower; all **rooms** have phone, TV, air conditioning
Facilities breakfast room
Credit cards AE, MC, V
Disabled not suitable
Pets not accepted
Closed Jan-Feb
Proprietors Sara and Simona Corsi

Le Cannelle
Town bed-and-breakfast

Le Cannelle's young proprietors Sara and Simona Corsi, have a father with a building business, so who better to restore these two old townhouses on Fiesole's main street, a little way north of the main square. Once finished, he handed over the management of the little bed-and-breakfast to his two daughters who have enthusiastically set about their new activity since opening in November 1999.

The cool hills surrounding Fiesole are studded with spectacular villas, and many of the hotels in the area are correspondingly expensive. We are therefore pleased to include Le Cannelle as a low-cost, but charming, alternative. It has been carefully decorated in simple, yet comfortable style. Bedrooms are quite spacious and one even has a duplex with two single beds at the top. Two offer lovely views of the hills to the north. Those on the somewhat noisy street have double glazing. The blue-and-white bathrooms are spotless. The pretty room where Sara and Simona prepare breakfast is, unfortunately, right on the street.

Via del Trebbiolo 8, 50060 Molino del Piano, Firenze

Tel 055 8300098
e-mail iltrebbiolo@libero.it
website www.iltrebbiolo.com

Nearby Fiesole (7 km); Firenze (11 km); Mugello.
Location 7 km north of Fiesole on Olmo road; after 7 km turn right for Monteloro. in own grounds with parking
Food breakfast, lunch, dinner
Price €€
Rooms 23; 19 doubles and twins, 2 singles, 2 apartments, all with bath or shower; all rooms have phone, TV, hairdrier; rooms in villa have minibar; rooms in annexe have air conditioning
Facilities sitting rooms, bar, restaurant, breakfast room, terrace, garden, swimming pool
Credit cards AE, DC, MC, V
Disabled adapted rooms **Pets** accepted if small **Closed** never; restaurant Tues lunch and Mon
Proprietors Roberto Bartolini

Il Trebbiolo
Country Guest House

After a long period of closure and a change of management, Il Trebbiolo has re-opened in a more relaxed, less up-market guise than before. The simple, ochre-coloured villa dates from the 1400s; it stands on a quiet hillside north of Fiesole, surrounded by acres of woodland, vines and olives. A large gravel terrace in front of the house looks out on to open countryside.

The building is flanked by two arched loggias under which tables and chairs are grouped; food is served here in the summer. Inside, paintwork in restful colours provides a good backdrop for some handsome antiques and oriental rugs. A bright sitting room is at guests' disposal for cooler weather (in summer, everyone sits outdoors) while a welcoming fire is lit in the lemon-painted restaurant where you can sample local specialities. Half the bedrooms are housed in the main villa. While spacious and comfortable, with big tiled bathrooms, they are quite simply furnished. A smartly-converted annexe houses more bedrooms, a couple of which have kitchennettes.

The new, young owners are enthusiastic and eager to please; thier guest house is comfortable yet unpretentious and enjoys a totally peaceful setting. The visitor's book is full of praise for the welcome and food.

Via Doccia 4, 50014 Fiesole, Firenze

Tel 055 59451
e-mail reservations@villasan-michele.net
website
www.orient/expresshotels.com

Nearby Roman theatre; cathedral; monastery of San Francesco.
Location on Florence-Fiesole road, just below Fiesole; car parking
Food breakfast, lunch, dinner
Price €€€€€€
Rooms 40; 25 double and twin, 15 suites, all with bath; all rooms have phone, air conditioning; TV and minibar on request
Facilities reading room/bar, piano bar, dining room with loggia/terrace, garden, swimming pool (open Jun-Sep)
Credit cards AE, DC, MC, V
Disabled access possible **Pets** small dogs accepted
Closed late Nov to mid-Mar
Manager Maurizio Saccani

Villa San Michele
Country villa

According to its brochure, the villa was designed by Michelangelo – which perhaps accounts in part for the high prices. The rooms are among the most expensive in Italy – only a fraction less than those at the hotel's more swanky sister, the Cipriani in Venice – and beyond the reach of most of our readers. But the guide would be incomplete without this little gem on the peaceful hillside of Fiesole – originally a monastery, built in the early part of the 15th century, enlarged towards the end of it, and much expanded recently, with 13 extra suites.

What you get for your money is not extravagant decoration or ostentatious luxury, but restrained good taste and an expertly preserved aura of the past. The rooms are furnished mostly with solid antiques including 17thC masterpieces (religiously maintained every winter, we are told); many of the bedrooms have tiled floors of notable antiquity. Bathrooms, on the other hand, are impressively contemporary. Views from the villa are exceptional. One of the great delights of the place is to dine in the loggia, gazing down slopes of olives and cypresses to the city below. The pool terraces share this glorious view. Breakfast is an American buffet feast; half board includes an *à la carte* meal, lunch or dinner.

Via Romana 43, 50125 Firenze

Tel 055 222402
e-mail info@hotelannalena.it **website** www.annalena.it

Nearby Pitti Palace; Boboli Gardens; Ponte Vecchio; Santo Spiritoi.
Location south of the river, 3 minutes' walk S of the Pitti Palace; public car parking nearby
Food breakfast
Prices €€
Rooms 20; 16 double and twin, 4 single, all with bath or shower; all rooms have phone, TV, air conditioning, minibar, safe, hairdrier
Facilities sitting room/bar/breakfast room
Credit cards AE, DC, MC, V
Disabled no special facilities
Pets accepted
Closed never
Proprietor Icilio Marazzini

Annalena
Town Guest house

One of Florence's traditional *pensioni* and, in spite of new owners, still very much in the old style, the Annalena is located opposite the back entrance to the beautiful Boboli gardens. Many of the bedrooms look out on to a horticultural centre next door; the best give on to a long veranda Luckily, none have windows on the busy Via Romana.

The 14th century *palazzo* has an intriguing past involving, in its early days, the tragic Annalena (a young noblewoman) and, during the war, foreign refugees fleeing from Mussolini's police. Today, while no luxury hotel, the Annalena offers solid comforts not without a hint of style, and at resonable prices. The huge public room (serving as reception, bar, sitting and breakfast rooms) is a bit dreary, but the bedrooms are lovely: spacious and full of light from tall windows which take full advantage of views of the garden below and the picturesque backs of neighbouring houses. Smart new fabrics and a lick of paint have done wonders for rooms that had been allowed to get a little shabby.

Guests lucky enough to have a room with a terrace should order breakfast there: so much nicer than a rather cramped table in the airless 'salon'.

Via Cavour 13, 50129 Firenze

Tel 055 211686
e-mail info@casci.com
website www.hotelcasci.com

Nearby San Lorenzo; Magi chapel;
Medici chapels; duomo.
Location on busy street N of
duomo; paid car parking nearby
Food breakfast
Price €€
Rooms 26; 14 double and twin, 4
single, 8 family, 7 with bath, 19 with
shower; all rooms have phone, TV,
air conditioning, hairdrier
Facilities breakfast room, bar, lift
Credit cards AE, DC, MC, V
Disabled one specially adapted
room
Pets small ones accepted
Closed Jan
Proprietors Lombardi family

Casci
Town hotel

Music lovers may get a thrill from the fact that the 15thC *palazzo* which now houses this hotel once belonged to Giacomo Rossini. Located on a busy main road just north of San Lorenzo, the Casci is an unpretentious family-run hotel where you can be assured of the warmest of welcomes from the helpful Lombardis.

The decoration is modern and functional, but painted ceilings in some of the public areas give a clue to the age of the building. The open-plan reception area is bright, cheerful and always busy. The first thing our inspector noticed were two bookcases overflowing with guidebooks and leaflets for guests' use. To the right is the breakfast room, and to the left a bar/sitting area both of which have painted ceilings. The rooms vary in size and shape (some sleep five), and are fairly spartan, but quite attractive with pale yellow walls and modern green wooden furniture.

Many of the bathrooms are new; some have tubs and all have heated towel rails, an unexpected bonus in a two-star hotel. The most peaceful rooms look over a garden at the back of the building; others have double glazing.

Florence

Viale Machiavelli 25, 50125 Firenze

Tel 055 229351

Nearby Pitti Palace; Piazzale
Michelangelo; Museo La Specola.
Location in residential area 5 min-
utes' walk from Porta Romana; car
parking
Food breakfast
Price €€
Rooms 20; 17 double and twin, 2
single, 1 suite, all with bath or show-
er; all rooms have phone, TV, air
conditiong, safe, hairdrier
Facilities breakfast room, conserva-
tory, garden
Credit cards AE, DC, MC, V
Disabled no special facilities
Pets accepted
Closed 2 weeks Aug
Proprietor Corinne Kraft

Classic
Town hotel

Standing in its own lush garden and rubbing shoulders with some of the most
impressive residences in Florence, this
pink-washed villa is on a leafy avenue just
five minutes from Porta Romana, the old
gate into the south of the city. A private
residence until 1991, the house was rescued from decay and turned into a comfortable and friendly hotel which maintains
admirably reasonable prices.

Bedrooms vary in size, but all are fairly
spacious, with parquet floors, original plasterwork, antique furniture and pretty bedspreads. Two have frescoes, and another
hosts an impressive fireplace. The high ceilings on the first floor allow for a duplex
arrangement with extra space for beds or
sitting areas on a higher level, while top
floor rooms have sloping, beamed attic
ceilings and air conditioning. A romantic
annexe suite tucked away in the garden,
complete with tiny kitchen area, offers
extra privacy for the same price as a standard double.

In warmer weather, breakfast is served
outside under a pergola, but even in winter the conservatory allows for a sunny –
possibly even a warm – start to the day.

Florence

Vicolo Marzio 1, Piazza del Pesce,
50122 Firenze

Tel 055 287216
e-mail
florence@hermitagehotel.com
website
www.hermitagehotel.com

Nearby Uffizi; Ponte Vecchio.
Location in heart of city, facing
river; garage
Food breakfast, snacks
Prices €€€
Rooms 28 double and twin, 24 with
bath, 4 with shower; all rooms have
phone, TV, air conditioning, hairdri-
ers, safe
Facilities breakfast room, bar/sitting
room, roof terrace
Credit cards MC, V
Disabled access difficult
Pets small dogs accepted
Closed never
Proprietor Vincenzo Scarcelli

Hermitage
Town hotel

The location, just north of the Ponte
Vecchio, is highly central, and highly
favoured: few hotels this close to
Florence's main drag could be described as
peaceful, but this Lilliputian-scale retreat is
not inappropriately named. There is an air
of tranquillity about it – helped by a judi-
cious, although not always sufficient,
amount of double glazing on the busier
riverside aspect.

Everything about the Hermitage is
small, like a doll's house – only upside
down, with neat, graceful bedrooms on the
lower floors, while the reception desk and
public rooms are on the fifth floor, overlooking the Arno. Both bar-sitting room
and breakfast room are delightfully
domestic, in cool lemony yellows made
intimate with flowers and pictures.

The Hermitage was once no more than
one of the typical, older-style *pension* that
are becoming rare in Florence. But it has
had a marked facelift and is now more
tasteful, well-kept – and expensive – than
average. It also has touches of luxury; most
rooms have Jacuzzi baths or showers. A
flower-filled roof terrace offers views
across Florence's red rooftops, the tower
of the *Palazzo Vecchio* and the *Ponte Vecchio*.
A recent visitor was overwhelmed by this
lovely hotel, commenting that it is clear
why people return here year after year.

Via di Mezzo 20, 50121 Firenze

Tel 055 2345005
e-mail jandj@dada.it
website www.hoteljandj.com

Nearby Duomo; church of Santa Croce.
Location E of duomo, N of Santa Croce; garage parking nearby
Food breakfast
Prices €€€€€
Rooms 19; 12 double and twin, 7 suites, all with bath; all rooms have phone, TV, air conditioning, mini-bar, hairdrier
Facilities sitting room, bar
Credit cards AE, DC, MC, V
Disabled no special facilities
Pets not accepted
Closed never
Proprietors Cavagnari family

J and J
Town hotel

A converted monastery provides the setting for this cool, chic hotel some distance east of the Duomo, on the way to the Sant' Ambroggio market. The street is comparatively quiet, and inside, the hotel feels a haven from heat and dust, so effective is its air conditioning and so peaceful is its ambience.

Many original features of the building are still intact – columns, vaulted ceilings, frescoes and wooden beams – and furnishings, though stylishly modern in places, are sympathetic to the spirit of the antique setting, and certainly not lacking in personality. A small, pretty patio garden at the rear of the hotel, with elegant white parasols and plants in tubs, tempts breakfast-eaters to venture out through the plate-glass doors, although the interior option, with its decorated, vaulted ceiling, is almost as inviting.

Bedrooms vary. All are of high standard; some exceptionally spacious, with split-level floors and seating areas, and high ceilings with exposed beams. A recent visitor felt that their eclectic style made them more like private rooms than hotel ones.

A word of warning; the stairs are very steep and there is no lift.

Piazza Santa Maria Novella 7, 50123
Firenze

Tel 055 2645181
e-mail info@JKPlace.com
website www.jkplace.com

Nearby Santa Maria Novella; Ponte
Vecchio; Uffizi; Palazzo Vecchio.
Location in the centre of town with
lift; private garage nearby
Food breakfast, snacks
Prices €€€€€
Rooms 20; 13 double and twin, 7
suites, all with bath or shower; all
rooms have phone, TV, DVD, CD,
air conditioning, minibar, safe, hair-
drier
Facilities sitting rooms, breakfast
room, bar, roof terrace
Credit cards AE, DC, MC, V
Disabled adapted rooms
Pets accepted if small
Closed never
General Manager Omri Kafri

J.K.Place
Town hotel

Occupying a tall, elegant town house
on Piazza Santa Maria Novella, and
opened in May 2003, J.K. Place is one of
Florence's newest and most captivating
boutique hotels. To the right is Alberti's
glorious symmetrical church façade; you
can almost ignore the shabbiness of the
square itself. Once inside the discreet
entrance, the cares of the world and the
dust of the city really do seem to fade into
the restful cream and grey colour scheme,
the soft music, the heady scent of flowers,
the flickering candle light and the bend-
over-backwards-to-help attention of the
charming staff. While not for those on a
lean budget, and much beloved by the fashion crowd, this hotel is not at all stuffy or
intimidating.

The decoration is a seductive contemporary take on neo-classical style. Rooms
are filled with comfortable furniture, interesting art and covetable objets. A fire
burns in the cosy sitting room where arm
chairs and sofas are draped with cashmere
throws. Breakfast is served at a big polished antique table in the glassed-in courtyard or in your room. Bedrooms continue
along the same stylish lines (although
some are very small) while bathrooms are
naturally magnificent. Views from the
rooftop terrace take in the whole city.

Piazza SS Annunziata 3, 50122
Firenze

Tel 055 289592
e-mail
info@loggiatodeiservitihotel.it
website www.loggiatodeiservitiho-
tel.it

Nearby Church of Santissima
Annunziata; Foundlings' Hospital.
Location a few minutes' walk N of
duomo, on W side of Piazza SS
Annunziata; garage service on
request
Food breakfast
Prices €€€
Rooms 29; 19 double and twin, 6
single, 4 suites, all with bath or
shower; all rooms have phone, TV,
air conditioning, minibar, hairdrier,
safe
Facilities breakfast room, bar
Credit cards AE, DC, MC, V
Disabled not suitable
Pets accepted
Closed never
Proprietor Rodolfo Budini-Gattai

Loggiato dei Serviti
Town hotel

One of Florence's newest charming
hotels is in one of its loveliest
Renaissance buildings, designed (around
1527) by Sangallo the Elder to match
Brunelleschi's famous Hospital of the
Innocenti, opposite. Until a few years ago
the building housed a modest *pensione* and
the beautiful square was a giant car park.
But the Loggiato is now elegantly restored
and, thanks to the city council's change of
heart, much more peaceful.

The decoration is a skilful blend of old
and new, all designed to complement the
original vaulting and other features with a
minimum of frill and fuss. Floors are terracotta-tiled, walls rag-painted in pastel
colours. Bedrooms are individually decorated with sympathy and flair. There is a
small, bright breakfast room in which to
start the day (with fruit juice, cheese and
ham, brioches, fruit and coffee) and a little
bar where you can recover from it, browsing glossy magazines and sipping a Campari.

A recent reporter praised the
'admirable' comfort and standards, 'individual' welcome and service, and 'calm, comfortable and quiet' atmosphere. They provided 'the best breakfast we have had in
Italy' and 'excellent' value for money. His
sole quibble was 'slightly gloomy lighting'.

Via Laura 50, 50121 Firenze

Tel 055 2344747
e-mail welcome@hotelmorandi.it
website www.hotelmorandi.it

Nearby Duomo; archaeological
museum; San Marco, Accademia.
Location in quiet street NW of
Piazza del Duomo with private
garage
Food breakfast
Price €€
Rooms 10; 6 double and twin, 2 single, 2 family, all with shower; all
rooms have phone, TV, air conditioning, minibar, hairdrier, safe
Facilities sitting room, breakfast
room
Credit cards AE, DC, MC, V
Disabled access difficult **Pets** small
well-behaved dogs accepted
Closed never
Proprietors Paolo Antuono

Morandi alla Crocetta
Town Guest hotel

Kathleen Doyle Antuono first moved into this lovely former convent in the 1920s; in the early '80s, she opened the house to guests. She, sadly, is no more (although her portrait as an 18-year-old beauty hangs in the breakfast room), but the hotel continues to be successfully run by her son Paolo.

Situated near Piazza Santissima Annunziata along with Brunelleschi's famous Spedale degli Innocenti, the house is decorated throughout with taste and care. Antique Tuscan furnishings, patterned rugs, interesting pictures and fresh flowers abound. You may spot corbels carved with coats of arms in the reception hall, ancient painted tiles or fragments of fresco in the bedrooms. A recent inspector was impressed not only by her lovely frescoed room, but by the attention to detail, such as the thoughtful lighting, heated towel rail and even a phone in the bathroom. Another recent visitor, however, complained about the 'businesslike' atmosphere and the 'disgraceful' breakfast. The latter is included in the room price, but is not obligatory; try instead the excellent Pasticceria Robiglio in nearby Via dei Servi. We like the unpretentious Morandi, and it is convenient for exploring Florence's centro storico. Be warned: the stairs up to the reception are steep, especially if you are carrying luggage.

Borgo San Frediano 5, 50124
Firenze

Tel 055 2399544
e-mail
info@palazzomagnaniferoni.com
website www.palazzomagnaniferoni.com

Nearby Pitti Palace; Santo Spirito;
Ponte Vecchio.
Location south of the river in centre
of own, west of Ponte Vecchio with
lift and private garage
Food breakfast, snacks
Price ⓔⓔⓔⓔⓔ
Rooms 11; 1 double and 10 suites all
with bath; all rooms have phone, TV,
air conditioning, minibar, safe, hair-
drier
Facilities sitting rooms, bar, break-
fast room, billiard room, gym, ter-
race
Credit cards AE, DC, MC, V
Disabled access difficult **Pets** not
accepted **Closed** never
Proprietor Alberto Giannotti

Pal. Magnani Feroni
Town hotel

If you want the romance and atmosphere
of a grand Renaissance *palazzo* combined
with the facilities of an upmarket hotel
(and you have a fat wallet), this could be
for you. Situated in the lively Oltrarno district south of the river, the *palazzo* was
home to the owner's family until he decided to convert it into a hotel. He has maintained all the characteristics of its noble
origins, however, and you will find grand
salons filled with fine family antiques and
pictures, elaborate frescoes, original boxed
ceilings, old terracotta floors and glittering
chandeliers.

There is no lack of communal space for
guests who can choose between a plant-
filled courtyard, a billiard room, various sitting rooms (including one on the top floor
with rather incongruous fake zebra print-
covered chairs) and a fabulous rooftop
terrace with views all over the city and
way beyond. The ten luxourious suites are
enormous; each has a seperate sitting
room furnished with squashy arm chairs
and sofas and a fair spattering of antiques
too. Our inspector particularly liked the
cheapest room in the place: a beautiful and
romantic little room with floor-to-ceiling
frescoes and a small private garden.
Bathrooms (complete with robes and slippers) are suitably opulent. You will even be
asked to choose which scent of soap you
desire on arrival.

Chiasso de' Baroncelli/Chiasso del
Buco 16, 50122 Firenze

Tel 055 2676239
e-mail info@relaisuffizi.it
website www.relaisuffizi.it

Nearby Ponte Vecchio; Palazzo
Vecchio; the Uffizi.
Location in a narrow lane off the
south side of Piazza Signoria with lift
and paid parking nearby
Food breakfast
Price €€€
Rooms 10 doubles and twins, 1 sin-
gle all with bath or shower; all rooms
have phone, TV, air conditioning,
minibar, safe (in some), hairdrier
Facilities sitting room/breakfast
room
Credit cards AE, DC, MC, V
Disabled adapted rooms
Pets accepted if small
Closed never
Proprietor Elisabetta Matucci

Relais Degli Uffizi
Town guest house

It is easy to get lost among the warren of
narrow passageways that lead off the
south side of Piazza della Signoria, and
there is no helpful sign to guide you to the
Relais degli Uffizi. Look out for a pale
stone arch that will lead you to its doorway, through which you will see a pretty
lunette fresco of a rooftop scene. Make
straight for the comfortable sitting room
which has a fabulous view over the piazza.
A few minutes of watching the comings
and goings in this historic square, sizing up
the vast outline of the Palazzo Vecchio, and
then pondering the extraordinary silhou-
ette of the cathedral dome to the north
will quickly give you a flavour of the city.

The ten bedrooms, each different from
the next, are arranged on two floors. All,
however, are tastefully decorated and furnished: pastel colours on the walls, a mix
of antique and traditional Florentine painted pieces, and original features such as
boxed ceilings, creaky parquet floors and
even an enormous fireplace that acts as a
bed head (this was the kitchen in the original 16th century house). Several rooms
have modern four-poster beds hung with
filmy white curtains. Bathrooms have
recently been re-vamped.

Via delle Cinque Giornate 12, 50129
Firenze

Tel 055 473377
e-mail cinquegiornate@johanna.it
website www.johanna.it

Nearby Santa Maria Novella;
Fortezza da Basso.
Location in residential area 15 min-
utes' walk NW of the station; limited
car parking
Food breakfast
Price €
Rooms 6; 5 double and twin, 1 fami-
ly, 1 with bath, 5 with shower; all
rooms have TV; 3 have air condi-
tioning
Facilities sitting room, small garden
Credit cards not accepted
Disabled no special facilities, but 3
ground floor rooms
Pets accepted
Closed never
Proprietor Lea Gulmanelli

Res. Johanna II
Town guesthouse

The Johanna is under the same ownership as the Johlea (see opposite page)
and offers the same excellent value for
money – of which we thoroughly approve.

Some way north-west of the centre of
the city, but on several bus routes, the
Johanna's existence is announced by a discreet brass plaque next to a solid iron
gate; the pleasant building stands in its own
small gravelled garden.

Inside, you find yourself in an elegant
private house, with cool, cream-coloured
walls, and high ceilings throughout giving a
sense of space. At the back of the house,
a comfortable sitting room doubles as the
guesthouse's reception.

The bedrooms are all fairly large (one
particularly so), and are furnished with
large beds and a mixture of antiques and
modern pieces. Tasteful fabrics, of predominantly pale green-and-cream stripes, add
style. The bathrooms vary in size, but even
the smallest is adequate. Each room has
the wherewithal for a simple DIY breakfast: electric kettle, coffee, tea, biscuits and
brioche.

Via San Gallo 76, 50129 Firenze

Tel 055 4633292
e-mail cinquegiornate@johanna.it
website www.johanna.it

Nearby Duomo; San Marco;
Accademia Gallery.
Location in centre of city, directly
north of the duomo with garage
parking nearby (extra charge); lift
Food breakfast (in room)
Price €
Rooms 6; 5 double and twin, 1 fami-
ly, 1 with bath, 5 with shower; all
rooms have TV; 3 have air condi-
tioning
Facilities sitting room, roof terrace
Credit cards not accepted
Disabled no special facilities
Pets accepted
Closed never
Proprietor Lea Gulmanelli

Antica Dimora Johlea
Town guesthouse

As we go to press for this new edition,
Antica Dimora Johlea, a long-standing
mainstay of our Florence guesthouses
selection, is preparing for major changes.
Its formula was to offer three-star comfort at one-star prices – quite a feat in this
city of sky high prices – but from 2007
onwards, although charges will probably
be fair, you will pay more and get more.

The hotel will still occupy its elegant
apartment in a solid *palazzo* north of the
Duomo; the atmosphere will still remain
that of a gracious private house. But
instead of taking breakfast in your room,
you will start the day in a new breakfast
room; and the six bedrooms will all have
four-poster beds, and be individually
designed with careful attention to detail,
including pastel colours on the walls and
expensive silk fabrics. We understand that
the small roof terrace with 360-degree
views of the city will remain and hope that
the cosy little sitting room will stay too.

This hotel, and the Johanna II look as
though they will remain major players in
the Florence guesthouses scene for the
foreseeable future, but we will welcome
readers reports on the changes at the
Antica Dimora Johlea.

Via Tornabuoni 3, 50123 Firenze

Tel 055 212645/268377
e-mail info@torabuonihotels.com
website www.tornabuonihotels.com

Nearby Santa Trinita; Ponte
Vecchio; Palazzo della Signoria.
Location in centre of town; garage
nearby
Food breakfast, dinner, snacks (in
summer)
Prices €€€
Rooms 28; 20 double and twin, 8
single, all with bath or shower; all
rooms have phone, TV, air condi-
tioning, minibar, hairdrier
Facilities sitting room, restaurant,
roof terrace
Credit cards AE, DC, MC, V
Disabled access difficult
Pets small dogs accepted
Closed never
Proprietor Francesco Bechi

Tornabuoni Beacci
Town guesthouse

One could not ask for more in terms of
location. Via Tornabuoni is one of
Florence's most elegant and central shopping streets, where leading designers such
as Gucci, Ferragamo, Pucci and Prada have
their stores, and within easy walking distance are all the main sights of the city. Yet
its position on the fourth and fifth floors
of the 15thC Palazzo Minerbetti Strozzi, at
one corner of Piazza Santa Trinita, makes it
a quiet haven from Florence's crowded,
noisy streets.

The *pensione* has a turn-of-the-century
atmosphere. Fans of E.M. Forster's A
Room with a View will find this a close
approximation of the Edwardian guesthouse described in the novel. Many of the
rooms have views, but none so fine as the
rooftop terrace, with its plants and pergola, which looks over the city to the towers
and villas of the Bellosguardo hill. Even in
the hot, still days of July and August, you
may catch a refreshing breeze here.

The decoration and furnishings are old-
fashioned but well maintained, like the
house of a maiden aunt. Parquet floors and
plain-covered sofas are much in evidence.
Rooms vary – some are quite poky – but
new management has been making
improvements.

Borgo SS Apostoli 8, 50123 Firenze

Tel 055 2396338
e-mail info@hoteltorreguelfa.com
website www.hoteltorreguelfa.com

Nearby Ponte Vecchio; Vecchio and
Pitti palaces.
Location in centre of town in traf-
fic-limited area; garage nearby
Food breakfast
Price €€
Rooms 16; 13 double and twin, 1
single, 2 family, all with bath or
shower; all rooms have phone, TV,
air conditioning, minibar, hairdrier
(some)
Facilities sitting room, breakfast
room, bar, terraces
Credit cards AE, EC, MC, V
Disabled one specially adapted
room
Pets small ones accepted
Closed never
Proprietor Giancarlo Avuri

Torre Guelfa
Town bed-and-breakfast

There can be few better spots in
Florence in which to enjoy a quiet
aperitivo after a hard day's sightseeing: this
is the tallest privately-owned tower in the
city, dating from the 13th century and
enjoying a 360° view over a jumble of
rooftops, taking in all the most important
landmarks and the countryside beyond.

The hotel is very popular, particularly
with the fashion crowd during trade fair
season. The Italian-German owners have
created a comfortable and unstuffy atmosphere rejecting a heavy, Florentine look for
a lighter touch. Bedroom walls are sponge-
painted in pastel shades and curtains are
mostly fresh, embroidered white cotton.
Furniture is a mixture of wrought iron and
prettily-painted pieces with some
antiques. Bathrooms are in smart grey
Carrara marble.

One room has its own spacious terrace
complete with olive tree; be prepared to
fight for it. A glassed-in loggia provides
space for a sunny breakfast room and the
double 'salon', with its boxed-wood ceiling
and little bar, is a comfortable and quiet
place in which to relax.

Florence

Viale Fratelli Rosselli 44, 50123
Firenze

Tel 055 214242
e-mail info@villa-azalee.it
website www.villa-azalee.it

Nearby Santa Maria Novella;
Ognissanti; San Lorenzo; duomo.
Location a few minutes' walk W of
the main station, towards Porta al
Prato; garage nearby
Food breakfast
Prices €€
Rooms 25; 23 double and twin, 2
single, all with bath or shower; all
rooms have phone, TV, air condi-
tioning, minibar, hairdrier
Facilities sitting room, bar, garden
Credit cards AE, DC, MC, V
Disabled 2 adapted rooms
Pets accepted by arrangement
Closed never
Proprietor Ornella Brizzi

Villa Azalee
Town hotel

Convenient for the station, but slightly
remote from the monumental district
(about 15 minutes by foot) Villa Azalee will
appeal to visitors who prefer family-run
hotels with some style to larger, more luxurious operations; and by the standards of
most hotels in Florence, prices are very
reasonable. The hotel consists of two
buildings: the original 19thC villa and,
across the garden, a new annexe, full of the
potted azaleas that give the place its name.

A highly individual style has been used in
the decoration and furniture: some will
find the results delightful, others exces-
sively whimsical. Pastel colours, frilly
canopies and matching curtains and bedcovers characterize the bedrooms. They
are all air conditioned, with spotless, new
bathrooms. The public rooms are more
restrained with an interesting collection of
the family's paintings. Breakfast is served
either in your room, in the garden (which
can be somewhat noisy) or in a separate
breakfast room.

One of the drawbacks of the hotel is its
location on the viali (the busy traffic artery
circling Florence). Sound-proofing has
been used, but rooms in the annexe, or
overlooking the garden, are preferable.

Via Benedetto Castelli 3, 50124
Firenze

Tel 055 222501
e-mail reception@villa-belvedere.com
website www.villa-belvedere.com

Nearby Pitti Palace; Boboli gardens.
Location 3 km S of city; car parking
Food breakfast, snacks
Prices €€
Rooms 26; 21 double and twin, 2 single, 3 suites, all with bath or shower; all rooms have phone, TV, air conditioning, safe, hairdrier
Facilities 2 sitting rooms, breakfast room, bar, TV room, veranda, garden, swimming pool, tennis
Credit cards AE, DC, MC, V
Disabled no special facilities
Pets not accepted
Closed Dec-Feb
Proprietors Ceschi-Perotto family

Villa Belvedere
Country villa

This family-run hotel lies in a pleasant hilly residential district on the southern outskirts of the city, commanding excellent views through classically Tuscan cypress trees when Florentine smog permits. The building itself is no great beauty, being practical and modern, but its well-kept gardens and small swimming pool are a great boon in hot weather, and its peaceful surroundings, away from any passing traffic, a relief from the city centre at any time of the year.

The Ceschi-Perotto family manage their business with welcoming enthusiasm and efficiency and have recently completed an ambitious programme of refurbishment. Bedrooms and bathrooms are traditionally decorated in a smart matching scheme of fleur de lys motifs, racing greens and high-quality solid wood furnishings. Bathrooms gleam, with white tiles offset by restrained geometric friezes. Public areas are light, spacious and comfortable – and the breakfast room makes the best of the villa's garden.

A limited evening snack menu is available until 8.30 pm – particularly useful after a tiring day's sightseeing, since there are few restaurants within easy walking distance.

Via San Matteo in Arcetri 24, 50125
Firenze

Tel 055 220016
e-mail
info@villapoggiosanfelice.com
website
www.villapoggiosanfelice.com

Nearby San Miniato, Piazzale
Michelangelo.
Location S of Porta Romana, follow
the signs for Arcetri; car parking
Food breakfast
Price €€€
Rooms 5; 4 double, 1 twin, 4 with
bath, 1 with shower; all rooms have
phone; hairdrier on request
Facilities sitting room, breakfast
room, terraces, garden, free shuttle
service to and from Ponte Vecchio
Credit cards AE, DC, MC, V
Disabled access difficult **Pets** small
pets accepted
Closed Jan-Mar
Proprietors Livia Puccinelli and
Lorenzo Magnelli

Villa Poggio San Felice
Hilltop villa

The hills immediately to the south of
Florence are full of grand and beautiful
villas, many of them erstwhile summer residences of wealthy Florentine families. The
15thC Villa Poggio San Felice is such a
house; perched on a little poggio or hill, it
could be in the heart of Chianti but is, in
fact, only ten minutes from the city centre.
The villa was bought by Gerardo Bernardo
Kraft – a Swiss hotelier – in the early 19th
century and was recently inherited and
restored by his descendants.

The mellow old villa is set in a lovely
garden designed by Porcinai in the late
1800s. Inside, the feeling is very much of an
elegant private house, but it is not at all
stuffy. Cheerful fabrics and interesting
colours give a young feel to the place
while blending nicely with family antiques
and pictures. The day starts in the long,
high-ceilinged breakfast room where
French windows open on to the garden.
For relaxation, there is a pretty, partially
arched loggia, plenty of seats dotted
around the grounds or a sitting room for
cooler weather. The comfortable and spacious bedrooms – each different from the
next – lead off a landing on the first floor;
two have working fireplaces. The suite has
a little reading room and a terrace overlooking the city.

Lecchi in Chianti

Loc.San Sano Gaiole in Chianti,
53010 Siena

Tel 0577 746130
e-mail info@sansanohotel.it
website www.sansanohotel.it

Nearby Radda in Chianti (9 km);
Siena (25 km); Florence (60 km).
Location hilltop hamlet in open
countryside with own car parking
Food breakfast, dinner
Price €€€
Rooms 14; 12 double and twins, 2
single, all with shower, 2 with bath;
all rooms have phone, TV, air condi-
tioning, minibar, hairdrier
Facilities sitting areas, breakfast and
dining room, garden, swimming
pool
Credit cards AE, DC, MC, V
Disabled 2 adapted rooms
Pets accepted
Closed mid-Nov to mid-Mar
Proprietors Marco Amabili

San Sano
Country hotel

The medieval hamlet of San Sano, a clut-
ter of stone houses with uneven terracotta roofs, has at its heart an ancient
defence tower, destroyed and rebuilt many
times. Now, in its latest incarnation, this
imposing structure forms the core of a
delightful, family-run hotel in a relatively
little visitied, authentic part of Chianti.

The various buildings surrounding the
tower (which houses some of the bedrooms; others have direct access to the
grounds) give the hotel a rambling character, connected by narrow passageways,
steep stairways and unexpected courtyards. The restoration has been meticulous and restrained. The decoration is in
classic, rustic Tuscan style but with individual touches: carefully chosen antiques,
colourful pottery and plenty of flowers
The dining-room, in the former stables,
spanned by a massive stone arch and still
with the feeding trough, is a cool haven
from the summer sun. Each bedroom has
its individual character (one with nesting
birds in its perforated walls, now glassed
off) and gleaming, almost surgical bathrooms. Outside is a stone-paved garden at
the foot of the tower and, at a slight
remove, a hill-side swimming pool.

Greve in Chianti

Greve in Chianti, 50022 Firenze

Tel 055 8544840
e-mail
agriturismo@vignamaggio.com
website www.vignamaggio.com

Nearby Greve (5 km); Florence (19 km); Siena (38 km).
Location 5 km SE of Greve on the road to Lamole from the SS222; car parking
Food breakfast; dinner 2 evenings a week
Price €€
Rooms 21 rooms, suites, self-catering apartments for 2-4 people, all with bath; all rooms/apartments have phone; air conditioning
Facilities sitting room, bar, gym, terrace, garden, 2 swimming pools, tennis court, children's playground
Credit cards AE, MC, V
Disabled one specially adapted apartment
Pets accepted
Closed mid Nov-mid Mar
Proprietor Gianni Nunziante

Villa di Vignamaggio
Country villa

Chianti has more than its share of hill-top villas and castles, now posing as hotels, or, as in this case, self-catering (agri-turismo) apartments. Vignamaggio stands out from them all: one of those rare places that made us think twice about advertising it. The villa's first owners were the Gherardini family, of which Mona Lisa, born here in 1479, was a member. This could even have been where she and Leonardo met. More recently, it was the setting for Kenneth Branagh's film of Shakespeare's Much Ado About Nothing.

Villa di Vignamaggio is a warm Tuscan pink. A small formal garden in front gives way to acres of vines. The pool, a short distance from the house, is among fields and trees. The interior is a perfect combination of simplicity and good taste, with the emphasis on natural materials. Beds, chairs and sofas are comfortable and attractive. Old wardrobes cleverly hide small kitchen units. The two public rooms are equally pleasing, and breakfast there or on the terrace is thoughtfully planned, with bread from the local bakery and home-made jam. The staff were charming and helpful when we visited. 'Service' is kept to a minimum ("This is not a hotel.").

Via Nuova per Pisa (SS 12 bis),
Massa Pisana, 55050 Lucca

Tel 0583 379737
e-mail elisa@relaischateaux.com
website www.locandalelisa.it

Nearby Lucca (3 km); Pisa (15 km).
Location 3 km S of Lucca on the
old road to Pisa; car parking
Food breakfast, lunch, dinner
Price €€€€
Rooms 10; 1 double, 1 single, 8
suites, all with bath or shower; all
rooms have phone, TV, air condi-
tioning, minibar, safe, hairdrier
Facilities sitting rooms, restaurant,
garden, swimming pool
Credit cards AE, DC, MC, V
Disabled ground floor rooms avail-
able
Pets small dogs accepted
Closed early Jan to early Feb
Manager Leonardo Iurlo

Locanda L'Elisa
Country villa

A French official of the Napoleonic
times who accompanied the
Emperor's sister, Elisa Baciocchi, to Lucca
acquired this 18thC villa for his own residence. Perhaps that accounts for the dis-
cernibly French style of the house that
makes it unique among Tuscan hotels. A
square building, three storeys high, painted
in an arresting blue, with windows and
cornices picked out in gleaming white, the
Locanda L'Elisa stands just off the busy old
Pisa-Lucca road.

The restorers have fortunately avoided
the oppressive Empire style (which, in any
case, the small rooms would not have
borne) and aimed throughout at lightness
and delicacy. The entrance is a symphony
in wood, with geometrically patterned parquet flooring and panelled walls, and the
illusion of space created with large mirrors. To the right is a small sitting room,
furnished with fine antiques and Knole
sofas. A round 19thC conservatory is now
the romantic restaurant; the food is unpretentious and excellent, with an emphasis
on fish. Each suite has been individually
decorated using striped, floral and small-
check patterns, canopied beds and yet
more antiques – no expense has been
spared. A glorious mature garden insulates
it from the main road.

Mercatale Val di Pesa

Via Grevigiana 80, 50024 Mercatale
Val di Pesa, Firenze

Tel 055 8218039
e-mail info@salvadonica.com
website www.salvadonica.com

Nearby Florence (20 km).
Location 20 km S of Florence, E of
road to Siena; car parking
Food breakfast
Price €€
Rooms 5 double, 10 apartments, all
with shower; all rooms have phone;
apartments have fridge
Facilities billiards room, TV room,
garden, swimming pool, tennis
Credit cards AE, DC, MC, V
Disabled one specially-adapted
room and one apartment
Pets if small (extra charge)
Closed Nov-Feb
Proprietors Baccetti family

Salvadonica
Country estate

This delightful assembly of rustic buildings amid olive groves and vineyards
will gladden the heart of any lover of
Tuscan scenery. Two entrepreneurial young
sisters have energetically converted a family home, on what was until recently a feu-
dal estate, into a thriving bed-and-breakfast and agriturismo business. Past visitors
have found the place enchanting.

Now the two main buildings of the farm
– one rich red stucco, the other mellow
stone and brick – offer five well-equipped,
comfortable guest rooms and ten apartments to let. They have clay-tiled floors
and wood-beamed ceilings, and range from
the merely harmonious and comfortable
to the positively splendid (in the case of a
brick-vaulted former cowshed).

From the paved terraces surrounding
the buildings, you look over an olive grove
to the neat swimming pool area with
Jacuzzi. A tennis court and riding stables
offer alternative pastimes. Breakfast, with a
changing variety of cakes and breads, is
served in a pleasant stone-walled dining
room or on a sunny terrace overlooking
unspoiled sweeps of countryside, where
the local Gallo Nero Chianti and excellent
olive oil are still produced.

Gargonza, 52048 Monte San Savino, Arezzo

Tel 0575 847021
e-mail gargonza@gargonza.it
website www.gargonza.it

Nearby Arezzo (25 km); Chianti; Val di Chiana.
Location 35 km E of Siena on SS73, 7 km W of Monte San Savino; car parking outside walls
Food breakfast, lunch, dinner
Price €€
Rooms 10 double in main guest-house all with bath or shower; 25 self-catering houses; all rooms have phone, hairdrier; main guesthouse rooms have minibar
Facilities sitting rooms, TV room, breakfast room, restaurant, meeting rooms, garden, swimming pool (open mid May-mid Sept)
Credit cards AE, DC, MC, V
Disabled access difficult **Pets** not accepted
Closed 3 weeks Nov
Proprietor Conte Roberto Guicciardini

Castello di Gargonza
Converted castle

Not so much a castle as an entire 13th century fortified hamlet, Gargonza was once a working farm where Dante Alighieri was a guest. Perched high above typical, unspoilt Tuscan landscape, it has been beautifully (but not overly) restored; the ancient walls encircle a cluster of buildings including a tower, a church and an octagonal well. Its paved alleyways are traffic free, although you can drive in with your luggage.

The foresteria, or guest house, has seven fairly Spartan rooms rentable for a minimum of three days in high season. Twenty five self-catering apartments (named after past occupants) have recently been refurbished; these are let on a weekly basis and offer good value for groups of families. They are comfortable and mostly spacious, with new bathrooms, pretty co-ordinating fabrics, working fireplaces and cleverly concealed kitchen units. Note that housekeepng is only available on request.

Breakfast is served in the frantoio (the old olive press) which also houses a sitting room graced with the only TV on the premises. Just below the walls, a rustic restaurant serves excellent local specialities including homemade pici with duck sauce and superb Chainina beef. The addition of a pool, on a terrace bordered by rosemary hedges, is welcome.

Montefiridolfi

Via Collina S Angelo 23,
Montefiridolfi, S. Casciano Val di
Pesa, 50020 Firenze

Tel 055 8244442
e-mail ilborghetto@studio-
cavallini.it

Nearby Florence (18 km); Siena (45
km); San Gimignano (40 km).
Location 18 km S of Florence, E of
Siena road, on right before village;
car parking
Food breakfast; lunch and dinner if
requested by enough people
Price €€€ (2-day minimum
stay)
Rooms 8; 6 doubles, 2 suites all with
shower
Facilities sitting room, dining room,
terrace, garden, swimming pool
Credit cards not accepted
Disabled one suitable room
Pets not accepted
Closed Nov-Mar
Manager Antonio Cavallini

Il Borghetto
Country villa

Discretion, taste and refinement are the key characteristics of this family guesthouse, much appreciated by a discerning (and returning) clientele that enjoys civilized living in this peaceful, bucolic setting.

A manicured gravel drive leads past the lawn, with its rose beds and cypress trees, to the main buildings, which include the remains of two 15thC military towers. From a covered terrace, where breakfast is improved by views of miles of open countryside, a broad-arched entrance leads to the open-plan ground floor of the main villa. Within, the usual starkness of the Tuscan style, has been softened by the use of muted tones in the wall colours and fabrics. Comfortable furniture abounds without cluttering the spacious, airy quality of the public areas. Upstairs, in the bedrooms (some of which are not particularly large), floral wallpaper and subdued lighting create a balmy, relaxed atmosphere. There are no intrusive phone calls or blaring televisions.

Even the refined like a swim; but for those who consider swimming pools raucous, there is a soothing water garden.

Cookery courses are organized here at certain times of the year.

Monteriggioni

Via 1 Maggio 4, 53035
Monteriggioni, Siena

Tel 0577 305009/305010
e-mail info@hotelmonteriggioni.net
website
www.hotelmonteriggioni.net

Nearby Siena (10 km); San
Gimignano (18 km); Florence (55
km); Volterra
(40 km).
Location within the walls of
Monteriggioni, 10 km N of Siena;
car parking available nearby
Food breakfast
Prices €€€
Rooms 12; 10 double, 2 single, all
with shower; all rooms have phone,
TV, minibar, air conditioning, safe
Facilities sitting area, breakfast
room, bar, garden, swimming pool
Credit cards AE, DC, MC, V
Disabled no special facilities
Pets not accepted
Closed Jan-Feb
Manager Michela Gozzi

Monteriggioni
Village hotel

Visitors to Tuscany have been increasingly keen to drop by well-preserved,
medieval Monteriggioni and spend a couple of hours relaxing in the piazza (where
a bar serves snacks), browsing the antique
shops or sampling the menu of Il Pozzo,
one of the finest restaurants in the Siena
area. Finally, somebody had the bright idea
that a small hotel would not go amiss,
especially since the town is peaceful and
well placed for exploring the locality.

A couple of old stone houses were
knocked together and converted with
sure-handed lightness of touch to make
this attractive hotel. The former stables
now make a large, light and airy public area
used as reception, sitting room and breakfast room.

At the back, a door leads out to a well-
tended garden running down to the town
walls and containing what is possibly the
smallest swimming pool in Tuscany. The
bedrooms are perfectly acceptable, furnished to a high rustic-antique standard
with stylish hypermodern bathrooms.

171

Monteriggioni

Pieve a Castello
Strada di Pieve a Castello
53013 Monteriggioni

Tel 0577 301034
e-mail pieveacastello@tin.it
website www.atg-oxford.co.uk

Nearby Monteriggioni (8 km), Siena
(15 km), San Gimignano (11 km).
Location In countryside, between
Strove and Scorgiano.
Food Breakfast, lunch, dinner.
Price €€€
Rooms 1 single, 7 double and twin,
2 junior suites.
Facilities 2 sitting rooms, library,
guests' kitchen, loggia, church,
chapel, terraces, several dining
rooms, swimming pool, garden,
parking
Credit cards AE, MC, V
Disabled not suitable
Closed Open all year
Proprietors Alternative Travel
Group (ATG)

Pieve a Castello
Town hotel

This stunning conversion of 8th century
ecclesiastical buildings on a hill-top site
to the north of the walled town of
Monteriggioni, near Siena, is used for
overnight stays by participants in organised trips run by owners, the Alternative
Travel Group; individual guests are now
welcome. The ten air-conditioned bedrooms, on the second and third floors of
the main building are well-equipped,
attractively furnished in local style, look
out over the central courtyard or the
grounds, and have charming modern bathrooms. On the first floor there is a sitting
room, a library opening onto an arched
loggia, and a small kitchen for the use of
guests. Another sitting room on the
ground floor looks over the courtyard to
the Baptistery, also used as a dining room,
from which an archway leads into a church
and a chapel (where concerts are often
held), and to a secluded terrace with magnificent views. Sunsets seen from here are
dramatic. There is a large, newly constructed, swimming pool in the grounds.

The food is excellent, with much use of
local produce; all vegetables and herbs
come from the garden. Meals may be taken
on a shaded terrace, in the courtyard or in
one of the dining rooms. Service is friendly, efficient and unobtrusive. Pieve a
Castello has a unique magical atmosphere,
more like an exclusive private home than
a hotel.

Montichiello di Pienza

53020 Montichiello di Pienza, Siena

Tel 0578 755133
e-mail info@olmopienza.it
website www.olmopienza.it

Nearby Siena (50 km); Pienza (7
km); Montepulciano (12 km).
Location 7 km S of Pienza; car
parking
Food breakfast, dinner on request
Price €€
Rooms 6; 1 double, 5 suites, all with
bath; all rooms have phone, TV,
minibar, hairdrier, safe; 1 apartment
Facilities sitting room,
breakfast/dining room, terraces, gar-
den, swimming pool
Credit cards AE, MC, V
Disabled one ground floor room
available
Pets not accepted
Closed mid Nov to end Mar
Proprietor Francesca Lindo

L'Olmo
Country guesthouse

The initial impression given by this solid
stone building set on a hillside overlooking the rolling hills of the Val d'Orcia
towards Pienza is a little stark. A few trees
would soften the lines. Once inside, however, the elegant, comfortable sitting room
with its oriental rugs, low beamed ceiling,
antiques and glass-topped coffee table
laden with books dispels any such feeling.
When we visited, there was a fire roaring
in the grate and Mozart playing softly in
the background.

The spacious bedrooms and suites (two
of which have fireplaces) are individually
and stylishly decorated in smart country
style with floral fabrics, fresh white cotton
bedcovers, botanical prints, soft lighting
and plenty of plants and dried flowers.
One room has the floor-to-ceiling brick-
grilled wall (now glassed in) that is so typical of Tuscan barns. The wrought-iron fixtures throughout are by a local craftsman.
Two suites have private terraces leading
on to the large garden.

The pool has a wonderful view and the
arched courtyard makes a pleasant spot
for an aperitif.

Panzano in Chianti

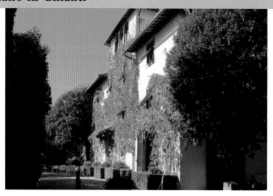

Via San Leolino 19, 50020 Panzano
in Chianti, Firenze

Tel 055 852621
e-mail info@villalebarone.it
website www.villalebarone.it

Nearby Siena (31 km); Florence (31
km).
Location 31 km S of Florence off
SS222; covered car parking
Food breakfast, lunch, dinner
Price €€€
Rooms 28; 27 double and twin, 22
with bath, 6 with shower, 1 single
with shower; all rooms have phone,
hairdrier; 15 rooms have air condi-
tioning
Facilities 3 sitting rooms, TV room,
self-service bar, dining room, break-
fast room, garden, table tennis,
swimming pool, tennis
Credit cards AE, MC, V
Disabled ground floor rooms
Pets not accepted
Closed Nov-Mar
Manager Caterina Buonamici

Villa le Barone
Country villa

Le Barone, the attractive 16thC country
house of the della Robbia family (of
ceramics fame), became a hotel in 1976,
but still feels very much more like a private home.

The small scale of the rooms helps, but
there are several other factors. The
antique furniture is obviously a personal
collection; reception amounts to little
more than a visitors' book in the hall;
there are plenty of books around – including English ones – and there are always
fresh flower arrangements in the elegant
little sitting rooms; and you help yourself
to drinks, recording your consumption as
you do so. In the past a minimum stay of
three nights has further contributed to the
low-key house-party atmosphere; but the
rule has now been dropped.

Guests who are not out on sightseeing
excursions have plenty of space to themselves in the peaceful woody garden or by
the lovely pool, which gives a glorious
panorama of the surrounding hills of
Tuscany.

The restaurant and some of the rooms
are in converted outbuildings. Recent
reports have praised the setting, the service and the food and concluded that the
price is justified.

Panzano in Chianti

Via S. Leolino 59, Panzano in
Chianti, Firenze

Tel 055 852577
e-mail info@resortvillarosa.it
website www.resortvillarosa.com

Nearby Florence (34 km); Siena (28
km).
Location 3 km SE of Panzano on
Radda road; car parking
Food breakfast, dinner
Price €
Rooms 16 double and twin with
bath or shower; all rooms have
phone, TV, minibar
Facilities sitting room, restaurant,
terraces, garden, swimming pool
Credit cards AE, DC, MC, V
Disabled one specially adapted
room, but access difficult
Pets accepted
Closed mid-Nov to just before
Easter
Proprietor Sabine Buntenbach

Villa Rosa
Country guesthouse

A recent addition to the countless
hotels and guesthouses in this part of
Chianti, Villa Rosa is a solid structure dating from the early 1900s. Looming over
the road from Panzano to Radda, its
appearance makes a refreshing change
from the usual rustic stone Tuscan farmhouse formula: it is painted bright pink.

Inside, a light touch is evident in the
decoration. The terracotta floors and
white walls downstairs are typical, but
bedrooms have pastel-coloured, sponged
paintwork, wrought-iron four poster beds
and a mixture of wicker furniture, together with antique pieces here and there. The
attractive, rather quirky, light fittings are by
a local craftsman. Bathrooms also have
touches of colour and heated towel rails
add a hint of luxury.

The building is too near the road to be
ideally situated, but at the back there is a
peaceful, partially shaded terrace for open-
air eating, while the garden slopes up the
hillside to a pleasant pool and open, vine-
striped countryside. Reasonable prices
and a relaxed style of management make
this hotel very popular; the food is good,
too. A recent report remarks on the 'interesting local fare' and 'good value'.

Panzano in Chianti

Piazza Bucciarelli 5, 50020 Panzano
in Chianti, Firenze

Tel 055 852461
e-mail villa.sangiovese@libero.it
website www.villasangiovese.it

Nearby Greve (5 km); Siena (31
km); Florence (31 km).
Location on edge of town, 5 km S of
Greve; car parking in front of hotel
Food breakfast, lunch, dinner
Price €€
Rooms 19; 16 double, 1 single, 2
suites, all with bath or shower; all
rooms have phone; rooms facing the
piazza have air conditioning, TV on
request
Facilities 2 sitting rooms, library,
dining room, bar, terrace, garden,
swimming pool
Credit cards MC, V
Disabled no special facilities
Pets not accepted
Closed 15 Dec-end Feb; restaurant
Wed
Proprietors Ulderico and Anna
Maria Bleuler

Villa Sangiovese
Country villa

The Bleulers have managed hotels in the
Chianti region since 1973, and opened
their doors in Panzano in 1988 after completely renovating the building, winning
high praise from our readers.

The main villa is a neat stone-and-stuc-
co house fronting directly on to a quiet
back street; potted plants and a brass plate
beside the doorway are the only signs of a
hotel. Attached to this house is an old,
rambling, stone building beside a flowery,
gravelled courtyard-terrace offering splendid views. The landscaped garden below
includes a fair-sized pool.

Inside, all is mellow, welcoming and stylish, with carefully chosen antique furnishings against plain, pale walls. Bedrooms,
some with wood-beamed ceilings, are spacious, comfortable, and tastefully
restrained in decoration. The dining room
is equally simple and stylish, with subdued
wall lighting and bentwood chairs on a
tiled floor.

A limited but interesting à la carte menu
is offered, which changes each night –
service on the terrace in summer. A
reporter praises the food and the wine.

Pelago

19-20 Ristonchi, 50060 Pelago, Firenze

Tel 055 8361387
e-mail ladoccia@tin.it
website www.ladocciawelcomes.com

Nearby Florence (27 km);
Vallombrosa (8 km).
Location 27 km E of Florence, 5 km
S of Pelago; car parking
Food breakfast; lunch and dinner by
arrangement
Price €€
Rooms 5 double, 4 apartments for
2-4 people, all with bath or shower
Facilities sitting rooms, dining
room, bar, terraces, garden, swim-
ming pool
Credit cards AE, MC, V
Disabled no special facilities
Pets accepted
Closed B & B rooms Dec-Feb;
apartments never
Proprietors Edward and Sonia
Mayhew

La Doccia
Country guesthouse

Edward and Sonia Mayhew opened their beautifully converted stone farmhouse to guests in May 1999. Stunningly situated high up in the hills in a refreshingly undiscovered corner of Tuscany, the style is comfortable rustic with handmade terracotta flagstones, beamed ceilings, stone staircases and brick arches. Warm colours on the walls make a welcome change from the usual stark white. The furniture is a successful mix of locally made pieces and the Mayhews' own English antiques while books, pictures on the walls and knick-knacks give it the feel of a private house. This style is continued in the comfortable bedrooms and self-contained apartments, which are carefully furnished and have particularly smart bathrooms; two of the appartments have open fires for added cosiness in winter.

There are two sitting rooms, both with fireplaces (one is enormous), and an honesty bar. Breakfast and dinner (the latter prepared by Edward) are served at a long communal table. The house stands at 630 metres above sea level, so the long stone terrace, shaded by large, white umbrellas and bordered by lavender and roses, has fabulous views over the hills and down to Florence far below.

Corso Rossellino 26, 53026 Pienza, Siena

Tel 0578 748400
e-mail ilchiostrocdipienza@virgilio.it
website www.relaisilchiostrodipienza.com

Nearby Palazzo Piccolomini; duomo; Siena (52 km), Montepulciano.
Location centre of town next to Palazzo Piccolomini; public car parking outside walls
Food breakfast, lunch, dinner
Price €€€
Rooms 37; 19 doubles and twins, 9 singles, 9 suites, all with bath; all rooms have phone, TV, air conditioning, minibar, safe, hairdrier
Facilities sitting rooms, bar, restaurant, garden, swimming pool
Credit cards AE, DC, MC, V
Disabled 2 adapted rooms
Pets accepted
Closed Jan-Mar; restaurant Mon
Manager Massimo Cicala

Il Chiostro di Pienza
Converted monastery

In the modest way of Renaissance popes, Pius II renamed his home town of Corsignano after himself and made it a model of 15thC urban planning. So it is appropriate that the modern tourist-pilgrim should find lodgings in this stylishly converted monastery. The entrance is located at the back of the austere white cloister that gives the hotel its name and on to which half the rooms look; the other half face away, over the serenely magnificent hills of Val d'Orcia.

Many of the original features of the monks' cells have been retained: frescoed, vaulted ceilings and tiled floors. The furniture, however, breaks with monkish antiquity and concentrates on modern comfort without sinning against the character of the building. Bathrooms, though hardly spacious, are fully equipped. The sitting rooms, with their old beamed ceilings, and the restaurant give on to a delightful terrace garden, where a pool has recently been built – a great bonus in a town. There could be no more agreeable place for an evening aperitif than its shady peace. A recent guest found the atmosphere, welcome and service fautless; 'I wouldn't mind moving in for life' she says.

Strada Statale 146, 53026 Pienza, Siena

Tel 0578 748022
e-mail info@lasaracina.it
website www.lasaracina.it

Nearby Pienza (7 km); Montepulciano (6 km).
Location on quiet hillside, 7 km from Pienza on Montepulciano road; car parking
Food breakfast
Prices €€€
Rooms 5; 2 double, 3 suites, all with bath or shower; all rooms have phone, TV, minibar; one self-catering apartment
Facilities breakfast room, garden, swimming pool, tennis
Credit cards AE, MC, V
Disabled no special facilities, but all rooms are on ground floor
Pets not accepted
Closed never
Proprietor Simonetta Vessichelli

La Saracina
Country guesthouse

By the time the McCobbs retired from La Saracina to return to the U.S.A. in 1996, they had created an extremely comfortable guesthouse. With the attention to detail that seems to be a characteristic of foreigners who go into the business, they turned an old stone farmhouse and its outbuildings, set in glorious countryside, into something special.

Refinement and good taste predominates: the bedrooms, all with their own entrance from out of doors, are spacious and elegant; suites have sitting areas. Antique furnishings mingle well with bright Ralph Lauren fabrics and there is a distinct leaning towards American country style. The luxurious bathrooms are fitted with marble sinks and Jacuzzis – several are enormous. Breakfast is served on the terrace in warm weather or in a neat breakfast room. There is an attractive swimming pool surrounded by smooth lawns.

We have no reason to believe that the new young owner has not maintained the high standards of this upmarket place and that her enthusiasm and fresh approach have not been winning through. More reports please.

Pietrasanta

Via Garibaldi 35, 55045 Pietrasanta,
Lucca

Tel 0584 793726
e-mail info@albergopietrasanta.com
website
www.albergopietrasanta.com

Nearby Pisa (25 km); Lucca (25 km);
beaches (4 km).
Location on pedestrian street in
town centre; private garage
Food breakfast
Prices €€€€
Rooms 19; 8 double and twin, 1 single, 10 suites, all with bath or shower; all rooms have phone, TV, minibar, air conditioning, safe
Facilities sitting rooms, bar, breakfast room/winter garden, gym,
Turkish bath, garden
Credit cards AE, DC, MC, V
Disabled 2 specially adapted rooms
Pets accepted by arrangement
Closed early Jan to Mar
Manager Marisa Giuliano

Albergo Pietrasanta
Town hotel

Pietrasanta (the 'Sainted Stone') has long been associated with the marble industry. The world-famous quarries at Carrara are nearby, and the attractive little town thrives on marble studios, bronze foundries, and a subculture of artists from all over the world. Recently, tourism here has moved upmarket, and the Albergo Pietrasanta is a response to this development. Opened in 1997, the hotel occupies elegant 17thC Palazzo Barsanti-Bonetti in the centre of town. The interior maintains many of the embellishments of a nobleman's house: intricate plasterwork, delicate frescoes, a couple of superbly-carved marble fireplaces, spacious rooms and antiques. However, the addition of the owners' contemporary art collection adds a totally new dimension.

The comfortable, unfussy bedrooms have warm, parquet floors, armchairs, smart fabrics and varying colour schemes. Thoughtful extras (cool linen sheets, plenty of mirrors, well-designed lighting and the tray of vin santo and biscuits) impressed our inspector. Downstairs, the winter garden doubles as breakfast room and bar while the pretty gravelled garden, dominated by three old palm trees, is a cool spot in summer.

Lungarno Pacinotti 12, 56126 Pisa

Tel 050 940111
e-mail mail@royalvictoria.it
website www.royalvictoria.it

Nearby Palazzo Reale; Piazza dei
Cavalieri; Leaning Tower.
Location on north bank of Arno
with private garage and lift
Food breakfast
Price €€
Rooms 48 doubles and twin, all but
8 with bath or shower; all rooms
have phone, TV, hairdrier on request
Facilities sitting room, breakfast
room, roof terrace
Credit cards AE, DC, MC, V
Disabled no special facilities
Pets accepted
Closed never
Proprietors Nicola and Maurizio
Piegaja

Royal Victoria
Town hotel

Famous worldwide for its now-not-so-leaning tower, Pisa has a long history as a tourist destination, having been an important stop on the Grand tour. These days, its hotels are disappointingly short on charm with the exception of the Royal Victoria, a relic of that golden age of travel which occupies a *palazzo* on the north bank of the Arno. It attraction lies in the rather funky retro atmosphere as opposed to its creatue comforts, but it has many fans and we are pleased to include it.

The hotel dates back some 160 years although the *palazzo* itself is very much older. The old fashioned lobby is adorned with potted palms and the walls are hung with framed letters from past guests who include Dickens, the Duke of Wellington and Ruskin. Upstairs, the bedrooms are fairly spartan with lumbering old furniture and 60s bathrooms (due to be renovated), but mattresses and fabrics are new. Room 202 is extraordinary, with creaky old parquet, floor-to-ceiling medieval-style trompe l'oeil frescoes and painted furniture. The breakfast room belongs to the same rather dreamy, bygone age. There are several sitting areas, but far the best place to relax with a book and an aperitivo is the plant-filled roof terrace.

Via di Pieve a Celle, 158 - 51030
Pistoia

Tel 0573 913087
e-mail info@tenutadipieveacelle.it
website www.tenutadipieveacelle.it

Nearby Pistoia (3 km); Montecatini
Terme (10 km); Florence (30 km).
Location 3 km NW of Pistoia in
own grounds with parking; take the
Abetone road from the autostrada,
come off at Pistoia Ovest, follow
signs to Montagnana; the entrance is
after 2 km on the right
Food breakfast, diner on request
Price €€€
Rooms 5 double, all with shower; all
rooms have TV, air conditioning,
hairdrier
Facilities sitting room, breakfast
room, terraces, garden, swimming
pool, mountain bikes
Credit cards MC, V
Disabled ground floor room Pets
not accepted
Closed never
Proprietors Fiorenza and Cesare
Saccenti

Pieve a Celle
Country guesthouse

Little visited Pistoia is a jewel of a town
which offers easy access to Florence,
Lucca and Pisa. This new agriturismo is situated near the zoo; at night the silence
may be broken by the incongruous sounds
of wild animal noises. Set in 1,700 acres of
land planted with olives, vines and woods
broken by walking paths and mountain
bike tracks, the house is a typically solid
Tuscan rural building. Inside, the usual rustic formula of terracotta floors, beamed
ceilings and so on has been brightened up
by warm colours on the walls and some
imaginative furnishings. An open fire burns
in the sitting room to welcome guests in
cold weather while upstairs, the bedrooms
are charmingly decorated with pretty fabrics (designed by the owner, who is in the
textile business) and mainly furnished with
antiques. Wrought-iron four poster beds
are hung with white linen while bright kil-
ims and African textiles sit well with warm
sand coloured walls.

Bordered by wooden decking, the sub-
stantial pool is surrounded by vineyards
and utterly peaceful views. The Saccentis'
style is very relaxed, and they are warm
hosts. Although there are good places to
eat in Pistoia, you should stay in at least
once to sample the delights of Fiorenza's
excellent cooking.

Pistoia

Villa di Piteccio, 51030 Pistoia

Tel 0573 42031
e-mail info@volpe-uva.it
website www.volpe-uva.it

Nearby Pistoia (6 km); Florence (35 km); Lucca (45 km).
Location 6 km N of Pistoia, take Abetone road from Pistoia and branch right; the hotel is 2 km above Piteccio
Food breakfast, lunch, dinner
Price €
Rooms 8 double and twin with bath (not all baths en suite)
Facilities 2 sitting rooms, games room, dining room, terrace, garden
Credit cards AE, DC, MC, V
Disabled no special facilities
Pets not accepted
Closed never
Managers the Bordonaro family

Villa Vannini
Country villa

We have received more reader's letters about Villa Vannini than any other hotel in the guide, and they have all been exuberant in their praise. Situated in a remote and delightfully peaceful setting high on the hill not far from the lively little town of Pistoia, access is via a narrow road which winds up through unspoilt countryside. The venerable Signora Vannini handed over the hotel several years ago to the charming Bordonaro family who offer a warm welcome and fabulous food. As we go to press we hear that they are leaving to run a hotel in the north, and, while no definite plans have been made, the future of the hotel is uncertain.

There are various little sitting areas with large vases of flowers, chintz-covered or chunky modern seats, prints and watercolours and the sort of antiques that complete a family home. The dining room, with its whitewashed walls, polished parquet and soft background jazz makes an elegant setting for Luigi Bordonaro and his daughter Francesca's 'inspirational and exquisitely fresh' cooking based on Tuscan specialities: there is nothing to be gained from eating out.

Bedrooms are beautifully and individually firnished with flowery fabrics and fine antiques; bathrooms are mainly spacious and old-fashioned. In front of the house, a simple terrace provides a haven after a day's sightseeing.

Prato

Via di Canneto 16, 59100 Prato,
Firenze

Tel 0574 460392
e-mail canneto@masternet.it
website www.toskana.net/villarucel-lai

Nearby Prato; Florence (20 km).
Location down a narrow street, in
Bisenzio river valley, 4 km NE of
Prato (keep parallel with river and
railway line on your left); car parking
Food breakfast
Price €
Rooms 11; 10 double and twin, 1
family, all with bath or shower
Facilities sitting room, TV room,
dining room, gym, terrace, garden,
swimming pool
Credit cards not accepted
Disabled not suitable
Pets not accepted
Closed never
Proprietors Rucellai Piqué family

Villa Rucellai
Country villa

This is a quintessential charming small hotel. Industrial Prato creeps almost to the doors of the mellow old villa, and the railway line skirts the property, but this should not stop you from visiting a very special place. Its origins date back to a medieval watchtower, and it has been in the venerable Rucellai family since 1740. The unsightly views from the lovely terrace – filled with lemon trees – and the loggia, are more than compensated for by the atmosphere of the house, the warm welcome and the modest prices. Behind the property rise the beautiful Pratese Hills, which can be explored on foot from the house.

Guests have the run of the main part of the house, with its baronial hall and comfortable sitting room, filled with pictures and books. Breakfast is self-service and is taken around a communal table in the homely dining room. The bedrooms are simply furnished and full of character; they reflect the rare attribute of the place – that of a well-run hotel which gives no hint of being anything but a cultivated family home. Recent algae problems in the swimming pool seem to have been solved.

Radda in Chianti

Via Pianigiani 15, 53017 Radda in Chianti, Siena

Tel 0577 738300
e-mail vignale@vignale.it
website www.vignale.it

Nearby Siena (31 km); Florence (52 km).
Location in middle of village, 31 km N of Siena; car parking
Food breakfast, snacks
Price €€€
Rooms 40; 31 double and twin, 4 single, 2 family rooms, 3 suites, all with bath or shower; all rooms have phone, air conditioning, minibar
Facilities 3 sitting rooms, breakfast room, bars, conference room, terrace, garden, swimming pool
Credit cards AE, MC, V
Disabled access difficult
Pets not accepted
Closed 3 weeks Dec, early Jan to mid-Mar
Manager Silvia Kummer

Relais Fattoria Vignale
Country hotel

This has always been a favourite with our inspectors, and recent visits have left their enthusiasm undimmed. The house is built on a slope down from the middle of the village. On the main 'ground' floor are four interconnecting sitting rooms, each on a domestic scale, and beautifully furnished with comfy sofas, antiques, muted rugs on polished terracotta floors, walls (either white and dotted with paintings or covered by murals) and one or two grand stone fireplaces. The bedrooms above are similarly classy, with waxed wooden doors, white walls and antique beds. The sitting rooms, the back bedrooms and the pool all share a grand view across the Radda Valley. Ten further rooms are housed in a heated annexe across the road.

A recent addition to the Relais Fattoria Vignale is the lovely breakfast terrace; in cool weather there is a neat breakfast room in a brick vault beneath the hotel, where an excellent buffet is set out, and coffee and extras are served by friendly waitresses. There is also a taverna providing light dinners.

Three hundred metres from the hotel (and under the same ownership) is the Vignale Restaurant which serves excellent (but pricey) creative Italian dishes.

Although they are tolerated, children will not be popular here unless they are as quiet as mice.

Reggello

Vággio 76, 50066 Reggello, Firenze

Tel 055 8656718/562
e-mail hotel@villarigacci.it
website www.villarigacci.it

Nearby Florence (30 km); Arezzo
(45 km).
Location 300 m N of Vággio, 30 km
SE of Florence (exit Incisa from A1);
car parking
Food breakfast, lunch, dinner
Price €€
Rooms 28; 20 double and twin, 3
single, 5 suites, all with bath or
shower; all rooms have phone, TV,
minibar, air conditioning
Facilities sitting rooms, library, din-
ing room, garden, swimming pool
Credit cards AE, DC, MC, V
Disabled not suitable
Pets small ones accepted
Closed never
Proprietors Frederic Pierazzi

Villa Rigacci
Hilltop villa

This creeper-covered 15thC farmhouse,
in the second decade since its transformation from private home to charming
small hotel, is in a beautiful secluded spot
– on a hilltop surrounded by olive groves,
pines, chestnut trees and meadows – yet
only a few kilometres from the Florence-
Rome autostrada, and a short drive from
Florence and Arezzo.

Many of the original features of the
house have been preserved – arched
doorways, beamed bedrooms, tiled or
stone-flagged floors – and it is furnished as
a cherished private house might be. The
sitting room has an open fire in chilly
weather. The bedrooms – the best (though
not all) of them gloriously spacious – are
full of gleaming antiques, and overlook the
gardens or swimming pool, which is of fair
size, with a pleasant tile-and-grass surround and woodland views. For relaxation,
there are plenty of quiet, shady spots in
the park, which contains some magnificent
trees.

These days, the food is predominantly
Tuscan with some French influences - it
used to be rather upmarket French, which
wasn't to everybody's taste. Families are
offered special rates and are well catered
for in that there is a small playground area
and part of the pool is given over to kids.

San Casciano dei Bagni

53040 San Casciano dei Bagni, Siena

Tel 0578 58174
e-mail info@settequerce.it
website www.settequerce.it

Nearby Thermal baths; Orvieto (40 km); Montepulciano (40 km).
Location on street just outside town; public car parking next door
Food breakfast
Price €€€
Rooms 9 suites with bath; all rooms have phone, TV, air conditioning, minibar, hairdrier
Facilities bar, restaurant, terraces
Credit cards AE, DC, MC, V
Disabled 2 specially adapted suites
Pets small ones accepted
Closed 2 weeks Jan
Proprietors Daniela, Maurizio and Silvestro Boni

Sette Querce
Village guesthouse

Several generations of Daniela Boni's family have run the local bar in this tiny spa town, located high in the hills in a remote corner of southern Tuscany. The family business expanded in 1997 to include this delightful and original hotel, and, most recently, the bar has extended into an excellent restaurant (located 100 m from the main building).

The name derives from the fact that the rambling townhouse backs on to an oak wood. The contemporary interior design is a refreshing change from the Tuscan norm. At ground level, earth tones, vivid reds and pinks prevail. Bedrooms on the second floor are in sunny yellows and greens, and, at the top, shades of blue predominate. The cheerful fabrics on chairs, curtains, cushions and duvets are by Designers Guild. The rooms are all dotted with ornaments (old irons, rustic ceramics, basket ware) while framed black-and-white photos depicting the history of the town hang on the walls. Each bedroom has a comfortable sitting area (compensating for the lack of public sitting room) and a cleverly-designed kitchenette. Bathrooms are immaculate and several have Jacuzzis.

San Casciano Val di Pesa

Via Collina 40, Loc. Montefiridolfi,
50026 San Casciano, Firenze

Tel 055 8244288
e-mail info@fattorialaloggia.com
website www.fattorialaloggia.com

Nearby Florence (18 km), San
Gimignano (40 km), Siena (45 km).
Location 18 km S of Florence, E of
road to Siena; car parking
Food breakfast
Prices €€
Rooms 4 double, 11 apartments for
2-6 people, all with bath or shower;
all rooms/apartments have phone,
fridge, safe, TV
Facilities garden, solarium, swim-
ming pool, table tennis, barbeque
Credit cards not accepted
Disabled one adapted apartment
Pets accepted by arrangement
Closed never
Proprietor Giulio Baruffaldi

Fattoria la Loggia
Country estate

Montefiridolfi is set in classic Chianti
countryside scattered with ancient
estates producing wine and olive oil. Many
of the mellow, stone farm buildings here-
abouts are being turned into tourist
accom-modation of one sort or another,
and Fattoria la Loggia is one of the most
successful of its type: a range of spacious
and attractive apartments agreeably
housed in a hamlet-like collection of rural
dwellings, in a hilltop setting with views
over gloriously peaceful surroundings. The
apartments are let daily or weekly. But this
is not simply a self-catering complex –
cooking lessons and dinners with wine
tastings are sometimes organized in the
cellar.

Each unit is carefully furnished with
country-style pieces and many personal
touches; kitchens and bathrooms, however, are efficiently modern, and are finished
to a very high standard. Visitors can swim,
ride, or walk on the estate, which produces its own wine and olive oil. La Loggia
has recently established an artists' studio,
with a permanent museum of contemporary art, as well as providing a venue for
concerts and theatre.

San Casciano Val di Pesa

Via Empolese 69, 50026 San
Casciano Val di Pesa, Firenze

Tel 055 828311
e-mail villailpoggiale@villailpog-
giale.it
website www.villailpoggiale.it

Nearby Florence (17 km); Siena (55
km); Chianti.
Location 2 km SW of San Casciano
off Empoli road in own grounds with
parking
Food breakfast, light lunch on
request when pool is open
Prices €€€
Rooms 21; 19 double and twin, 2
suites and 3 self-catering apartments
all with bath or shower; all rooms
have phone, TV, air conditioning,
fridge, kettle, safe, hairdrier
Facilities sitting rooms library,
breakfast room, terraces, garden,
swimming pool
Credit cards DC, MC, V
Disabled access difficult **Pets** not
accepted
Closed Feb **General manager**
Caterina Piccolominii

Villa il Poggiale
Country villa

Family home of one of the owners until
quite recently, Il Poggiale is a pale
salmon-coloured villa dating from the 16th
century. At the front of the house, a gracious Renaissance loggia overlooks an
expanse of green lawn protected by
ancient cypress trees. It opened as a hotel
in April 2003 after careful restoration, but
still maintains the feeling of a private
house.

On arrival, guests are shown into a spacious, elegant salon dominated by a vast
chandelier; family portraits hang on the
walls while soothing classical music plays in
the background. Drinks are laid out on a
table to which guests can help themselves
and sign a chit. Generous breakfasts (with
home-made breads, cakes and jams) are
served in a pretty dining room with pink
and white striped tablecloths.

The bedrooms, each different from the
next, are beautifully furnished and roman-
tically decorated (several have four
posters) in dusty blues and pinks with
filmy white curtains and colourful bedspreads and rugs. Bathrooms are gorgeous
too; one (entirely frescoed) has a claw-
foot bath. Outside, a long terrace runs
along the west wall of the villa. Breakfast is
served here in summer, but it is also a glorious spot from which to enjoy spectacular sunsets.

San Gimignano

Via San Matteo 87, 53037 San Gimignano, Siena

Tel 0577 942014
e-mail info@anticopozzo.com
website www.anticopozzo.com

Nearby duomo; Museo Civico; Torre Grossa.
Location on pedestrian street in centre of town; public car parking (300 m)
Food breakfast
Price €€
Rooms 18; 17 double and twin, 1 single, all with bath or shower; all rooms have phone, TV, air conditioning, minibar
Facilities bar, breakfast room, terrace, lift
Credit cards AE, DC, MC, V
Disabled 2 specially adapted rooms
Pets not accepted
Closed 6 weeks in winter
Proprietor Emanuele Marro

L'Antico Pozzo
Town guesthouse

The ancient brick well in question (pozzo means well) is in the entrance hall of this fine, 15thC townhouse situated on one of the pedestrian streets leading up to San Gimignano's central Piazza del Duomo. The building was beautifully restored in 1990, and is now, in our view, possibly the best hotel in town.

A stone staircase leads up to the large first floor bedrooms and the breakfast room, the latter known as the sala rosa, thanks to its deep pink walls. The waxed and worn terracotta tiles on this floor are original, as are the high, beamed ceilings. Several rooms have delicate frescoes; in one, the walls and ceiling are entirely painted with garlands of flowers and elegant, dancing figures.

Rooms on the upper floors are smaller, but still most attractive. Those at the top have attic ceilings and views of the famous towers or countryside to compensate for their small size.

The furnishings throughout are in simple good taste; carefully-chosen antiques mix well with the wrought-iron beds; colours are muted. A pretty, walled terrace is an added bonus.

Recent reports on Il Pozzo have been generally very positive although several mention steep stairs (there is also a lift) and a lack of public sitting areas.

San Giovanni d'Asso

Via Sant'Emidio 10,
Monterongriffoli, 53020 San
Giovanni d'Asso, Siena

Tel 0577 802 943
e-mail info@ankhura.com
website www.ankhura.com

Nearby Montalcino, Montepulciano
Val d'Orcia sights; Pienza,
Montepulciano.
Location between San Giovanni
D'Asso and Torrenieri, take the
gravel road signposted
Monterongriffoli, hotel is inside the
hamlet, with parking next to the
church
Food breakfast, dinner, lunch on
request – residents only
Price €
Rooms 4, all with bath or shower
Facilities sitting room, garden
Credit cards not accepted
Disabled not suitable
Pets by arrangement
Closed never
Proprietor Christopher and
Tina Tung

Ankhura
Country guesthouse

This place is so discreet that at first we couldn't find it. Located up a half-mile gravel track in a semi-inhabited medieval hamlet, hidden behind the church, with no signposts and only a small carved stone plaque to identify it, Ankhura gives real meaning to the over-used term 'retreat' as applied to Tuscan rural hideaways. Owners Christopher and Tina left Wall Street and started a new life here in 2001, converting a village house into a simple public space with just four bedrooms. It's all fresh and clean, and while certainly comfortable enough, it isn't luxurious. Guests share a large fridge for drinks on the first floor, and in warm weather can eat out on the terrace which overlooks a charming little wooded valley, and leads the eye to the classic Tuscan landscape beyond.

This is Italy's best truffle country, and Ankhura's unique selling point is the activities it offers guests: not just cooking classes and wine tours, but truffle hunts with a local *tartufaio* and his dog; and guided walks with an expert on local flora. This is a guesthouse, albeit a charming variation on the usual theme. If you eat in, it'll be with the other guests at a single table. But, if you want, you could have complete privacy, hardly meeting the owners or guests: there's a separate guest entrance and you're given a key. Christopher and Tina's easygoing charm and dedication to their new lifestyle ensure that it's an unusual, perhaps even exclusive experience.

San Gusme

Loc. Arceno, San Gusme, 53010
Castelnuovo Berardenga, Siena

Tel 0577 359292
e-mail mail@relaisvillarceno.com
website www.relaisvillarceno.com

Nearby Siena (25 km); Florence (85
km).
Location 30 km NE of Siena; car
parking
Food breakfast, light lunch, dinner
Price €€€€
Rooms 16; 12 double, 4 suites, all
with bath; all rooms have phone, TV,
air conditioning, minibar
Facilities sitting rooms, restaurant,
garden, tennis, swimming pool,
mountain bikes
Credit cards AE, DC, MC, V
Disabled not suitable **Pets** small
dogs accepted by arrangement
Closed mid-Nov to Mar
Proprietor Gualtiero Mancini

Villa Arceno
Country villa

Villa Arceno originally served as a hunting lodge for a Tuscan noble family, but
'lodge' is too humble a word to describe
this aristocratic building. A long, private
road winds through the thousand-hectare
estate (which has many farmhouses converted into apartments) to the square,
rigidly symmetrical villa with its overhanging eaves, surrounded by lawns, gravel
paths and flower-filled terracotta urns. In
front of the villa is a separate, walled park
in the Romantic style, with shady paths
leading down to a small lake.

Inside, a cool, elegant style prevails: off-
white walls and vaulted ceilings contrast
with the warmth of terracotta floors
(strewn with Persian carpets), reproduction antique furniture and light yellow
drapes. The atmosphere is formal, but not
stiffly so: the highly professional staff make
guests feel more than welcome.
Upstairs, the guest rooms, which are all
light and spacious, have been individually
decorated. Particularly attractive is the
suite, which has a bay of three arched windows. Some rooms have their own terraces. You should also ask to see the spiral
stairway of the central tower that finishes
in a rooftop gazebo.

The hotel does not accept children
under 12.

Via Poliziano 18, 53027 San Quirico
d'Orcia, Siena

Tel 0577 899028
e-mail info@palazzodelcapitano.com
website
www.palazzodelcapitano.com

Nearby Pienza, Montepulciano
Location near town centre in pedes-
trian zone
Food breakfast, lunch, dinner
Prices €
Rooms 16 double and twin, all with
bathm phone, TV, safe
Facilities bar, dining room, sitting
room, large garden, swimming pool,
laundry service, boutique, wine tast-
ing, horse riding, taxi service, quad
rental, massages, bike service
Credit cards V, MC
Disabled not suitable
Pets accepted
Closed never
Proprietor Genovese Roberto

Palazzo del Capitano
Town hotel

San Quirico is charming, well kept and
unspoiled; and you could say the same
of this (fairly recently) opened town hotel
a few minutes from the main square. The
public spaces downstairs are simple but
full of character: a roomy entrance lobby
and a spacious bar-dining room under a
vaulted ceiling. Up a flight of stairs cheer-
fully decorated corridors lead to bedrooms carved out of interesting spaces; in
one, the bathroom, on a much higher level,
is reached by a steep staircase – almost a
ladder. But the clinching factor here is the
large, well-tended garden. Plenty of shade,
and plenty of space for lounging in the sun,
and a collection of curious lights. A great
place to come and relax in after exploring
the Val d'Orica's sights.

Another significant bonus is that the
hotel is in the same ownership as Al
Vecchio Forno, San Quirico's best restaurant, which has a solid reputation among
the locals.

Scansano

Scansano, 58054 Grosseto

Tel 0564 507219
e-mail info@anticocasaledis-
cansano.com **website** www.antico-
casalediscansano.com/cucina.uk.html

Nearby Thermal spa of Saturnia;
Argentarian coast.
Location in countryside 30 km SE
of Grosseto; car parking
Food breakfast, lunch, dinner,
snacks
Price €€
Rooms 32; 21 double, 6 single, 1
family room all with shower, 4 suites
with Jacuzzi bath; all rooms have
phone, TV, air conditioning, mini-
bar, hairdrier
Facilities sitting room, dining room,
bar, terrace, swimming pool, horse
riding **Credit cards** AE, DC, MC, V
Disabled 2 adapted rooms
Pets accepted if well behaved
Closed never; restaurant closed mid
Jan-mid Feb
Proprietor Massimo Pellegrini

Antico Casale di
Scansano **Country hotel**

Two widely-travelled readers wrote in
enthusiastic terms to draw our attention to this captivating hotel in the coastal
region of Tuscany known as the Maremma,
south-east of Grosseto. We can scarcely
improve on their verdicts: 'Rooms sweetly
decorated with country antiques and a
lovely restaurant with terrace overlooking
a spectacular green valley with vineyards
and olive groves; a truly relaxing experience.' And: 'In four months touring the
country, we thought this hotel number
one; we were impressed by the welcome
and hospitality, the surroundings – even
the beds were the best we encountered in
Italy.' A recent report praised the food,
which is 'local and delicious'.

The Antico Casale is a beautifully
restored, 200-year-old farmhouse which
retains more of its origins than most such
places. The Macereto estate of which it is
part produces a range of grappa, olive oil
and wines (including the Morellino di
Scansano DOC); many surrounding farms
produce olive oil, and the Casale's stables
are in very active use: riding holidays are
offered (with instruction if you need it),
and the hotel even offers special 'DB&B
and horse' rates. Wine-tasting and cookery courses too.

Pian dei Mantellini 34, 53100 Siena

Tel 0577 280462
e-mail bureau@palazzoravizza.it
website www.palazzoravizza.it

Nearby Duomo; Ospedale Santa
Maria della Scala.
Location just SW of town centre in
residential street; car parking
Food breakfast, dinner
Price €€
Rooms 40; 30 double and twin, 3
single, 7 suites, all with bath or
shower; all rooms have phone, TV,
minibar, hairdrier
Facilities sitting rooms, bar, restau-
rant, garden
Credit cards AE, DC, MC, V
Disabled adapted room
Pets accepted
Closed never
Proprietor Francesco Grotanelli de
Santi

Palazzo Ravizza
Town hotel

Siena is notorious for its dearth of decent hotels in the centre of town, so we were delighted to see that Palazzo Ravizza has undergone a facelift and is now a very pleasant place in which to stay. Fortunately, the old-fashioned, slightly faded charm has not been sacrificed to modernization. The bedrooms still have their heavy – at times quirky – period furniture and polished parquet or terracotta floors, but the fabrics have been smartened up and bathrooms are all shining new with heated towel rails. Some even have double Jacuzzis.

Downstairs, the public rooms (in part with smart black and white floor tiles) have pretty painted ceilings and comfortable armchairs and sofas. There is a cosy library, as well as a smart new bar and an elegantly-appointed (now independent) restaurant; the 'obligatory half board in high season' rule no longer applies.

The garden at the back is a great asset and has recently been re-designed in formal Italian style: it provides a cool and shady respite from the city heat, and tables are laid outside for breakfast and dinner in the summer.

Sinalunga

53048 Sinalunga, Siena

Tel 0577 679497
e-mail locanda@amorosa.it
website www.amorosa.it

Nearby Siena (45 km); Arezzo (45 km); Chianti.
Location 2 km S of Sinalunga; car parking
Food breakfast, lunch, dinner
Price €€€€€
Rooms 25; 17 double, 8 suites, all with bath or shower; all rooms have phone, TV, air conditioning, minibar
Facilities sitting room, dining room, bar
Credit cards AE, DC, MC, V
Disabled access difficult
Pets not accepted
Closed mid-Jan to mid Mar; restaurant Mon, Tue
Manager Carlo Citterio

Locanda dell'Amorosa
Country inn

The Locanda dell'Amorosa is as romantic as it sounds. An elegant Renaissance villa-cum-village, within the remains of 14thC walls, has been converted into a charming country inn.

The old stables, beamed and brick-walled, have been transformed into a delightful rustic (but pricey) restaurant serving refined nouvelle-style versions of traditional Tuscan recipes, using ingredients from the estate, which also produces wine.

Only a fortunate few can actually stay here – either in apartments in the houses where peasants and farmworkers once lived, or in ordinary bedrooms in the old family residence. The bedrooms are cool, airy and pretty, with whitewashed walls, terracotta floors, antique furniture and Florentine curtains and bedspreads – and immaculate modern bathrooms.

To complete the village there is a little parish church with lovely 15thC frescoes of the Sienese school. While certainly not an authentic feature, the recently installed pool, surrounded by vineyards and enjoying marvellous views of the rolling countryside, is a great asset. With discreet, attentive service, the Locanda is a paradise for connoisseurs of Tuscany, for gourmets and for all romantics. It is, however, popular with up-market tour groups.

Piazza Cairoli, 58010 Sorano,
Grosseto

Tel 0564 632010
e-mail fortezza@fortezzahotel.it

Nearby Pitgliano (9 km); Lake
Bolsena (20 km).
Location 9 km NE of Pitigliano, on
edge of town; car parking
Food breakfast
Price €€€
Rooms 16; 14 double and twin, 2
suites, all with bath; all rooms have
phone, TV, minibar, hairdrier
Facilities breakfast room, sitting
room, terraces
Credit cards AE, MC, V
Disabled one specially adapted
room
Pets small ones accepted
Closed early Jan to Mar
Proprietor Luciano Caruso

Hotel della Fortezza
Castle guesthouse

For enthusiasts of archaeology, this remote corner of the Maremma – with its abundance of Etruscan remains – is a dream. The ancient, picturesque town of Sorano is built on a tufa outcrop and is surrounded by the hills of the Alta Maremma. The imposing 11thC Orsini fortress is dramatically situated on the edge of the town and now partially occupied by a stylish hotel. After dark, the place is floodlit, and the approach to the hotel across an old suspension bridge and through several courtyards is like taking a step back into the Middle Ages.

Once inside, however, the comforts are very much of this century although the tasteful and careful restoration has been carried out with full respect for the building's origins. The solid walls are pale throughout, warmed by soft lighting while beamed ceilings and terracotta floors are in tone with the surroundings. A collection of 19thC antiques blend well with fine reproduction pieces and fabrics in deep blue and gold. There are some wonderful old beds in the comfortable bedrooms which vary enormously in shape and size. All have fabulous views over the rooftops of unspoiled countryside.

Sovicille

Loc. Pretale, 53018 Sovicille, Siena

Tel 0577 345401
e-mail info@borgopretale.it
website www.borgopretale.it

Nearby Siena (20 km); San
Gimignano (28 km).
Location 20 km SW of Siena on
quiet hillside; car parking
Food breakfast, lunch (buffet by
pool Jun-Sep), dinner
Price €€€
Rooms 35; 32 double, 3 suites, all
with bath or shower; all rooms have
phone, TV, air conditioning, mini-
bar, safe
Facilities sitting room, restaurant,
bar, sauna, garden, swimming pool,
tennis, archery, gym, mountain bikes
Credit cards AE, DC, MC, V
Disabled not suitable **Pets** not
accepted
Closed Nov to early Apr
Manager Daniele Rizzardini

Borgo Pretale
Hillside hamlet

A long, winding, unsurfaced road through
wooded hills brings you to this group
of grey stone houses clustered around a
massive 12thC watchtower. Local histori-
ans claim that it was part of a system of
such towers, spread across the Sienese
hills, all within line of sight, to communi-
cate quickly any news of approaching
invaders and to provide protection against
their rampages. Nowadays, this civilized
retreat offers a haven from the stresses of
modern life.

Every detail has been considered in the
restoration and decoration. The harshness
of the medieval structure has been less-
ened by the use of well-chosen antiques,
mellow lighting and rich, striped fabrics. A
serenely beautiful 15thC carved wooden
Madonna, bearing the Infant Christ, stands
in a brick-framed niche.

Every bedroom contains a different
blend of the same artful ingredients, each
splendid in its own way, though we particularly liked those in the tower. The stylish
restaurant serves a limited choice of dishes (but all well prepared) and has an
extensive wine list on which a sommelier
can offer advice. And tucked away, close to
the edge of the woods, is an inviting pool.

Vicchio

Via di Campestri 19, 50039 Vicchio
di Mugello, Firenze

Tel 055 8490107
e-mail villa.campestri@villacam-
pestri.it
website www.villacampestri.it

Nearby Florence (35 km).
Location in countryside 3 km S of
Vicchio, 35 km NE of Florence; car
parking
Food breakfast, dinner; snacks
Price €€€
Rooms 21; 14 double and twin, 1
single, 6 suites, all with bath or
shower; all rooms have phone, TV,
minibar
Facilities sitting room, dining room,
garden, swimming pool
Credit cards MC, V
Disabled 4 specially adapted bed-
rooms
Pets accepted by arrangement
Closed mid Nov-mid Mar
Proprietor Paolo Pasquali

Villa Campestri
Country villa

Get clear directions before you set off
for this hilltop villa: it is in an isolated
location, some way south of the village of
Vicchio di Mugello.

The house looks classically Renaissance,
but actually dates back to the 13th century. It overlooks sloping hillsides of mown
grass, and miles of unspoiled countryside –
much of it part of the villa's own estate.
Inside, many original features remain: an
old chapel, 14thC frescoes, massive interi-
or doors, and timbered ceilings.
Furnishings blend with this venerable setting, including some valuable antiques,
notably a vast and regal four-poster bed
and an 18thC sofa. Plain white walls offset
the dark wood of beams and furniture.
Most of the bedrooms are handsomely
furnished and spacious – some might find
them too grand for comfort. Although one
satisfied guest found them 'very comfortable indeed' and 'well worth' the high
prices. Bathrooms are beautifully tiled in
blue and white. The open-plan sitting room
and dining room are traditionally furnished
and fairly formal; the restaurant is
renowned, and local dignitaries make the
long trek to enjoy its food. Breakfast was a
disappointment for one visitor, though. The
staff are kind and welcoming, and if you're
lucky the owner may entertain you with a
little piano music after dinner.

Loc. Montanino, Volpaia, 53017
Radda in Chianti, Siena

Tel 0577 738832
e-mail info@lalocanda.it
website www.lalocanda.it

Nearby Florence (48 km); Siena (38 km).
Location 4 km W of Volpaia (signed from piazza in the village) follow signs to the hotel; car parking.
Food breakfast, dinner on request
Price €€€€
Rooms 7; 6 double and twin, 1 suite, all with bath; all rooms have phone, TV, hairdrier, safe
Facilities sitting rooms, bar, dining room, terraces, garden, swimming pool
Credit cards AE, DC, MC, V
Disabled ground floor rooms available
Pets not accepted
Closed mid-Nov to mid-Mar
Proprietors Guido and Martina Bevilaqua

La Locanda
Country guesthouse

The Bevilaquas (he Neapolitan, she Milanese) began their search for the ideal spot in which to set up their guesthouse four years ago. In April 1999, what was once a collection of ruined farm buildings high up in the Chianti hills finally opened for business, and you would be hard pressed to find a more beautiful setting. At 600 m above sea level, views from the terraces, garden, pool and some of the rooms are of layers of hills, striped with vines and shaded with woods; in the foreground is the mellow old fortified hamlet of Volpaia.

The restoration of the pale stone buildings has been done with unerring good taste. Interiors, while maintaining many of the rustic features, have a refreshingly contemporary look with an imaginative use of colour throughout to offset plenty of terracotta and wood.

The comfortable bedrooms have an uncluttered feel, and the bathrooms are spacious and gleaming. One end of the long, sunny living room is dominated by a massive stone fireplace, and filled with colourfully-upholstered sofas and armchairs.

Barberino Val d'Elsa

Loc. San Filippo, 50021 Barberino
Val d'Elsa, Firenze

Tel 055 8059218 **Fax** 055 8059231
e-mail ilparetaio@tin.it
website www.ilparetaio.it
Food breakfast, dinner
Price €€
Closed never
Proprietors Giovanni and Cristina
de March

Il Paretaio
Country guesthouse

A great address for those interested in horse riding but not to be dismissed by any traveller in search of the country life. Strategically located between Florence and Siena, in hilly surroundings, Il Paretaio is a 17thC stone-built farmhouse on its own large estate. The accommodation is simple but attractive. The ground floor entrance and sitting area was originally a work room, and still retains the old stone paving. A huge brick arch spans the central space and brick-vaulting contrasts with the plain white walls. Upstairs, the rustic style is continued in the exposed-beam ceilings and worn terracotta floors.

Castellina in Chianti

Via Ferruccio 26, 53011 Castellina
in Chianti, Siena

Tel 0577 741186 **e-mail**
info@palazzosquarcialupi.com
website
www.palazzosquarcialupi.com
Food buffet breakfast; bar snacks
Price €€
Closed Nov to mid-Mar
Proprietors Targioni family

Palazzo Squarcialupi
Town hotel

P alazzo Squarcialupi is set in the medieval village of Castellina in Chianti, and when our reporter first came here, she was struck by the friendly, peaceful atmosphere and the lovely rooms. It is a 14thC stone building with arched doors and windows, which was formerly an imposing farmhouse. It has been renovated in a simple, stylish way, while retaining its traditional farm character. There are 17 large bedrooms and suites with plain white walls, beamed ceilings and dark wooden furniture. Downstairs there is a rustic sitting room in muted tones of white, cream and terracotta, and another elegant room with frescoes.

Castelnuovo Berardenga

Loc. Curina, 53019 Castelnuovo
Berardenga, Siena

Tel 0577 355630
e-mail info@villacurina.it
website www.villacurina.it
Food breakfast, dinner
Price €€€
Closed Nov-Mar/Apr
Manager Andrea de Agostini

Villa Curina
Country villa

A vivacious, convivial atmosphere per-vades this hotel-and-apartment complex set in low, rolling countryside north of Siena. When we visited, it was full of activity, with people enjoying themselves in the pool, playing tennis or setting off for bike rides. The main villa, surrounded by ornamental gardens and trees, is a large, cream-coloured, 18thC building and contains the guest bedrooms as well as the principal public rooms. Most of the apartments are in three old stone farmhouses with small, brown-shuttered windows and connected by pathways of Siena brick. An attractive restaurant, spanned by strong brick arches, serves fresh produce from the estate.

Gaiole in Chianti

Gaiole in Chianti, 53013 Siena

Tel 0577 749483
e-mail info@spaltenna.it
website spaltenna.it
Food breakfast, lunch, dinner
Prices €€€
Closed early Jan to late Mar
Manager Guido Conti

Castello di Spaltenna
Castle hotel

A dramatically situated, fortified monastery on a hilltop next to the medieval church of Santa Maria di Spaltenna, built round a central courtyard. The present management has been in place for some years now and has carried out extensive redecoration and renovation. Cosy standard rooms are in what were the monk's cells, while suites and de luxe rooms (done out in up-market country style) are housed in various outbuildings. There is a plethora of facilities (pools, sauna, gym, Jacuzzis and so on) but a dearth of atmosphere. The food, served in a rather formal room, is good but expensive.

Gaiole in Chianti

Gaiole in Chianti, 53013 Siena

Tel 0577 746067
e-mail info@castelloditornano.it
website www.castelloditornano.it
Food breakfast, lunch, dinner
Price €€€
Closed never
Proprietor Francesco Giuffrede

Castello di Tornano
Castle hotel

One of the countless defence and watchtowers that dot Tuscany and solidly built in grey stone with commanding views of the surrounding countryside, the Castello di Tornano has undergone something of a transformation recently. There are still self-catering apartments for rent in an adjoining farmhouse, but these are rather drab compared to the luxourious rooms that are now available in the castle and tower itself. The style is rather theatrical with a medieval feel; deep red brocaded fabrics, mezza corona beds, elaborated wrought iron light fittings, luxourious (unmedieval) bathrooms. The restaurant serves Tuscan specialities and there is a hot tub on the top of the tower.

Greve in Chianti

Via San Cresci 31/32 - Mezzuola - Greve in Chianti

Tel 055 8840004
e-mail info@villabordoni.com
website www.villabordoni.com
Food breakfast, lunch, dinner
Price €€
Closed 8th Jan-28th Feb
Proprietors David and Catherine Gardner

Villa Bordoni
Town hotel

Emily Fitzroy of Bellini Travel who organizes art tours in Italy (ideal for CSH readers) recommends this new hotel at Greve in Chianti – and her advice is good. David Gardner and his wife Catherine ran Baldovino and Beccofino restaurants in Florence before turning to this ambitious new restoration. Two restaurants occupy the whole ground floor and open onto a lovely garden. Original features are preserved with flair and respect. Upstairs, decoration is bolder (a sitting room in manganese black and ivory) while bedroom collour schemes are inspired by tints in the unique hand painted Vietri tiles. High-tech LCD screens are integrated into antique mirrors: everywhere, artful marriage of past and present. Spot the thistle in the hotel's insignia? The Gardners are Scots.

Isola del Giglio

Località Cala degli Angeli,
Isola del Giglio, Grosseto

Tel 0564 809034
e-mail info@hermit.it
website www.hermit.it
Food breakfast, lunch, dinner
Price €€ (half board
compulsory: minimum 3 nights.)
Closed 15 Oct-20 March
Proprietor Federigo Pardini

Pardini's Hermitage
Seaside hotel

If you are looking for a simple island hide-away, Pardini's might be it. It is situated on Giglio, part of the Tuscan Archipelago which lies off the southern Tuscan coast and is only accessible by boat from Giglio Porto. The setting is idyllic; a '50s villa in beautiful terraced gardens which tumble down to the sea where flat rocks make good sun-bathing spots and the swimming is fabulous. Courses are offered in painting, yoga, pottery and cooking or you can just laze around. The food is excellent. Rooms are Spartan yet comfortable (and air-conditioned), but you are unlikely to spend much time in them.

Lucca

Via degli Angeli 23, 55100 Lucca

Tel 0583 469204
e-mail
info@allacortedegliangeli.com
website
www.allacortedegliangeli.com
Food breakfast
Price €€
Closed never
Manager Pietro Bonino

Alla Corte Degli Angeli
Castle hotel

The lovely walled town of Lucca makes an excellent base for a few days: you can explore the town itself, visit nearby villas, drive up to the verdant Garfagnana or spend a day on the beach. This small, upmarket guest house is one of the few 'charming' places to stay within the walls. Downstairs, a reception area includes a small dining room (it must be said that we have had one negative comment about the breakfast) while on the upper floor, the six bedrooms (named after flowers) are elegantly and comfortably furnished and painted in pastel shades. Bathrooms all have Jacuzzi tubs.

Massa e Cozzile

Villa Pasquini
Country villa

Via Vacchereccia 56, Margine
Coperta, 51010 Massa e Cozzile,
Pistoia

Tel 0572 72205
Food breakfast, dinner
Price €€
Closed late Nov to mid-Mar
Proprietors Innocenti family

Stay at Villa Pasquini and you step back into the 19th century. Little has changed here, either in furnishings, or decoration, since then. Until seven years ago, it was the autumn retreat of an aristocratic Roman family, the Pasquinis; then it was bought, fully furnished, by the present incumbents, who have lovingly preserved it, combining a family home with a most unusual hotel. The bedrooms are, of course, all different, some quite grand with canopied beds. Bathrooms are old-fashioned, but well equipped. In the attractive dining room – originally the entrance hall – the emphasis is on traditional recipes. Our reporter chose the fixed-price menu (five delicious courses) and thought the price very reasonable.

Pieve Santo Stefano

Locanda la Pergola
Country inn

Via Tiberina 177, Pieve Santo
Stefano, 52036 Arezzo

Tel 0575 797053
Food breakfast, lunch, dinner
Price €
Closed never; restaurant closed Wed
Proprietors Marida Gorini and
Loreana Marini

A useful address for anyone taking the road from central Tuscany to Ravenna, this local inn is run by three capable women; Marida, Oriana and Valeria. Previous owners restored the house with real panache in classy country style: rustic antiques and painted reproduction pieces sit on polished tiled floors in the bedrooms. Shower rooms are compact but smart. The dinng room shows the same simple good taste, but the real attraction here is Marida's exquisite country cooking which includes a daily batch of superb ravioli made with local ricotta. The busy new superstrada across the narrow valley doesn't seem to be a major problem.

Radicofani

Loc. Le Vigne, Celle sul Rigo, 53040
Radicofani (Siena)

Tel 0578 55771
e-mail info@fattorialapalazzina.com
website
www.fattorialapalazzina.com
Food breakfast
Price € (minimum 3 nights in high
season)
Closed 1 Nov-mid Mar
Proprietor Nicoletta Innocenti

La Palazzina
Country guesthouse

A 17th century hilltop hunting lodge, La Palazzina is situated on a big farm in the remote and captivating south-eastern corner of Tuscany amidst rolling hills. Approached by an alley of cypress trees, the house is set in manicured gardens with a pristine swimming pool to one side overlooking wide vistas. Inside, pale pastel colours and smart black and white tiled floors downstairs give a clean cool look, while antiques and carefully chosen fabrics add style. The bedrooms have beamed ceilings and wrought-iron beds; a few have their own terraces. A generous breakfast includes produce from the farm.

San Gimignano

Loc. Pancole, 53037 San
Gimignano, Siena

Tel 0577 955044
e-mail lerenaie@iol.it
website www.hotellerenaie.com
Food breakfast, lunch, dinner
Price €€
Closed Nov
Proprietor Leonetto Sabatini

Le Renaie
Country hotel

A simple, well-run country hotel – built up over the years by the present owners from a bar and restaurant – which makes a respectable base within a short drive of San Gimignano. The building is no architectural masterpiece, but a typical example of a modern rustic construction. Inside, modern terracotta flooring and cane furniture make for a light, fresh atmosphere. The restaurant, Da Leonetto, is popular with locals (especially for large functions) but gets mixed notices from reporters. Upstairs are the bedrooms, which have a mixture of modern, built-in furniture and reproduction rustic. Guests seem to appreciate the peaceful location, services (including a swimming pool and access to a tennis court).

Sassetta

Tenuta La Bandita
Country hotel

This elegant, 18th century villa is set in 150 acres of grounds and lies in unspoilt, wooded countryside inland from the 'Etruscan Coast', an area famous for its archaeological remains, beautiful scenery and excellent food and wines. La Bandita produces its own olive oil, pork, wild boar and poultry, all of which you can sample in the restaurant. The house has grand proportions (there is a lovely, vaulted *salone* with a huge fireplace), but feels lived-in and prices are reasonable. Bedrooms vary from the small and quite simple to larger rooms with canopied beds. In fine weather, guests can lounge by the pool or enjoy views of the open countryside from the terrace.

Via Campagna Nord 30
57020 Sassetta, Livorno

Tel 0565 794224
e-mail bandita@tin.it
website www.labandita.com
Food Breakfast, light lunch, dinner
Price €
Closed Nov-March
Proprietors Dino and Daniela Filippi

Sesto Fiorentino

Villa Villoresi
Town villa

The aristocratic Villa Villoresi looks rather out of place in what is now an industrial suburb of Florence, but once in the house and gardens you suddenly feel a million miles away from the modern, bustling city. Contessa Cristina Villoresi is a warm hostess who has captured the hearts of many transatlantic and other guests. It is thanks to her that the villa still has the feel of a private home – all rather grand, if a little faded. Bedrooms are remarkably varied – from the small and quite plain to grand apartments with frescoes and Venetian chandeliers. Some look over the courtyard, others on to the pool and garden. We are assured that the food is now better than it was.

Via Ciampi 2, 50019 Colonnata di Sesto Fiorentino, Firenze

Tel 055 443212
e-mail cvillor@tin.it
website www.villavilloresi.it
Food breakfast, lunch, dinner
Price €€
Closed never
Proprietor Contessa Cristina Villoresi

Siena

Via della Sapienza, 53100 Siena

Tel 0577 222073
e-mail relais@camporegio.com
website www.camporegio.com
Food breakfast
Price €€€
Closed never
Manager Elena Frati

Relais Campo Regio
Town Hotel

Another recommendation from Emily Fitzroy (see also page 203), and a very useful new addition to our Siena hotels selection: 'elegant', 'comfortable', 'friendly', 'pristine rooms' say reporters. Fresh whites dominate in the bedrooms, with artfully placed antiques here and there, together with decorative luxurious touches. 'We had such an amazing time' says a another guest. Views of historic Siena.

Sovicille

Loc. Toiano, 53018 Sovicille, Siena

Tel 0577 314639
e-mail toiano@hotelmodernosiena.it
website www.hotelmodernosiena.it
Food breakfast, snacks
Price €€€
Closed Nov-Mar
Manager Pierluigi Pagni

Borgo di Toiano
Country hotel

Most of the abandoned rural hamlets (borgi) that once housed small farming communities and have since been converted into distinctive hotels were located on steep hills or jumbled together behind secure walls. Borgo di Toiano, by contrast, has a pleasant open aspect: a few old stone houses, superbly restored, are spread out across acres of stone and terracotta terraces. The main public rooms also have a spacious, uncluttered feel. Bedrooms have the same mixture of rustic and modern. Swimming pool.

Piazza Tannucci 85, 52017 Stia, Arezzo

Tel 0575 504569
e-mail info@albergofalterona.it
website www.albergofalterona.it
Food breakfast
Price €
Closed never
Manager Sergio Bresciani

Albergo Falterona
Country hotel

Lying north east of Florence, the hilly, wooded area known as the Casentino lies far from the main tourist itineraries and yet offers much for the visitor (unspoilt countryside with wonderful walking, Romanesque churches, historic monasteries and numerous castles), but few good places to stay. The pink-washed Falterona lies on delightful, sloping Piazza Tannucci in the pretty little town of Stia which is famous for its production of wool fabric. It has 15, really quite smart rooms with tiled floors, beamed ceilings (one has a fresco) and good bathrooms. There's a pleasant courtyard for summer breakfasts. A good base for exploring the area and only a bare hour's drive from Florence.

Visitors are discovering that there is more to Umbria than Assisi; but it nonetheless remains the main tourist highlight of the region. Choices of hotel here are strictly limited: there are many that are mediocre, and some of the more comfortable are too big for a full entry here; of these, the **Subasio** (tel 075 812206) is a 70-room, polished, rather formal place, but notable for the views from its better bedrooms and beautiful flowery terraces. We continue to recommend **L' Orto degli Angeli** in Bevagna (page 213).

Perugia is not nearly so well known as Assisi, but well worth a visit if you can penetrate the infuriating defences of its traffic system. Since its massive expansion to over 90 bedrooms, we have dropped our entry for the **Brufani** (tel 075 5732541), though it's worth knowing about, if expensive. Just along from the Brufani is **La Rosetta** (tel 075 5720841); though also large, it is not worryingly impersonal, and better value. Another possibility as a base for exploring the area is the **Da Sauro** (tel 075 826168), a family hotel on the peaceful island of Maggiore in Lake Trasemino. We have a new recommendation for the centre of Orvieto, and there's plenty of choice for relaxing hotels in the Umbrian countryside.

Marche's coast, like the rest of the Adriatic, offers large resorts with plenty of hotels, but not many suitable for this guide. Pesaro, though a big town, is a more interesting mixture of old town and beach resort than many along this coastline; along with the **Villa Serena** (page 225) we have added **Villa La Torraccia** (page 230), and we might also mention the **Vittoria**, a stylish, well-equipped hotel on the seafront (tel 0721 34344). Ancona, regional capital of the Marche and a big seaport, is definitely not the place to stay but 12 km down the coast, at the popular resort of Portonovo, we have the **Emilia** and, as a back-up address can also suggest the **Hotel Monteconero** (tel 071 9330592). this hotel is built around a 11thC Benedictine monastery and perched on a cliff, 550 m above the sea in the middle of the Monteconero national park. Further south at Numana, the **Eden Gigli** (tel 071 933 0652) is a smart, modern hotel in a beautiful setting overlooking the sea.

Inland from Pesaro, the Renaissance art city of Urbino is an essential place to visit, and we have the **Locanda di Valle Nuova**. If you want to stay in the centre of things, however, our best suggestion is the **Raffaello** (tel 0722 4896), a straightforward 19-room place; it has no restaurant but this is not a problem since it is right in the middle of the town.

Gubbio is an equally compelling place to visit: try the **Bosone** (tel 075 9220688), or alternatively the **Torre dei Calzolari Palace** (tel 075 925 6327), which is some 7 km away. Also slightly out of town are the **Villa Montegranelli** (tel 075 9220185), a severe stone-built villa in hillside grounds, or the extravagant **Park Hotel ai Cappuccini** (tel 075 9234).

Loc. Asproli 7, 06059 Todi, Perugia

Tel 075 8853385
e-mail poggiodasproli@email.it

Nearby Todi (7km); Oriveto (29 km).
Location country house in its own grounds
Food breakfast, dinner on request
Price €€
Rooms 7 double, 2 suite all with shower or bath, phon, heating
Facilities pool, garden, terrace, sitting room
Credit cards AE, MC, V
Children not suitable
Disabled difficult
Pets not accepted
Closed mid-Jan to mid-Mar
Proprietor Bruno Pagliari

Poggio D'Asproli
Country guest-house

If you are tired of Naples, you may not be tired of life – just in need of peace and quiet. Such was the case with Bruno Pagliari, so he sold his large hotel in southern Italy to continue his career as an artist in the tranquility of Umbria's leafy valleys. But the tradition of hospitality remained, and he has opened up his hillside farmhouse so that his guests can also enjoy this oasis.

The rambling building of local stone is packed full of an arresting mixture of antiques and Bruno's own modern art. The main sitting room, with its great fireplace and white couches, is flanked by a long terrace where one can eat or just relax, listening to birdsong from the wooded hills.

In the rest of the house, stone and brick arches frame decoratively painted doors and parchment-shaded lights illuminate old coloured wooden carvings. The bedrooms will inspire many a pleasant dream.

The atmosphere is hushed, but in a relaxed rather than reverent manner and, birdsong aside, the only sound is of operatic arias gently playing in the background.

Loc. Armenzano, 06081 Assisi, Perugia

Tel 075 8019000
e-mail info@lesilve.it
website www.lesilve.it

Nearby sights of Assisi.
Location in countryside 12 km E of Assisi, between S444 and S3; ask hotel for directions; ample car parking
Food breakfast, lunch, dinner; room service
Price €€€
Rooms 13, 5 deluxe, 7 doubles, 1 single, all with bath; all rooms have phone, TV, minibar, safe **Facilities** 2 sitting rooms, dining room, bar, terrace, swimming pool, tennis, sauna, riding, archery, mini-golf, motorbike
Credit cards AE, DC, V **Disabled** 2 rooms available
Pets accepted
Closed mid-Nov to mid-Mar
Managers Sirignani family

Le Silve
Country hotel

Even if you are not planning to stay at this sophisticated gem, the road up to Le Silve is worth exploring for its own rewards – or perhaps avoiding if you are the nervous sort. It winds up over a series of hills until you reach the house, set on its own private hill-ridge, 700 m above sea level and views are wonderful.

Le Silve is an old farmhouse (parts of it very old indeed – 10th century) converted to its new purpose with great sympathy and charm. There is a delightfully rambling feel to the place, with rooms on a variety of levels. The rustic nature of the building is preserved perfectly – all polished tile floors, stone or white walls, beamed ceilings, the occasional rug – and it is furnished with country antiques. Public rooms are large and airy, bedrooms stylishly simple. The self-contained suites are in villas about 1.5 km from the main house.

We have had conflicting reports of the food, which uses produce from the associated farm. Recently, a reader praised the 'very modern Italian cooking' (also pointing out that portions were small) while a previous guest complained about the 'pretentious cuisine minceur at astronomical prices'. What do you think? Le Silve is close enough to Assisi for sightseeing expeditions but remote enough for complete seclusion – and with good sports facilities immediately on hand (fair-sized pool). But it's not for vertigo sufferers.

Via Dante Alighieri, 06031 Bevagna, Perugia

Tel 0742 360130
e-mail ortoangeli@ortoangeli.it
website www.ortoangeli.it

Nearby Assisi (24 km); Perugia (45 km); Spello (13 km).
Location 8 km SW of Foligno, in centre of town; public car parking 100 m
Food breafast, lunch, dinner
Price €€€
Rooms 14; 5 double and 9 suites, 7 with bath, 7 with shower; all rooms have phone, TV, air conditioning, minibar, safe, hairdrier
Facilities breakfast room, restaurant, sitting room, reading room, garden
Credit cards AE, DC, MC, V
Disabled not suitable
Pets accepted on request
Closed mid-Jan to mid-Feb
Proprietors Tiziana and Francesco Antonini Angeli Nieri Mongalli

L'Orto degli Angeli
Town hotel

Bevagna is another of those sleepy little Umbrian places full of artistic gems, this time on the old Via Flaminia. Situated in the centre of town, l'Orto degli Angeli is a 17thC property which is remarkable for two features. The delightful hanging garden occupies the site of a Roman amphitheatre, and one rough stone wall of the pretty, lemon-painted restaurant is a remnant of a first century temple to Minerva.

The grandly-named Antonini Angeli Nieri Mongalli family have restored their fascinating home with much care. Its dimensions are grand, too, complete with frescoes, aged terracotta floors and vast stone fireplaces are still there, but it manages to be homely and comfortable too – anything but overwhelming. The bedrooms are imaginatively decorated with great style; smart fabrics blend with the original terracotta floor tiles, gorgeous family antiques and painted woodwork. Modern equipment is carefully hidden from view. The menu in the restaurant changes every week, and Tiziana Antonini oversees the cooking. She bakes fresh bread daily, and even grinds her own flour. The jams and cakes served at breakfast are home made.

Campello sul Clitunno

Loc.Pissignano, Via del Tempio 34,
06042 Campello sul Clitunno,
Perugia

Tel 0743 521122
e-mail vecchiomolino@perugiaon-line.com
website www.perugiaonline.com

Nearby Spoleto (11 km); Perugia (50 km).
Location 50 km SE of Perugia between Trevi and Spoleto; in own grounds by the Clitunno river; ample car parking
Food breakfast
Price €€€
Rooms 13; 6 double, 2 single, 5 suites, all with bath or shower; all rooms have phone, minibar, air conditioning
Facilities sitting rooms, bar, TV room, gardens
Credit cards AE, DC, MC, V
Disabled access difficult
Pets accepted
Closed Nov-Mar
Proprietor Paolo Rapanelli

Il Vecchio Molino
Converted mill

It is a mystery how this inn, so close to the busy Perugia-Spoleto road, remains so peaceful. Almost the only sound is of gurgling brooks winding through the leafy gardens. As befits an old mill, all the buildings live in close harmony with the river: the drive sweeps around the mill pond to a creeper-covered building against which old grinding-stones rest. The gardens are a spit of land, with weeping willows dipping into streams on both sides. Water even runs through some of the old working parts, where the mill machinery has been built into the decorative scheme.

There seems to be no end to the number of public rooms, all furnished in a highly individual manner: elegant white sofas in front of a big brick fireplace, surmounted by carved wooden lamps; tables with lecterns bearing early editions of Dante's Purgatorio; mill wheels used as doors. The bedrooms were, we were relieved to note, pleasingly dry and decorated in a restrained manner with fine antiques, the white walls lit up by parchment-shaded lamps; TV's are absent as a matter of principle.

It's worth remembering that the hotel is popular in the wedding season and during the Spoleto festival.

Via Rigone 1, 06060 Castel Rigone, Lago Trasimeno, Perugia

Tel 075 845322
e-mail info@relaislafattoria.com
website www.relaislafattoria.com

Nearby Perugia (27 km); Assisi (35 km); Gubbio (50 km).
Location 27 km NW of Perugia, in centre of town; car parking nearby
Food breakfast, lunch, dinner
Price €€
Rooms 29; 23 double, 3 single, 3 junior suites, all with bath or shower (suites with Jacuzzis); all rooms have phone, TV, minibar
Facilities sitting room, restaurant, terrace/garden, swimming pool
Credit cards AE, DC, MC, V
Disabled no special facilities
Pets accepted
Closed hotel never; restaurant only, Jan
Proprietorss Pammelati family

Relais La Fattoria
Town hotel

On the hills behind Lake Trasimeno lies the small medieval town of Castel Rigone, a mere handful of houses grouped about a handsome piazza. Right at its centre is this pleasant, family-run hotel occupying what was once a manor house.

You feel a sense of welcome the moment you step inside the reception area, which has a wooden ceiling, stone walls and comfortable Knole sofas. Keen young staff are on hand to make you feel at home. The public rooms are tastefully decorated, with Persian rugs on the polished cork floors and bright modern paintings on the white walls. The only addition to the building that has been allowed by the Italian Fine Arts Ministry is a restaurant perfectly in keeping with the original style. Dishes include fresh fish from the lake.

Bedrooms have been designed with an eye more to modern comfort than to individual style and some have lake views. The bathrooms are bright and new.

Along the front of the house is a terrace with sitting areas and a small swimming pool. An excellent, extensive buffet breakfast (home-made bread and jams, cheeses and cured meats) is served here in fine weather.

Castel Ritaldi

Cole del Marchese 60, 06044 Castel
Ritaldi, Perugia

Tel 0743 254068
e-mail benvenuti@lagioia.biz
website www.lagioia.biz

Nearby Assissi (35km); Spoleto
(13km); Todi (35km); Terni (45km).
Location 13 km NW of Spoleto; in
ample grounds with car parking
Food breakfast, dinner; light lunch
on request
Price €€€ half board
Rooms 12; 11 double, 1 single, all
with bath or shower; all rooms have
phone, TV, safe, hairdrier
Facilities bar, sitting room, library,
restaurant, terraces, garden, swim-
ming pool
Credit cards MC, V
Disabled adapted rooms
Pets accepted
Closed Nov, Jan-Feb
Proprietors Marianne and Daniel
Aerni-Kühne

La Gioia
Country House hotel

Having run her own interior decorating
business in Zurich, Marianne Aerni-
Kühne was in an ideal position to restore
this 300-year-old oil and grain mill and
indeed, she and her husband Daniel have
done a beautiful job. La Gioia is situated in
gentle countryside near several of
Umbria's bigger towns, but also within
easy reach of such undiscovered gems as
Bevagna and Montefalco. The pale stone
building stands in its own extensive
grounds, which include an attractive pool,
lawns, terraces and plenty of sitting areas
where big white umbrellas provide shade.
Inside, typical rustic features (cotto floors,
beamed ceilings, exposed brickwork and
so on) have been tastefully enhanced by
the use of earthy, Mediterranean colours, a
mix of old and new furniture, bright fabrics
and soft lighting. The bedrooms have been
individually decorated with much attention to detail: underfloor heating and
duvets on the beds make them very cosy
in cooler weather. Some are split level with
either a bed or sitting area on the top
level, while others have a private terrace
overlooking the garden.

At La Gioia, food and wine are considered to be an important part of your stay
(the chef uses home-grown or local produce), and half board is encouraged, especially during high season.

06134 Loc. Cenerente, Perugia

Tel 075 690125
e-mail info@oscano.com
website www.oscano.com

Nearby Perugia (5 km); Assisi (28 km); Gubbio (40 km).
Location on a hillside in its own grounds; ample car parking
Food breakfast, dinner
Price €€€–€€€€
Rooms 11 double (Castello), 8 double, 2 single (Villa Ada), all with bath or shower; all rooms have phone, TV, air conditioning, minibar, hairdrier, safe
Facilities sitting rooms, dining room, library, bar, gardens, swimming pool
Credit cards AE, DC, MC, V
Disabled 1 suitable bedroom
Pets on request
Closed never; restaurant only, mid-Jan to mid-Feb
Manager Michele Ravano

Castello dell'Oscáno
Castle villa

At first sight Castello dell'Oscáno appears like a fairytale medieval castle: ivy-clad turrets, battlements and crenellated towers rise above a steep, hillside pine forest. The two main towers date from the 15thC; they were incorporated into the 18thC re-building by an American tycoon.

The interiors are finely proportioned, spacious and light. The hall rises the entire height of the castle, with an imposing carved stairway, polished wood floors and neo-Gothic windows. One public room leads into another, all filled with the castle's original furniture: a library which will entrance any bibliophile with its carved classical bookcases and 18thC volumes; sitting rooms with wooden panelling, tapestries and sculpted fireplaces; a dining room with old display cases full of Deruta pottery.

Upstairs, the floors are of geometrically patterned, black-and-white marble. There are only ten bedrooms in the castle, each with its own antique furnishing. The remainder, in the Villa Ada next door, are less exciting and cheaper. The most spectacular (but strictly for the agile) is in the turret, with a four-poster bed and a door to the ramparts which look over the romantic gardens below.

Montecastello Vibio

Loc. Buchella 1a, 9-Doglio, 05010
Montecastello Vibio, Perugia

Tel 075 8749607
e-mail info@fattoriadivibio.com
website www.fattoriadivibio.com

Nearby Todi (15 km); Orvieto (30
km), Perugia (40 km).
Location on quiet hillside off S448
road between Todi and Orvieto;
ample car parking
Food breakfast, lunch, dinner
Price €€; half board obligatory;
1-week minimum stay in Aug and
over Easter
Rooms 14 double and twin, all with
bath or shower; TV, phone; 2 self-
catering cottages
Facilities sitting room, dining room,
terrace, garden, swimming pools,
bicycles, riding, fishing, archery, ten-
nis
Credit cards AE, DC, MC, V
Disabled one suitable room
Pets accepted
Closed Jan and Feb
Proprietors Gabriella, Giuseppe &
Filippo Saladini

Fattoria di Vibio
Farm guesthouse

Occasionally, the whole atmosphere of a place is captured by a small detail: here it is the hand-painted pottery used to serve Signora Saladini's delicious food which sums up the relaxed elegance of this renovated 18thC farmhouse. The style is modern rustic Italian, with pleasing open spaces, defined by white walls that contrast with the colourful fabrics and ceramics. Light, airy and well proportioned, there is an feeling of effortless simplicity which, you quickly realize, required a great deal of taste and effort. Most of the bedrooms, of similar style, are in the house next door.

The Saladini family are serious about their visitors' comforts and well-being, starting in the kitchen. Much of what goes into the guests comes out of the farm or the market garden and the preparation is a spectacle in itself, open to all. The mandatory half board should not prove a penance. If you need to lose calories, you can swim (even in winter thanks to the new indoor pool) , play table tennis, ride or walk in the magnificent countryside around. Or just relax in the quiet of the garden. Otherwise, there is not much to do – but then that is the whole point of this soothing guesthouse.

Viale della Vittoria 20, 06036
Montefalco, Perugia

Tel 0742 379417
e-mail info@villapambuffetti.it
website www.villapambuffetti.com

Nearby Montefalco; Assisi (30 km);
Todi (30 km).
Location just outside Montefalco, in
its own grounds; with ample car
parking
Food breakfast, dinner
Rooms 15; 11 double and twin, 1
single; 3 suites, 2 with bath, 13 with
shower; all rooms have phone, TV,
air conditioning, minibar, hairdrier
Price €€€
Facilities sitting room, bar, restau-
rant, loggia, garden, swimming pool
Credit cards AE, DC, MC, V
Disabled 2 rooms on ground floor
Pets not accepted
Closed never
Managers Argentina, Alessandra
and Mauro Pambuffetti

Villa Pambuffetti
Villa hotel

Like Hemingway in Spain, the poet
D'Annunzio seems to have stayed
everywhere in Italy; however, in the case of
Villa Pambuffetti the claim is better justified than most. Not only did he dedicate a
poem to the delightful medieval walled
town of Montefalco (a 5-min walk), from
where the views are breathtaking, but the
villa itself has a turn-of-the-century elegance that fits the poet's legend.

Ten thousand square metres of shady
garden surround the main building. Inside,
furniture and decoration have been kept
almost as they were at the start of the
1900s when the Pambuffetti family began
taking 'paying guests': floors and panelling
of seasoned oak, bamboo armchairs,
Tiffany lampshades and old family photographs in art nouveau frames pay tribute
to a century that started optimistically.
Many of the bedrooms are furnished with
the family's older and finer antiques and all
have bathrooms which, though recent, are
stylistically nearly perfect. If you like a
room with a view, try the tower, which has
one of the six-windowed, all-round variety.
The food, based proudly on local seasonal
ingredients, is excellent. All in all, a gem.

SS Flaminia, Strada per Itieli

Tel 0744 722495/335 5738210
e-mail costaromana@virgilio.it
website
www.poderecostaromana.com

Nearby Narni (3km); Terni (15km);
Todi (40km).
Location in open countryside off the
SS3 (to Rome) south of Narni
Food breakfast
Rooms 6 self-catering apartments
sleeping from 2-5, all with bath or
shower; all rooms have TV
Price €€, minimum two nights
Facilities sitting room, garden, ter-
races, swimming pool
Credit cards not accepted
Disabled access difficult
Pets not accepted
Closed never
Proprietor Anna Maria Giordano

Podere Costa Romana
Country apartments

Anna Maria Giordano decided in the
late Nineties to swap the chaos of her
native Naples for the peace of this south-
western corner of Umbria. She brought
and lovingly restored an 18thC stone
farmhouse, keeping a piece for herself and
conveting the rest into apartments, which
she opened to guests in 2002. The property is immersed in a wooded hillside just
outside the fine old town of Narni, once
an important station on the Roman Via
Flaminia. Inside the house, the large communal sitting room, with its open fireplace,
allows guests to mingle. There is a garden,
too, for general use and a pool overlooking the hills.

The apartments, sleeping up to five, are
carefully decorated in comfortable rustic
style: warm pastels on the walls, dark
wood floors and beamed ceilings,
wrought-iron fittings, old country furniture and thoughtful lighting. Each has a
kitchenette and some kind of private outside space.

Loc. La Badia, 05019 Orvieto, Terni

Tel 0763 301959
e-mail labadia.hotel@tin.it
website www.labadiahotel.it

Nearby Orvieto (5 km); Todi (40 km); Viterbo (45 km).
Location on quiet hillside, 5 km S of Orvieto; own car parking
Food breakfast, lunch, dinner
Price €€€
Rooms 28; 21 double, 7 suites, all with bath or shower; all rooms have phone, air-conditioning, minibar, hairdrier, TV
Facilities sitting room, breakfast room, bar, restaurant, tennis, swimming pool **Credit cards** AE, V, MC
Disabled ground floor rooms
Pets not allowed
Closed Jan, Feb
Proprietor Luisa Fiume

La Badia
Converted abbey

Arriving at twilight at La Badia is like landing in a scene from a Gothic novel: ruined arches, rooks cawing from a crenellated bell tower, dark cypresses silhouetted against the sky and, across the valley, the evening profile of Orvieto's cathedral, secure on its fortress crag. But the golden stone monastery on the hill, surrounded by Umbria's intense green countryside, soon reveals itself as an outstanding hotel that would have delighted any Renaissance cardinal.

Restraint is the hallmark of this fine building's conversion into a distinctive hotel. The robust architecture of the old abbey is always allowed to speak for itself, and modern embellishments have been kept to a minimum. The heavy wooden period furniture goes well with the massive stone walls; wrought-iron lights illuminate vaulted ceilings; floors are either of plain or geometrically-patterned terracotta. Here and there, an unexpectedly-placed church pew reminds the guest of what once was.

On the hill behind is a pool fit for a pope. In front of the abbey, beside the famous 12-sided tower, is a peaceful garden where the meditative visitor can contemplate the view of Orvieto.

Piazza Ranieri 36, 05018 Orvieto,
Terni

Tel 0763 341743
e-mail
piccolomini.hotel@orvienet.it
website www.hotelpiccolomini.it

Nearby cathedral; underground
caves.
Location on the S side of town near
Porta Romana; public car parking
200 m away
Food breakfast
Price €€
Rooms 31; 22 double and twin, 6
single, 3 suites, all with shower; all
rooms have phone, TV, air condi-
tioning, minibar, hairdrier
Facilities breakfast room, sitting
room, bar, lift
Credit cards AE, DC, MC, V
Disabled some adapted rooms
Pets accepted
Closed 1 week Jan
Manager Liliana Achilli

Palazzo Piccolomini
Town hotel

At last a decent hotel has been created in the centre of this remarkable town which sits on a pedestal of tufa some 300 m above sea level. Orvieto is a charming place with a fabulous, candy-striped cathedral, an atmospheric centro storico, a choice of restaurants serving fine, regional food and last, but not least, an excellent local white wine.

Pale pink Palazzo Piccolomini (so-named after the family who built it at the end of the 16th century) is situated at the heart of the old city and was beautifully restored as a hotel in 1998. Inside, there is a wonderful sense of calm throughout the cool, vaulted rooms, which have been furnished with what some might call Spartan good taste. In the spacious salon, wrought-iron candelabras and white covers on sofas and chairs are stylish against white walls and polished terracotta floors; filmy white curtains ripple in the breeze and filter the sunlight. The bedrooms, although varying in shape and size, are similar, with modern, dark wooden furniture and the odd splash of deep blue. Some have rooftop views. You eat breakfast in a vaulted basement room which has Etruscan origins.

Loc. Ciconia, Via dei Tigli 69,
Oriveto, 05018 Terni

Tel 0763 305582/3
e-mail info@hotelvillaciconia.com
website www.hotelvillaciconia.com

Nearby Oriveto (3km); Todi (33 km); Perugia (78 km).
Location just outside Oriveto in its own grounds, ample car parking
Food breakfast, lunch, dinner
Price €€€
Rooms 9 double, 1 single, all with bath (one with Jacuzzi), phone, satellite TV, minibar, air-conditioning
Facilities sitting rooms, dining room, breakfast room, garden, swimming pool
Credit cards AE, DC, MC, V
Children welcome
Disabled not suitable
Pets please check first
Closed mid-Jan to mid-Feb; restaurant only, Mon Languages English
Proprietor Valentino Petrangeli

Villa Ciconia
Country villa

Protected from the nearby busy road and the encroachments of Oriveto's new suburbs by its tree-filled gardens, La Ciconia is a small, attractive 16thC grey stone villa with two bays of windows flanking an arched entrance. Inside, you'll find a variety of styles, from the spacious ground floor public rooms with geometric, polychrome tiled floors, massive stone fireplaces and frescoed friezes to the simpler but more restful sitting rooms on the upper floor, where leather couches add a zestful note of modernity.

The bedrooms are in a more rustic style, with wrought-iron or four-poster beds and antique chests that combine well with the exposed roof-beams and warm, terracotta floors. Bathrooms are spanking new and most have a shower rather than a bath.

The gardens are a delight, bounded by two streams and there is now a pool, but suffer unfortunately, from some noise from the road outside. The restaurant serves Umbrian specialities with oil and wine from the owner's farms - popular for weddings, so it may get busy at weekends.

A pleasant alternative to La Badia (page 221) if the latter is full or you find it too expensive.

Panicale

Loc. Colle San Paolo, 06070
Panicale, Perugia

Tel 075 832376
e-mail info@villamontesolare.it
website www.villamontesolare.it

Nearby Panicale (12 km); Città della
Pieve (24 km); Perugia (25km).
Location 3 km N of the SS220,
direction Colle S. Paolo; ample car
parking
Food breakfast, lunch, dinner
Price €€€
Rooms 28 rooms; 21 doubles and 7
suites, all with bath or shower; all
rooms have air conditioning, hairdri-
er, phone, minibar (not in main
villa), TV, safe
Facilities 2 dining rooms, sitting
room, bar, 2 swimming pools, tennis
court
Credit cards AE, DC, MC, V
Disabled one suitable apartment
Pets accepted
Closed never
Proprietor Rosemarie Strunk and
Filippo Iannarone

Villa di Montesolare
Country villa

High walls keep out the arid scenery
around, enclosing the stuccoed villa in
a green oasis. The present building dates
back to 1780, although the 16thC chapel in
the garden suggests a much earlier house
was on the site. When the present owners
bought it, they set about restoring the
19thC garden (and the secret garden
behind it), building the swimming pool a
discreet distance away, and converting the
villa without interfering with its patrician
character.

The result is one of the most comfortable country retreats of the Trasimeno
area. The bedrooms of the villa retain their
original character – beamed ceilings, quar-
ry tile floors and whitewashed walls, furnished in squirely fashion with turn-of-the-
century high-backed beds, cabinets and
wardrobes. The cool blue sitting room on
the piano nobile certainly is noble, while
the dining rooms and the bar are situated
more humbly, downstairs. Since 1994
Rosemarie Strunck and her husband
Filippo have converted several 'case
coloniche' and other outbuildings which
stand outside the walls by the hotel's second swimming pool. These contain suites
and superior doubles which are furnished
in country style.

Via San Nicola 6/3, 61100 Pesaro

Tel 0721 55211
e-mail info@villa-serena.it
website www.villa-serena.it

Nearby Pesaro (4 km); Urbino (40 km).
Location 4 km SE of Pesaro and beach, in a large wooded park on hillside, with private car parking
Food breakfast, lunch, dinner
Price €€€
Rooms 9 double and twin, 1 suite, all with bath or shower; all rooms have phone and hairdrier
Facilities sitting rooms, dining room, bar, terrace, swimming pool
Credit cards AE, DC, V
Disabled access difficult
Pets accepted
Closed 2 weeks early Jan
Proprietor Renato Pinto

Villa Serena
Country villa

The Adriatic coast south of Rimini is not short of hotels, but it is very short of our kind of hotel, which makes this one a real find – a handsome 17thC mansion with some token castellations, standing in a wooded park high above the hubbub of the coast.

The villa has always belonged to one family – the counts Pinto de Franca y Vergaes, who used it as a summer residence until, in 1950, they turned it into a small hotel to be run like a family home. A natural host, Renato Pinto does the cooking, producing delicious, well-presented dishes (order in advance out of high season). Stefano and Filippo see to guests and reception, while their mother, Signora Silvana, busies herself in the house and garden, with its terracotta pots and orange trees; all the family are reassuringly down-to-earth. The emphasis is on character, simplicity and peace, not luxury. There are salons of baronial splendour, and corridors delightfully cluttered with bric-à-brac and potted plants. A few faded corners reinforce the villa's appealing air of impoverished aristocracy. No two bedrooms are alike, but antiques and fireplaces feature in most. A couple could do with painting and some trees could well be lopped to let in light.

Via del Ponte 6, 06049 Spoleto, Perugia

Tel 0743 223447
e-mail info@hotelgattapone.it
website www.hotelgattapone.it

Nearby Assisi (48 km); Todi (42 km); Perugia (63 km).
Location on hillside, just outside historic centre of Spoleto; no private car parking facilities
Food breakfast
Price €€
Rooms 14; 7 double and twin, 7 junior suites, all with bath or shower; all rooms have phone, TV, air conditioning, minibar
Facilities sitting room, breakfast room, bar, terrace
Credit cards AE, DC, MC, V
Disabled no special facilities
Pets accepted
Closed never
Proprietor Pier Giulio Hanke

Gattapone
Town villa

There are two things you can do in this hotel just outside Spoleto's centre. The most obvious is to gape at the unparalleled views of the 13thC Bridge of Towers spanning the Tessino Valley. The other is to enjoy the quaintness of its Sixties jet-set decoration, all wood, glass, chrome and leather. If you tire, as some do, of the oh-so-prevalent rustic antique look, then you will enjoy the now dated, but meticulously maintained 'modern' style of the much-loved Gattapone.

The hotel is a favourite of the Spoleto Festival crowd, and the walls of the American Bar are festooned with pictures of the famous and would-be famous who throng its salons late into the evening. Even if you do not stay at the Gattapone, you will notice it. From the outside it looks like a solid, two-storey villa with classic ochre walls and green shutters. Inside, one becomes aware how the original building and its more modern extension have been constructed downwards to exploit the hillside position. Many of the bedrooms have large picture windows to capture the panorama.

We have visited the hotel in low season and enjoyed the peace and quiet. During the Festival (Jun-Jul), rooms here are hard to get.

Via Garibaldi 48, 06089 Torgiano, Perugia

Tel 075 9880447
e-mail 3vaselle@3vaselle.it
website www.3vaselle.it

Nearby Deruta (5 km); Perugia (8 km); Assisi (16 km).
Location in quiet street in village of Torgiano, 13 km SE of Perugia; car parking in nearby piazza
Food breakfast, lunch, dinner; room service
Price €€€
Rooms 61; 52 double and twin, 2 singles, 7 suites, most with bath, some with shower; all rooms have phone, TV, air conditioning, hairdrier
Facilities sitting rooms, dining rooms, breakfast room, bar, lift, terrace, swimming pool, sauna
Credit cards AE, DC, MC, V
Disabled access possible
Pets not accepted
Closed never
Manager Giovanni Margheritini

Le Tre Vaselle
Village hotel

Three monastic wine jugs discovered during the restoration of the original 17thC *palazzo* are what give this exceptional hotel its name and its theme: wine. Owned by the Lungarotti family, makers of Umbria's finest vintages, the *palazzo* is packed with still lifes of grapes, prints of the gods carousing and statues of Bacchus. However, nothing but sober professionalism characterizes the day-to-day management of this hotel.

Bedrooms, some in a more modern building behind the main one and others in a luxury annexe a short walk away, are all furnished to the highest standards: comfortable striped sofas, antique chests, individually chosen prints and lamps give an air of unrushed elegance. Public rooms are open and spacious, spanned by sweeping white arches and softly lit. Breakfast, an extensive buffet, is served on a secluded back terrace. The restaurant is outstanding, with a wine list the size of a telephone directory.

A recent visitor to Le Tre Vaselle could report only improvements. It could not be more professional; you could not feel more at home.

Baschi

Loc. Pomurlo Vecchio, 05023
Baschi, Terni

Tel 0744 950190/950475
Food lunch, dinner
Price €; minimum stay 1 week in
Aug
Closed never
Proprietor Lazzaro and Daniela
Minghelli

Pomurlo Vecchio/Le Casette **Country guesthouse**

Lazzaro Minghelli's 350-acre farm estate stretches from the shores of Lago di Corbara almost to Baschi. His romantic family home, Pomurlo Vecchio, is an eccentric 12thC tower, jutting out of a wooded hillock. It also has four small apartments: they are homely, though when we last visited we felt they were rather frayed at the edges. The principal guest accommodation, Le Casette, stands on the other side of the estate. Three stone cottages have been rebuilt around a swimming pool. Though lacking the patina of age, they provide a summer oasis particularly suitable for families. Rooms are simply decorated. The restaurant, overseen by daughter Daniela, is noteworthy.

Narni

Vicolo del Comune 4, Narni, 05035
Narni, Terni

Tel 0744 726843
e-mail loggiadeipriori.it
website info@loggiadeipriori.it
Food breakfast, lunch, dinner
Price €
Closed never
Proprietor Maurizio Bravi

Dei Priori
Town hotel

Tucked away in a quiet alley in the medieval heart of one of southern Umbria's unsung towns, this friendly small hotel provides an ideal staging post for travellers who prefer the 'backroads' route along the via Flaminia to Rome. As well as the magnificent Piazza dei Priori, the town's Romanesque duomo and the 14thC Palazzo del Podestà provide ample reason for an overnight detour. A lift, or a grandiose black oval staircase, takes you up to the comfortable modern bedrooms which look out into the central courtyard or over the pantiled roofs of the medieval borgo. A few have small balconies. Downstairs, the "La Loggia" restaurant spills out into the courtyard in the summer months. Its menu is mainly Umbrian and includes truffles in season.

Narni

La Cappella 14, Sagrata di
Fermignana, 60133 Pesaro-Urbino

Tel 0722 330303
e-mail info@valenuova.it
website www.vallenuova.it
Food breakfast, dinner
Price €
Closed mid Nov-mid June
Proprietor Savini family

Locanda di Valle Nuova
Farm Guesthouse

The Savini family moved to Umbria from Milan 20yrs ago because they loved the area; now, their 185 acre organic farm is thriving as is their delightful little guesthouse. Set in rolling hills just outside Urbino, the farm prodces its own wine, wheat, fruit and veg plus beef, pork and poultry, much of which features in the delicious meals prepared by mother and daughter. The six simple but stylish bedrooms are named after their colour schemes; all have a little sitting area. This is a relaxing place with a nice pool; there is horse riding on the property, and sightseeing nearby. Neither smokers nor credit cards are accepted.

Ospedalicchio de Bastia

Piazza Bruno Buozzi 3, 06080
Ospedalicchio de Bastia, Perugia

Tel 075 801 0323
e-mail info@lospedalicchio.it
website lospedalicchio.it
Food breakfast, lunch, dinner
Price €
Closed never
Manager Signor Costarelli

Lo Spedalicchio
Medieval manor

Despite the attractions of Assisi, for the touring motorist there is much to be said for staying out of town. This one is the best around: a four-square manor house on the road to Perugia. The ground-floor rooms have high, vaulted brick ceilings and tiled floors with the occasional rug. The restaurant (which enjoys a high local reputation) is on one side – stylishly set out; in contrast, the sitting room-bar area is traditionally sparse with exposed stone walls. Bedrooms vary widely – some high-ceilinged, some two-level affairs with sitting space. The staff are courteous and helpful; their French is better than their English. We are pleased to hear that the noisy church bells are now stopped during the night.

Pesaro

Strada Torraccia 3, 61100 Pesaro

Tel 0721 21852
e-mail info@villatorraccia.it
website www.villatorraccia.it
Food breakfast
Price €€
Closed never
Proprietor Antonio Galeazzi

Villa La Torraccia
Country villa

Villa La Torraccia is an unusual structure: a solid, rectangular house with a tower which seems to grow out of its middle. The 13thC building was constructed as a watchtower and later used as an of inland lighthouse which lit the way to Pesaro. This spot could make an ideal base for anyone who wants a bit of culture (Urbino and other art sights are within easy reach) combined with a bit of beach (coast, 4 km). Extensive restoration work was done in 1994 using traditional building materials. The rather intimidating dimensions of the house are softened by comfortable furnishings and some clever duplex arrangements in the spacious bedroom suites. These are all different, furnished with antiques and rustic pieces.

Portunuovo

Collina di Portonuovo 149/A,
Portonuovo, 60020 Ancona

Tel 071 801145
e-mail info@hotelemilia.com
website www.hotelemilia.com
Food breakfast, lunch, dinner
Price €€€
Closed Nov-Mar
Proprietor Rafaella Fiorini

Emilia
Seaside hotel

We have had mixed reports about the Emilia recently, but have decided to keep it because of its wonderful position above the Adriatic, its relaxed atmosphere and the 'excellent seafood' served in the restaurant. The building itself is modern and undistinguished, but has a distinctive appeal inside thanks to the scores of paintings adorning the walls, left by artists in lieu of payment. The décor is bright, sunny and modern with big windows taking full advantage of views across verdant lawns to the sea. many of the bedrooms share this view and each has a balcony. Jazz and classical concerts are held on the lawn in summer.

Spoleto

Via Interna delle Mura 21, 06049
Spoleto, Perugia

Tel 0743 223399
e-mail sanluca@hotelsanluca.com
website www.hotelsanluca.com
Food breakfast
Price €€
Closed never
Proprietor Daniela Zuccari

San Luca
Town hotel

When Pope Innocent II came to this spot in 1198, his presence is reputed to have caused a fountain to begin spouting, giving renewed strength to himself and his retinue. Today the site is occupied by an impressive 19thC building, with soft yellow painted exterior walls, which was transformed into an elegant hotel in 1995. The yellow colour scheme continues inside in the light, sunny hallway and sitting areas. Several of the pastel-toned bedrooms have a balcony or terrace; all of them are soundproofed and have a large bathroom. Right in the centre of Spoleto, but peacefully set in lush gardens, the San Luca also has a roof garden and a spacious courtyard, filled with flowers and olive trees.

Although Rome is a city of grand hotels rather than small and charming ones, we have recently made several interesting discoveries. These are the stylish **Locanda Cairoli**, in a converted *palazzo* (page 237), the pretty **Sant' Anna**, conveniently near the Vatican and with the bonus of an attractive courtyard garden (page 259), **Casa Howard** (page 238), **Lord Byron** (page 245) and **Santa Maria** (page 251). A recent inspection confirmed that many of our favourites are going from strength to strength: among them, the delightful **Due Torri** (page 241) and its smart sister, **Fontanella Borghese** (page 242), friendly **La Residenza** (page 250), and the newly refurbished **Scalinata di Spagna**. We have not included **Caesar House** (tel 06 6792674), a new and very sophisticated boutique hotel in Via Cavour, certainly less impersonal than most smart Rome hotels, but still impressively ritzy. If you want to rub shoulders with the glitterati, the **de Russie** (tel. 06 328881), off Piazza del Popolo, is the place to stay. One-time haunt of well-to-do Russians, it opened after a total revamp in 2000; pricey but with fabulous terraced gardens and a spa.

Only 38 km north-west of Rome in Anguillara Sabazia, **I Due Laghi** is a friendly country four-star hotel (page 258). Also within easy driving distance of Rome to the north just outside Poggio Mirteto Scalo is the country-club-style **Borgo Paraelios** (page 235), and, on the coast outside Palo Laziale, **Posta Vecchia** is the 17thC mansion that once belonged to Jean Paul Getty (page 258). A stay here surrounded by the fabulous artworks and faded grandeur is an expensive but unique experience. Within day-trip range of the capital to the east are **Palestrina** (birthplace of the 16thC composer) and **Tivoli** (villas of Emperor Hadrian and the 16thC Cardinal d'Este). If you want to stay overnight in Palestrina, go for the **Stella** – an excellent, modern restaurant with clean spacious bedrooms (tel 06 9538172).

North of Rome is the pretty wooded countryside around the ancient city of Viterbo and Lago di Vico, the homeland of the Etruscans. East of Rome, **Antico Borgo** is a simple bed-and-breakfast in the medieval village of Fumone (page 226), and further north-west near Farnese, **Il Voltone** retains its appeal, set in gloriously unspoiled country (page 233). To the south, on Lazio's coast at San Felice Circeo, there's **Punta Rossa** (page 257), a pleasant holiday hotel, and on the nearby island of Ponza, **Gennarino a Mare** (page 236) is a delight.

Abruzzo is a wild and wooded mountainous region, forming part of the Apennine mountains. Charming small hotels are thin on the ground here and you might do best to explore the area from a base nearer Rome. Nevertheless you could try the tiny **Villa Vignola** on the coast at Vasto (tel 0873 310050); in Scanno, the friendly chalet, **Mille Pini** (tel 0864 74387), or **Del Lago** (tel 0864 74343), in a lakeside setting 3 km outside the town.

L'Aquila, the capital of the region, is a big town further north but still in the heart of the mountains. Though mainly a business centre today, the surrounding mountains and the imposing historical buildings within the town itself still make it an interesting place to stay. Try the **Grand Hotel del Parco** (tel 0862 413248), which with 36 rooms is smaller and less business-oriented than most of the hotels in the town.

Il Voltone, 01010 Farnese, Viterbo

Tel 0761 422540
e-mail info@voltone.it
website www.voltone.it

Nearby Farnese (12 km); Lake Bolsena.
Location N of Farnese off the Ischia di Castro-Latera road; car parking
Food breakfast, lunch, dinner
Price €€
Rooms 30 double and twin, triple and family, all with bath or shower; all rooms have phone, TV, hairdrier
Facilities sitting room, breakfast room, terrace, garden, swimming pool
Credit cards MC, V
Disabled ground floor room with special facilities
Pets accepted by arrangement
Closed early Nov to early Apr
Proprietors Daniela and Donatella Parenti

Il Voltone
Country hotel

Hardly anyone arrives at Il Voltone without getting lost (make sure you have precise directions and don't give up on a road that seems never-ending); or without falling in love at first sight with this charming, individual hotel. A clutch of beautifully restored 17thC buildings – including a small church – colour-washed in pinks, yellows and creams, it stands high in the middle of a 465-hectare estate. Rolling hills, vineyards, woods and fields stretch out on three sides – scenery you can admire from reception rooms, bedrooms and even the swimming pool.

The unfussy decoration is more Tuscan than Roman with warm, fresh colours that echo the exterior. Floors are terracotta-tiled, scattered with the occasional Persian carpet. Almost everywhere table lamps cast a warm, flattering light. Bedrooms are graced with a few handsome pieces of furniture, and some have lovely old beams.

In the dining room, choose from a range of local dishes, made from the freshest ingredients, and drink wine from the estate's own vineyards. For relaxing outside, there is a terrace with tables and chairs, shaded by horse chestnuts and parasols. There is so much to see locally that the thoughtful Parenti sisters have planned itineraries for those guests who want to explore.

Via del Fico 5, 3010 Fumone, Frosinone

Tel 0775 49791
e-mail lisaeagles@infinito.it
website ww.italiaabc.it/az/anti-coborgo

Nearby Frosinone (21 km); Lake Canterno.
Location in centre of Fumone, 12 km N of Ferentino; public car park outside fortress walls.
Food breakfast 50E
Price €
Rooms 8; 7 double and twin, 1 with bath, 6 with shower, 1 single with shower; all rooms have TV
Facilities sitting/breakfast room
Credit cards not accepted
Disabled access difficult **Pets** not accepted
Closed Nov to Mar
Proprietor Lisa Eagles

Antico Borgo
Village bed-and-breakfast

Little seems to have changed over the centuries in the charming medieval fortress village of Fumone (the name means 'big smoke', after the smoke signals sent up from here to warn Rome of imminent invasion from Naples). No cars are permitted inside the old walls, still intact and with only two entrances: one facing Rome, the other, Naples. So if you arrive by car, you must park outside and walk through the labyrinthine streets until you reach this simple, friendly B&B in one of the ancient village houses. Once inside, all is airy and bright. Upstairs and down, the plain white-walled rooms are lifted by warm terracotta floors and attractive timberwork. There are wooden panels on the bar, wooden stairs, doors and even ceilings.

Don't worry about the lack of a dining room. There is a choice of restaurants and pizzerias in the village, two of them only a couple of minutes' walk away. Guests will be helped and advised by their delightful English host, Lisa Eagles, who, with her Italian husband Giampaolo, provides a very personal service. They will even pick up and drop off at Rome airport or local stations. In an area where this guide has no other hotels, we feel that Antico Borgo is a real find.

Valle Collicchia di Poggio
Catino, 02040 Poggio Catino,
Rieti

Tel 0765 26267
e-mail info@borgoparaelios.it
website www.borgoparaelios.it

Nearby Rome (40 km);
Marmore Falls; Lake
Piediluco.
Location 4 km N of Poggio
Mirteto off SS313; car parking
Food breakfast, lunch, dinner
Price €€€€
Rooms 18; 16 double and
twin, 2 suites, all with bath or
shower; all rooms have phone,
TV, air conditioning, hairdrier
Facilities sitting rooms,
restaurant, games rooms, meet-
ing room, spa, garden, indoor
and outdoor swimming pool,
tennis, golf
Credit cards AE, DC, MC, V
Disabled access difficult
Pets small dogs accepted
Closed never; restaurant Tues
Proprietors Salabe family

Borgo Paraelios
Country villa

A 19thC villa is at the heart of this attractive country club-style development in the hills halfway between Rome and Rieti, with most of the immaculately
furnished rooms and suites spread around the beautiful gardens and courtyards,
ensuring peace and seclusion for their occupants. Each room also has its own terrace. Decoration varies from room to room, but the predominant style is Italian
'rustic chic' – a blend of warm colours, chintzes and period furniture. Some also
have exposed rafters and brass beds. The numerous public rooms are grander: don't
be surprised to spot a Canaletto or an Attardi among the fine paintings on their
walls. This show of wealth is not off-put-
ting, however, and the place exudes warmth and hospitality, thanks in great
measure to the friendly staff.

One of the most relaxing places to sit is the huge covered terrace with splendid
views of the hills and masses of padded wicker chairs. Whenever possible, food is
served outside, and consists largely of sim-
ple but tasty local specialities.

An excellent range of facilities includes indoor and outdoor pools, sauna, Turkish
bath and a minibus service to Rome.

Via Dante 64, 04027 Ponza , Latina

Tel 0771 80071/80593
e-mail
gennarinoamare@yahoo.it

Nearby Chiaia di Luna beach; Pilatus caves.
Location on waterfront opposite harbour; garage for 30 cars
Food breakfast, lunch, dinner
Price €€€
Rooms 12 double and twin with bath; all rooms have phone, TV, minibar
Facilities sitting room, restaurant, bar
Credit cards AE, DC, MC, V
Disabled access difficult
Pets not accepted
Closed never
Proprietor Francesco Silvestri

Gennarino a Mare
Restaurant-with-rooms

The *raison d'être* of the Gennarino a Mare is its popular, buzzing restaurant, spread out over a covered timber deck, perched on piles, jutting into the sea. There are no prizes for guessing what the cuisine is based on – seafood, including fish and shellfish of all descriptions. The Gennarino provides moorings so, in the holiday season, hotel guests rub shoulders with yachties who come ashore to sample the daily catch.

A small blue-painted box-shaped building, with a backdrop of Ponza's colourful houses climbing the cliffside, the hotel is modest but full of sunlight. White-walled rooms are simply furnished with ceiling fans, brightly co-ordinating curtains and bedspreads, and balconies overlooking the sea; the best have large terraces with table and deckchairs.

The hotel had its genesis in the tiny *pensione* run by the parents of the present owner Francesco Silvestri, who has lived here all his life. A charming man, for whom nothing is too much trouble, he will direct you to the island's many natural treasures: beaches, cliffs, caves and grottoes. There are other hotels on Ponza but this one has the edge, combining a terrific restaurant, character and unbeatable prices.

Piazza Benedetto Cairoli 2,
00186 Roma

Tel 06 68809278
e-mail cairolo@tin.it

Nearby Campo di Fiori;
Pantheon; Trastevere.
Location SE of Campo di
Fiori, on the SW side of Lago
Argentina; public car parking
nearby
Food breakfast
Price €€€
Rooms 13; 11 double, 4 with
bath, 7 with shower, 2 single
with shower; all rooms have
phone, TV, video, air-condi-
tioning, hairdrier
Facilities sitting/breakfast
room, communal minibar, lift
Credit cards AE, DC, MC, V
Disabled no special facilities
Pets not accepted
Closed never
Proprietor Luciano Chasini

Locanda Cairoli
Town hotel

The cold staircase inside the entrance
to this *palazzo* doesn't prepare you for
such a charming hotel on the first floor.
'Welcome Home' heads the brochure,
which says it all: this *locanda* is deeply comfortable and fitted out in serious style.
Opened in 2000, it was designed and is
clearly loved by its architect owner Signor
Chasini, who lives in part of the building.
The atmosphere is bright and warm and
the staff are welcoming and professional.

Opposite reception is a funky, small
kitchen – all granite surfaces and 'Smeg'
appliances. In the stunning room next-
door, a simple breakfast is served at a long
glass dining table, in front of a huge and
beautiful hand-painted dresser. There are
pale sofas, fresh flowers, and an impressive
contemporary collection of art and sculpture, including works by the owner's family. All the woodwork is natural, and complemented by terracotta floors and tapestry rugs. Bedrooms are smart, with crisp
monogrammed linen, navy and white furnishings, Aubusson carpets, and high-spec
bath and shower rooms.

It may not be ideal for families, but this
little hotel is a comfortable and sophisticated address in central Rome.

149 Via Sistina (Piazza di Spagna),
Roma

Tel 06 69924 555
e-mail info@casahoward.it
website www.casahoward.com

Nearby Spanish Steps, Trevi
Fountain, Via Condotti.
Location City Centre. 150 metres
from the Spanish Steps.
Food breakfast
Price €€€€
Rooms 5; 4 doubles, 1 triple. 1 with
balcony (Zebra); all with ensuite
bathrooms, 1 with wet-room. All
rooms have flat-screen TV, wy-fi
internet, air-conditioning, hairdryer,
tea and coffee-making facilities.
Facilities library corner, self-service
fridge, Turkish steam bath, Edgar's
little black book.
Credit cards AE DC MC V
Disabled not suitable
Pets no
Closed never
Proprietor Massimiliano Leonardi
and Jenifer Howard

Casa Howard
Town hotel

Two minutes' walk down Via Sistina
from the hectic Spanish Steps is the
unmarked door of a secluded 19th century *palazzo*. If you didn't know Casa
Howard was here, you'd walk right past.
This "in-the-know" ethos is not accidental.
Aristocratic owner Massimiliano Leonardi
and his half-English wife Jenifer Howard
want their guesthouses (another is round
the corner, a third in Florence) to be
homes-from-home. So there's no concierge at the second-floor apartment, just
'house-genie' Edgar, who shows you the
'honesty fridge' packed with cokes and
juices; and will bring you breakfast in bed.

The stunning mirrored hallway was
designed by Howard as a cage for the
porcelain monkey she found at a Paris flea-
market which hangs from the ceiling. It
sets the tone: chic and personal. The rest
of the shared space is limited to a book
corner and an amazing *hammam* – rather
extravagantly priced at 50 euros. Designed
by Tommaso Ziffer, the five bedrooms are
all different. From the Zebra Room with
its 70s New York vibe to the Indian
Room's colonial grace, the feel is high-style
but never flash. Beautifully chosen *objets
d'art*, furniture and prints make the best of
the relatively small spaces. Comfort is at a
premium. A word of warning to the stat-
uesque: the baths are on the short side.

Via SS Quattro 35/C, 00184 Roma

Tel 06 70495333
e-mail info@hotelcelio.com **website**
www.hotelcelio.com

Nearby Colisseum, Roman forums.
Location central Rome, near
Colisseum
Food breakfast
Price €€€€
Rooms 19 doubles and suites, all
with en suite bath, shower; all rooms
have phone, TV, hairdryer, air-con-
ditioning
Facilities roof terrace with pool for
children, wellness area, breakfast
area, sitting area
Credit cards AE, DC, MC, V
Disabled no lift
Pets small ones by
arrangement
Closed never
Proprietor Roberto Quattrini

Celio
Town hotel

The massive bulk of the Colisseum
stands guard at the end of the quiet,
largely residential street where stands
the Hotel Celio. Those two reasons – the
quiet, and the proximity of the amazing
ancient arena (plus important nearby
remains of the ancient city), make the
Celio a prime base in central Rome. Ease
of parking (own small drive, and a garage
nearby), is a bonus, too, and driving in
from Ciampino airport is no big deal – as
quick as half an hour on the Via Appia.
The rooms aren't large, but they are
rather fun if you don't mind deep red
brocade on the walls, and paintings and
mirrors created by an artist from Brescia
to look at least 200 years older than they
actually are. The floors are wonderful:
high-quality imitation ancient mosaic,
designed by the owner, Roberto
Quattrini. There is no lift to the bedrooms, and it is a moderate climb to the
roof where guests can sunbathe and
where there is a penthouse suite, complete with own roof terrace and views
across Rome to St Peter's. Breakfast is
served in fine weather in a courtyard
imaginatively roofed in with a tent.

Via Mario De' Fiori 37, 00187 Roma

Tel 06 6794661
e-mail
info@hotelcondotti.com
website
www.hotelcondotti.com

Nearby Spanish Steps; Via del Corso; Villa Borghese.
Location between Via del Corso and Piazza di Spagna; public car park nearby
Food breakfast
Price €€€
Rooms 17 double and twin, 12 with bath, 5 with shower; all rooms have phone, TV, air conditioning, minibar, hairdrier
Facilities reception, breakfast room, lift
Credit cards AE, DC, MC, V
Disabled access difficult
Pets not accepted
Closed never
Proprietor Massimo Funaro

Condotti
Town hotel

The owners continue to make improvements to this appealing little hotel located in an attractive street in the heart of Rome's chicest shopping zone. The warmly-lit reception hall looks inviting from the street side of the double glass doors; guests are greeted at an antique table, often by a professional and helpful Canadian. The public rooms have been recently restored, and the reception area has a white and gold marbled floor - perhaps a bit gaudy for some tastes. Down a marble staircase is the attractive breakfast room where cream-coloured walls, touches of blue and soft lighting make the very best of a windowless basement. Here, unfortunately our inspector ate a disappointingly minimalist breakfast.

All of the bedrooms (divided into two categories – standard and superior) have been recently refurbished, and now look tasteful and smart, though some of the standard ones are smallish and bland. The superior rooms are more appealing, with much larger bathrooms and terraces. Blue and gold predominate (a favourite colour scheme in Roman hotels) on fabrics and carpets while furniture and bedheads are in rich cherry wood. Five rooms in an annexe round the corner help satisfy demand for this rightfully popular hotel.

Vicolo del Leonetto 23, 00186 Roma

Tel 06 68806956
e-mail hotelduetorri@mclink.it
website www.hotelduetorriroma.com

Nearby Piazza Navona; Piazza di Spagna; Via del Corso.
Location in quiet side street just N of Piazza Navona; public car park nearby
Food breakfast
Price €€€
Rooms 26; 15 double and twin, 7 single, 4 family, all with shower; all rooms have phone, TV, air conditioning, minibar, hairdryer
Facilities sitting rooms, breakfast room, lift/elevator
Credit cards AE, DC, MC, V
Disabled no special facilities
Pets accepted
Closed never
Proprietor Cinzia Giordani Pighini

Due Torri
Town guesthouse

This stylish little hotel in a quiet, cobbled lane just north of Piazza Navona is a real discovery. The fresh, painted façade offers a foretaste of the neat interior where the spacious reception area leads into a series of comfortable public rooms. Marble floors gleam and provide a suitable setting for some lovely antiques while chairs and sofas are upholstered in red velvet or smart red and beige, a colour scheme which is continued throughout the house. There are some fine antique mirrors (including a huge one on each landing), old lamps and attractive prints, all of which are offset by cool, cream walls.

The bedrooms (each with its own brass doorknocker) are arranged on five floors and reached by an elegant marble staircase with *fin-de-siècle* iron banister (or there's a lift). None of them is very large (one or two are, in fact, quite small), but all are pretty and comfortable. Bedheads, valances, curtains and bedcovers are all in co-ordinated red and beige; attractive but never fussy. Some rooms have great views over rooftops and terraces, excellent for an inside glimpse of Roman domestic life. Four – including a single – have terraces.

A recent report describes the Due Torri as 'spotless and professionally run... guests receive very personal service'.

Largo Fontanella Borghese 84,
00186 Roma

Tel 06 68809504
e-mail fontborghese@mclink.it
website
www.fontanellaborghese.com

Nearby Augustus Mausoleum;
Piazza di Spagna; Pantheon.
Location N of the Pantheon
between Via del Corso and Via
di Ripeta; public car park
nearby
Food breakfast
Price €€€
Rooms 29; 21 double and
twin, 5 single, 3 suites, all with
bath or shower; all rooms have
phone, TV, air conditioning,
minibar, hairdrier
Facilities sitting room, break-
fast room, lift
Credit cards AE, DC, MC, V
Disabled access possible
Pets accepted
Closed never **Proprietor**
Cinzia Giordani Pighini

Fontanella Borghese
Town guesthouse

Occupying the top two floors of a
graceful 16thC building, which once
belonged to the Borghese princes, this elegant, modern hotel is under the same
ownership as the more modest Due Torri
(see page 241). A neoclassical courtyard
separates it from the busy road and a discreet lift whisks you up to the hotel.

The open-plan reception area gives a
taste of the style of the establishment:
smart marble floors, cool cream walls,
leafy pot plants, some fine antiques and
plenty of light. The space is dominated by a
sweeping, open staircase in wrought iron,
brass and marble, and behind this are several comfortable sofas which make a sunny
spot for relaxing with a magazine. The
owner has kept the decoration of the stylish bedrooms simple; co-ordinating fabrics
(in green and cream on the lower floor,
blue and cream upstairs), dark parquet
floors, neutral cream walls, brass light fittings, some antique furniture and prints on
the walls. Our latest inspector noticed
some rather tired-looking decoration, but
was assured that there is an ongoing programme of refurbishment. Bathrooms (off-
white with the appropriate-coloured trim)
are smart and well equipped.

A classy, inviting hotel, with an enthusiastic owner and loyal clientele, which
offers reasonable prices.

Via Gregoriana 18, 00187
Roma

Tel 06 6797988
e-mail info@hotelgregoriana.it
website
www.hotelgregoriana.it

Nearby Spanish Steps; Via del
Corso; Trevi Fountain.
Location City Centre. Just SE
of Spanish Steps
Food breakfast; room service
Price €€€
Rooms 22: 19 doubles, 3 suites
with bath or shower; all rooms
have flat-screen TV, internet
access, air-conditioning, safe,
hairdrier
Facilities room service,
lift/elevator, umbrellas, break-
fast room and terrace under
construction
Credit cards AE DC MC V
Disabled no special facilities
Pets accepted
Closed never
Proprietor Maria Novella
Panier Bagat

Gregoriana
Town guesthouse

Hidden in a shuttered former convent, a mere 30 seconds from the top of the Spanish Steps, the first-rate Gregoriana is a real find. The hotel is reasonably priced despite both its position in the priciest district of Rome and its emphasis on low-key deco luxury. A highpoint is the welcome from wonderful head concierge Aldo Basso Bandini, in charge for the last thirty years. Ask him about his time at the Savoy in the Sixties and don't leave without his recipe for pressed duckling. Anything you need to know about the Eternal City, Signor Bandini can tell you.

The 4-storey Gregoriana reopened in April 2005 after a total renovation. Gone are the deep pink carpets and ubiquitous bamboo. In their place understated decadence, monochromatic colour-schemes and well-hung prints. The rooms (three with private terraces) come with excellent Irish bedlinen, well-sprung mattresses and huge fluffy towels. Stairwells and landings have been refitted with inlaid marble; and the bedrooms lettered (not numbered) with Aubrey Beardsley-like illustrations. The balance between style and warmth is perfectly struck.

Croissants, great coffee and jams are served with a flourish in the rooms – the hotel is still awaiting its breakfast area.

Via della Penna 22, 00186
Roma

Tel 06 3610841
e-mail info@hotellocarno.com
website
www.hotellocarno.com

Nearby Piazza del Popolo;
Villa Borghese; Via del Corso.
Location in side street just N
of Piazza del Popolo; public car
parking nearby
Food breakfast, lunch, dinner
Price €€€
Rooms 65; 51 double and
twin, 13 single, one suite, all
with bath or shower; all have
phone, TV, air conditioning,
minibar, hairdrier; de luxe
rooms have video and stereo
Facilities sitting room, breakfast room, dining room, bar,
meeting room, lift, roof garden, terrace, free bicycles
Credit cards AE, DC, MC, V
Disabled some rooms **Pets** not
accepted **Closed** never
Proprietor Maria-Teresa Celli

Locarno
Town hotel

To step inside the fine *fin-de-siècle* doors
of this stylish, wisteria-clad hotel just
north of the Piazza del Popolo is to enter
a time warp, somewhat faded, but with a
dark, mysterious appeal that makes it a
perennial favourite with musicians, artists
and film-makers. The ground floor public
rooms house the owner's impressive collection of original art nouveau and art
deco pieces; fabulous lamps, Thonet bentwood furniture, old posters and, in reception, a grandfather clock with a resonant
chime. The bar leads into a spacious sitting
room where a fire burns in winter.

A birdcage lift creaks up to the bedrooms, each one different from the next,
but all furnished with antiques, original
lamps and rich fabrics. The spotless bathrooms are mostly in marble. New rooms
and suites in the 1905 villa next door are
more luxurious with opulent fabrics and
more marble, though some guests might
miss such modern practicalities as reading
lights and power showers.

There is plenty of outside space, too; in
warm weather, breakfast is served until
11.30 am either on the stunning roof terrace or in the pretty garden. And a fleet of
bicycles is available for guests' use. The
laid-back feel to this hotel and its understated glamour ensure that it is almost
always full, even in winter.

Via Giuseppe De Notaris, 5 - 00197 Roma

Tel 06 3220 404
e-mail
info@lordbyronhotel.com
website
www.lordbyronhotel.com

Nearby Villa Borghese, Galleria Borghese, Via Veneto, Casa Guilia.
Location N side of Villa Borghese in Pairoli district
Food breakfast, lunch, dinner
Price €€€€–€€€€€
Rooms 32; 20 guest rooms, 6 junior suites, 6 senior suites; most with balcony and/or terrace, all have TV, minibar, safe, phone, internet, air conditioning
Facilities bar, restaurant, breakfast room, patio
Credit cards AE, DC, MC, V
Disabled not suitable
Pets not accepted
Closed never
Proprietor Amadeo Ottaviani

Lord Byron
Town hotel

As you leave Centro Storico and wind north through Villa Borghese, Rome's largest park, two things happen: the constant cacophony of car horns fades to birdsong and a sense of escape creeps over you. The five star Hotel Lord Byron is an elegant white 1910 villa with wrought iron balconies in a posh and bosky district. Owned by Roman mover-and-shaker Amedeo Ottaviani, the hotel is packed with 1930s art and treasures from his private collection, deco lamps jostling for position in the second floor salon.

The public areas are all clad in deco-style heavily-veined white marble and smoked glass mirrors. Fiendishly efficient front desk manager Melita Marrak will turn a blind eye to guests whose luggage includes a "very small" dog. The fractionally over-lit bar – with jolly pianist playing souped-up lounge melodies on a Casio keyboard – serves a dynamite whisky and ginger. Breakfast is first-rate, particularly the bacon and freshly-squeezed blood orange. Rooms, all 30s style, are slowly being refurbished: go for one on the 3rd floor that hasn't yet been touched. They're smaller but the jumbled aesthetic is more characterful. Huge vintage marble baths big enough for two on the more neutral renovated floor, though, are a triumph, as is the service.

Via dei Greci 23b, 00187
Roma

Tel 06 36001915
e-mail info@hotelmozart.com
website www.hotelmozart.com

Nearby Piazza di Spagna;
Piazza del Popolo; Villa
Borghese.
Location in side street
between Via del Corso and Via
del Babuino; public car parking
nearby
Food breakfast
Price €€€
Rooms 56; 45 double and
twin, 9 single, 2 suites, all with
bath or shower; all rooms have
phone, TV, air conditioning,
minibar, hairdrier
Facilities sitting room, break-
fast room, bar, roof garden
Credit cards AE, DC, MC, V
Disabled some adapted rooms
Pets not accepted
Closed never
Proprietor Antonella De
Gregorio

Mozart
Town hotel

Ideally placed for shopaholics on one of
the narrow, cobbled streets that run
between Via del Corso and Via del
Babuino, the Mozart is one of the pleasan-
test of the numerous hotels in the area. It
expanded a few years ago into the adjacent building, so there is an 'old' part and
a 'new' part, two sets of stairs and lifts, and
rather confusing warren-like corridors.

The lobby is a calm expanse of cool,
creamy archways, marble floors and stylish
parlour palms. On the first floor, a long,
comfortable sitting room has pale yellow
walls, dark hardwood floor broken by oriental rugs, invitingly squashy sofas, and
handsome antique furniture. An open fire
cheers up chilly evenings. Although small,
the bedrooms are well-equipped, with pale
terracotta floors and dark cherry wood
furniture as well as the odd antique piece;
the pokey singles are best avoided. In the
bathrooms, chrome fittings gleam; one
even opens on to a little terrace. The
suites also have their own spacious terraces, and there is a delightful roof garden
on two levels, equipped with stylish garden
furniture, from where you can see most of
Rome. There is a little bar up there, too.

Signs requesting that guests refrain from
lingering over breakfast made our recent
inspector worry that the hotel might have
outgrown itself.

Via delle Convertite, Roma
00187

Tel 06 6792082
e-mail
hotelparlamento@libero.it
website
www.hotelparlamento.it

Nearby Via del Corso; Spanish
Steps; Pantheon.
Location between Via del
Corso and Piazza San Silvestro;
public car park nearby
Food breakfast
Price €–€€
Rooms 25; 15 double and
twin, 4 single, 6 family, all with
bath or shower; all rooms have
phone, TV, hairdrier; some
have air-conditioning
Facilities breakfast room,
communal minibar, roof gar-
den **Credit cards** AE, DC, MC
Disabled not suitable
Pets accepted
Closed never
Proprietor Plinio Chini

Pensione Parlamento
Town guesthouse

One of a handful of two-star establishments that we feature in Rome, this
friendly family-owned *pensione* on the
third and fourth floors of a 17thC *palazzo*,
has an excellent central location for those
on a budget. Anyone interested in the con-
tortions of Italian politics can stroll over
to the Quirinale in nearby Piazza del
Parlamento to watch the comings and
goings of politicians and officials.

On our latest visit, we were particularly
impressed by the infectious enthusiasm of
the Chini family and their staff. Their front
door opens on to the tiled reception,
where collages of postcards from grateful
clients cover the walls. Murals brighten the
next-door breakfast room, where the odd
elegant touch (such as a glittering chandelier) softens the modern decoration.
Bedrooms – where pale, dusty pink predominates – vary in size from quite large
to tiny. Bedcovers are monogrammed, furniture is simple reproduction. Singles are
amongst the best we have seen in Rome
(try for Nos 92 or 109), and double windows keep the street noise at bay.

Some changes have recently been made,
including the transformation of the scruffy
roof terrace, and the creation of some
new bedrooms opening on to it. Not ritzy
or glitzy, but comfortable and clean, and
perfect for families.

Via dei Portoghesi 1, 00186
Roma

Tel 06 6864231
e-mail info@hotelportoghe-
siroma.com **website**
www.hotelportoghesiroma.com

Nearby Piazza Navona;
Pantheon; Castel Sant' Angelo.
Location in a side street just N
of Piazza Navona; public car
parking nearby
Food breakfast
Price €€€
Rooms 28 double and twin,
single and suites, 5 with bath,
23 with shower; all rooms have
phone, TV, air conditioning,
hairdrier
Facilities breakfast room, roof
garden, lift
Credit cards MC, V
Disabled access difficult **Pets**
not accepted
Closed never
Proprietors Claudio and
Marco Trivellone

Portoghesi
Town hotel

Just north of lovely Piazza Navona and
situated in the heart of what was the
Portuguese quarter of 17thC Rome, the
Portoghesi has an attractively old-fashioned look to it from the outside. Until a
few years ago, it was pretty old-fashioned
on the inside too, but major refurbishment
has brought increased comfort although
possibly at the expense of character.

Bedrooms (a few are large enough to be
called suites) are modernized with quality
reproduction furniture mixed with some
antiques, padded bedheads, pleasant wallpapers and co-ordinated fabrics in rich
colours. The new bathrooms sparkle.
Depending on which floor you are on,
views may include the neighbour's washing
hanging out to dry or little terraces tucked
away among the rooftops. The pretty
glassed-in breakfast room, decked out in
sunny fabrics, adjoining a flower-filled terrace are at the top of the building, and
look on to the ancient 'Torre della
Scimmia' or 'Tower of the Monkey', so
named from a legend which claims that a
baby was rescued and carried to the top
by a monkey in the 17th century.

A reader recently wrote to praise this
small hotel's 'central yet quiet location'
and 'delightful, sunny breakfast room',
where she enjoyed a delicious breakfast.

Largo Febo 2, 00186 Roma

Tel 06 682831
e-mail info@raphaelhotel.com
website www.raphaelhotel.com

Nearby Piazza Navona;
Palazzo Altemps; Santa Maria
della Pace.
Location at the N end of Via
dell' Anima behind Piazza
Navona; public car park nearby
Food breakfast, lunch, dinner
Price €€€€€
Rooms 56; 49 double and
twin, 7 suites, all with bath; all
rooms have phone, TV, air
conditioning, minibar, hairdri-
er; some rooms have stereo,
safe
Facilities breakfast room, din-
ing room, bar, conference
room, fitness centre, roof din-
ing terrace **Credit cards** AE,
DC, MC, V
Disabled 2 adapted rooms
Pets accepted **Closed** never
Proprietor Roberto Vannoni

Raphaël
Town hotel

Cloaked in stalactites of ivy, the Raphaël
stands back from the bustle of Piazza
Navona and belongs, instead, to the quiet
refinement of the antiques and antiquarian
bookshops and local *trattorias* of Via dei
Coronari which runs beside it. The discreet façade conceals one of the most
evocative and theatrical lobbies in the city.
The dazzling white marble floor provides a
dramatic contrast with the Byzantine
icons, Old Master paintings, prints by the
Italian Futurists and ceramics by Picasso
displayed in baroque furniture; modern
sofas add comfort. The dining room is
equally immaculate, and the German manager has introduced an impressive new
breakfast buffet. Nothing disappoints here.

Bedrooms are constantly being updated, and some of the smaller ones have
been combined to make fewer, more spacious, rooms. Older bedrooms drip in
paisley fabrics, with co-ordinated padded
headboards and bedspreads, and parquet
floors. Newer ones are modern and mini-
mal, but not so beautiful, with bedcovers
and sofas in Fendi's deep purple and black
stripes and well-lit pale walls. Bathrooms,
new and old, in white marble, are all stunning. Its final incomparable asset is the roof
terrace, which offers magnificent views
over almost the entire city. Book early to
dine up here in the summer months.

Via Emilia 22, 00187 Roma

Tel 06 4880789
e-mail la.residenza@thegiannet-
tihotelsgroup.com **website**
www.thegiannettihotelsgroup.c
om

Nearby Spanish Steps; Villa
Borghese; Via del Corso.
Location in side street off Via
Veneto; limited car parking
Food breakfast
Price €€€€
Rooms 29; 17 double and
twin, 7 suites, all with bath, 5
single with shower ; all rooms
have phone, TV, air condition-
ing, minibar, hairdrier, safe
Facilities sitting rooms, break-
fast room, bar, lift, patio,
terrace
Credit cards MC, V
Disabled access difficult **Pets**
small ones accepted
Closed never
Manager Paolo D'Angelo

La Residenza
Town hotel

Fashionable Via Veneto is home to some of Rome's grandest hotels. La Residenza is not one of these, but its posi-tion, just a block away from the sweeping, tree-lined avenue, is only one of its advan-tages. It is a traditional, well-managed, good value hotel with an impressive entrance and exceptionally welcoming and profes-sional staff. A bar and sitting rooms lead off the front hall on the elevated ground floor. Smartly kitted out in a deep-pink striped fabric, with cream on the walls, these have a mixture of modern and antique furni-ture, sofas, attractive paintings and a calm atmosphere. But in the stylish downstairs breakfast room our inspector found the service rather slow and the food a little tired-looking.

Bedrooms are very comfortable with huge beds. Some have a glassed-in bath which might challenge the physically less agile. There are some homely personal touches, such as a fruit bowl and tea and coffee making facilities. The singles are very small and tend to be dingy. The larger dou-bles or suites are ideal for families; some have fair-sized terraces.

Unfortunately, due to new laws, the air-conditioning system has been relocated to the roof terrace, and almost entirely blocks what used to be a stunning view over Rome.

Vicolo del Piede 2, 00153 Roma

Tel 06 589 4626
e-mail
info@hotelsantamaria.info
website
www.hotelsantamaria.info

Nearby Santa Maria Di
Trastevere, Isola Tiberina,
Piazza Campo de' Fiori.
Location W of Centro
Storico. Seconds from Piazza
Di Santa Maria
Food breakfast, afternoon
buffet
Price €€€€
Rooms 18, 8 doubles, 4 triples,
6 family rooms. All rooms have
flat-screen TV, air-condition-
ing, hairdryer, phone, mini-bar
Facilities breakfast room, 2
courtyards, bar, games chest,
internet, bicycles **Credit cards**
AE, DC, MC, V **Disabled** one
room **Pets** not accepted
Closed never **Proprietor**
Paolo Vetere

Santa Maria di Trastevere
Town hotel

If location really is everything, then this
three star hotel in the medieval heart of
Rome has it all. Trastevere is Rome's best-
kept secret. Just a short stroll across the
Tiber from all the big-name sights, it's
where hip Romans want to hang out. The
beautiful higgledy-piggledy streets have
been enthusiastically graffitied, but don't
let that put you off.

Built in 2000 on the site of a demolished
16th century convent just behind the lively Piazza Di Santa Maria, Hotel Santa Maria
is a single-storey mock-up arranged
around two leafy courtyards. In summer
the excellent breakfast of croissants, cakes,
ham and 'scrumbled eggs' is served by
cheerful staff under the orange trees.
Otherwise guests eat in the convent's former kitchen, which also acts as bar, internet café and the venue for a tasty and free
afternoon buffet. Another thoughtful
touch is the provision of bicycles.

Front-of-house manager Stefano Don-
ghi doubles as a guide and is generous with
his local knowledge. Rooms are large, basic
and clean. The beds are comfortable, the
bathrooms small but perfectly formed. If
you can get past the peach rag-rolling and
cheap iron bedsteads, the doubles are a
good no-frills option. Rather more characterful, however, are the split-level suites.

Piazza Trinità dei Monti 17,
00187 Roma

Tel 06 6793006
e-mail
info@hotelscalinata.com
website
www.hotelscalinata.com

Nearby Piazza di Spagna; Villa
Medici; Villa Borghese.
Location at top of Spanish
Steps; public car parking
nearby
Food breakfast
Price €€€€
Rooms 15 double and twin,
one triple, all with bath; all
rooms have phone, TV, air
conditioning, minibar,
hairdrier, safe
Facilities sitting room, break-
fast room, roof terrace
Credit cards AE, DC, MC, V
Disabled no special facilities
Pets accepted
Closed never
Proprietor Renato Bellia

Scalinata di Spagna
Town guesthouse

For many visitors to Rome, the Spanish
Steps represent the heart of the city, a
popular, lively rendezvous. At their summit
stand two hotels which represent the epit-
omes of their respective markets: the
Hassler, one of the city's grandest establishments, and this individual little *pensione*
which, now more than ever, wins our accolade for genuine charm.

Recent redecoration, by the proprietor's daughter, Claudia, has brought about
some very pleasing changes. Rooms are
now coated in pretty blue and gold floral
fabrics and illuminated by Murano chandeliers. Neoclassical scroll sofas and small
tables enhance a mood of comfort and
intimacy. Although every room is done out
in the same fabrics and colour scheme,
individual pieces of furniture, large oil
paintings and gilded mirrors make each
seem distinctive. The new bathrooms are
modern and well-equipped. Inevitably,
prices have risen and are now among the
highest of hotels in this category.

The breakfast area has also been refurbished, and here, on a recent visit, our
reporter enjoyed a variety of fresh pastries, juices, fruit and coffee, although she
was slightly disappointed that there was
nobody on hand to make her a *cappuccino*.
There are just 16 rooms, so book ahead.

Largo del Pellaro 8, 00186
Roma

Tel 06 6872812
e-mail hotel.teatrodipom-
peo@tiscali.it **website**
www.hotelteatrodipompeo.it

Nearby Campo dei Fiori;
Piazza Navona; the Vatican.
Location just E of Campo dei
Fiori; car parking nearby
Food breakfast
Price €€€
Rooms 13; 12 double and
twin, 6 with bath, 6 with show-
er, 1 single; all rooms have
phone, TV, air conditioning,
minibar, hairdrier
Facilities sitting rooms, break-
fast room, bar, lift
Credit cards AE, DC, MC, V
Disabled no special facilities
Pets not accepted
Closed never
Proprietor Lorenzo Mignoni

Teatro di Pompeo
Town guesthouse

Tucked away in a little frequented corner off the rather shabby but nonetheless picturesque Campo di Fiori, this is a
relaxed, but very efficient, modest family-
run hotel, where Paolo Cavarocchi,
nephew of the owner, Lorenzo Mignoni,
has taken over as manager. It has one
unique and extraordinary feature: it is built
on the site of the Teatro di Pompeo which
dates from 55 B.C., and the breakfast
room is hewn from the ancient tufa walls.
The adjoining sitting room shares the
same setting but is rather spoiled by ugly
lighting; however, a table is thoughtfully
laden with guidebooks, novels and
magazines.

Upstairs, the bedrooms are simple,
homely and appealing; padded bedheads
and bedspreads in attractive fabrics, the
odd antique combined with good reproduction furniture and filmy white curtains
add a touch of style to white walls and
standard terracotta flagstones. However a
recent visit revealed some bedrooms and
bathrooms in need of a lick of fresh paint
in places. Rooms on the top floor are
cosier, with beamed, attic ceilings and
those at the front of the building have a
bird's-eye view, through efficiently double-
glazed windows, of the sometimes noisy
comings-and-goings in the *piazza* below.

Via Nomentana 28, 00161
Roma

Tel 06 4403036
e-mail
villa.florence@flashnet.it
website www.hotelvillaflo-
rence.it

Nearby Villa Borghese; Via
Veneto; Piazza di Spagna.
Location about 1 km NE of
Via Veneto, NE of Porta Pia;
private car parking in garden
Food breakfast
Price ⓔⓔⓔ
Rooms 32; 27 doubles, 2 sin-
gles, 3 family, all with bath or
shower; all rooms have phone,
TV, air conditioning, minibar,
hairdrier
Facilities sitting room, break-
fast room, bar, lift, roof terrace,
garden
Credit cards AE, DC, MC, V
Disabled ground floor rooms
available **Closed** never
Proprietors Fabio Capelli

Villa Florence
Town villa

This popular hotel, located in a 19thC house on the busy Via Nomentana just beyond Porta Pia to the north-east of the centre of Rome, has emerged sparkling from a major refurbishment. Not only are the rooms now freshly and stylishly deco-rated but air conditioned and sound-proofed, with a number of new features such as modem plugs, trouser presses and Jacuzzis.

The newly-pointed façade is now an ele-gant pale yellow. The public areas have been refitted in a traditional style, suited to the period of the villa, with brocade wallpaper and heavy curtains. The bed-rooms, once merely functional, are now considerably more elegant and comfort-able, decked in richly-coloured, elegant fabrics (on walls, beds and curtains) with the colour schemes changing depending on the floor. The furniture is mostly good quality neoclassical-style reproduction which blends well with original features such as fine walnut bedroom doors. The smart bathrooms are also new.

There is a small, secluded terrace behind the house, on to which some of the bedrooms (in outbuildings) have direct access, and where breakfast is served on warm days. The private car parking – albeit limited – is a big plus in this city.

Via Nomentana 110, 00161
Roma

Tel 06 44237773
e-mail info@hotelvilladelpar-
co.it
website www.hotelvilladelpar-
co.it

Nearby Villa Torlonia; Villa
Borghese; Catacombe of S.
Agnese.
Location in residential area,
NE of city centre (Porta Pia);
public car parking nearby
Food breakfast
Price €€
Rooms 29; 15 double and
twin, 14 single, all with bath or
shower; all rooms have phone,
TV, air conditioning, minibar,
hairdrier **Facilities** 2 sitting
rooms, breakfast rooms, bar,
lift, garden **Credit cards** AE,
DC, MC, V **Disabled** ground
floor room available **Pets**
accepted **Closed** never
Proprietor Elisabetta
Bernardini

Villa del Parco
Town villa

Our inspector was full of enthusiasm after her visit to this mellow, 1910 villa situated in a little oasis of calm off the busy Via Nomentana and a 20-minute bus ride from the centre of Rome. It was worth the journey: she had found a delightful hotel with a truly warm welcome and very reasonable prices.

The pretty walled gardens to either side (where breakfast is served in summer) only partially protect against traffic noise, but once inside, all is peaceful and elegant. The reception lobby emanates a cosy glow with deep yellow sofas and armchairs grouped around a coffee table laden with magazines. An old grandfather clock, some fine oil portraits and a collection of covetable antiques add to the feeling of well-being. From here, steps lead down to a series of sunny rooms: a bar, two breakfast rooms and a sitting area. The ambience, here too, is both restful and tasteful; more antiques, green fabrics, plants and a mass of nicely-framed pictures. Bedrooms vary in size: some are quite small, others larger but all have touches of elegance. Six attic rooms were added a few years ago, and they are charmingly decorated in fresh greens and cream. Excellent value.

Via Vicenza 5,00185 Roma

Tel 06 4451788
e-mail info@villadellerose.it
website www.villadellerose.it

Nearby Termini station; Villa
Borghese; Roman Forum.
Location in a residential street
just N of Termini station; lim-
ited free car parking
Food breakfast
Price €€
Rooms 37; 28 double and
twin, 3 single, 6 family, all with
bath or shower; all rooms have
phone, TV, air-conditioning,
hairdrier, safe
Facilities sitting room, break-
fast room, bar, lift, garden
Credit cards AE, DC, MC, V
Disabled ground floor rooms
available **Pets** accepted
Closed never
Proprietors Claude and Frank
Filippo

Villa delle Rose
Town villa

The area round Termini train station is
scruffy, but Via Vicenza is a once-ele-
gant street lined with mellow old villas set
in attractive gardens. Despite the presence
of a few shady-looking characters, the
location of Villa delle Rose is convenient
for those who arrive in Rome by train. The
warmth and enthusiasm of the Filippo family give it a friendly atmosphere and, ambitious for their hotel, they are continually
improving its comfort and style. The bar-
sitting room is surprisingly grand, with
marbled columns, elaborate plasterwork
and a frescoed ceiling. The basement
breakfast room is somewhat stark, but is
due to be updated this year, and serves a
better-than-average buffet.

Recent improvements have brought two
of the 37 rooms up to a much higher standard (Nos 110 and 111). More luxurious
than the rest, they have green carpet,
padded headboards and matching covers,
large sofas and modern desks. The new
bathrooms are tiled in co-ordinating
colours. The other bedrooms vary (some
have balconies), but they, their bathrooms
and the corridors all have a lingering
Sixties decoration that cries out for updat-
ing: apparently this is planned to take place
over the next year or two. The pretty garden is a welcome and unusual feature so
close to the station.

Latina, 04017 San Felice
Circeo

Tel 0773 548085
e-mail punta_rossa@iol.it
website www.puntarossa.it

Nearby Terracina (20 km);
Circeo national park.
Location 4 km W of San
Felice, isolated on rocky shore;
private car parking
Food breakfast, lunch, dinner
350E
Price €€€
Rooms 34; 27 double, 7 suites,
all with bath or shower; all
rooms have phone, TV, air-
conditioning, minibar
Facilities bar, dining room,
spa, terrace, garden, swimming
pool
Credit cards AE, DC, MC, V
Disabled access difficult
Pets not accepted
Closed never
Manager Maria Fiorella
Battaglia

Punta Rossa
Seaside hotel

San Felice is an amiable village at the foot of the 550-metre Monte Circeo, which is an isolated lump of rock at the seaward point of a flat area, once marshland but now drained, except for zones which have been declared a national park. The Punta Rossa curves around the mountain in a secluded setting above an exposed and rocky shore, laid out like a miniature village. Reception is in a lodge just inside an arched gateway, and beyond that is a little *piazza* enclosed by white-walled buildings in rough Mediterranean style. Public rooms are light and beautifully decorated. Bedrooms are spread around in low buildings at or near the top of a flowery garden which drops steeply to the sea. All of them are pleasant, with balconies and sea views; but sizes vary, and, at our last inspection, some of the colour schemes looked dated. The main attraction of the suites is their generous size. The restaurant (food is 'exceptional' according to our latest report) is some-way down the garden towards the sea and glorious sea-water pool. In another rave report, a guest says his only regret was 'not to stay longer'.

Anguillara Sabazia

I Due Laghi
Country hotel

If you want to be within striking distance of Rome but based in the countryside, with a swimming pool in the garden and riding, tennis, golf and sailing on your doorstep, consider this friendly rural hotel. Originally a simple *agriturismo*, it has grown into a fully-fledged hotel, which still feels relaxed despite its four stars. It has a delightful hands-on owner, willing staff, and a reputation for excellent food, served in a large homely dining room or on a leafy terrace. The bedrooms tend to be uniform, with unexciting decoration but lovely views over the surrounding woods and fields. In addition to the 25 bedrooms, there are seven suites which open on to the garden.

Loc. Le Cerque, 00061
Anguillara Sabazia

Tel 06 99607059
e-mail info@iduelaghi.it
website www.iduelaghi.it
Food breakfast, lunch, dinner
Price €€
Closed never
Proprietor Mrs Alba Cella
Nizza

Palo Laziale

Posta Vecchia
Country villa

The Tyrrhenian seafront mansion that belonged to John Paul Getty and which he filled with fabulous artworks and antiques makes one of Italy's most remarkable hotels. Staying here, surrounded by priceless *objets* but with none of the formality that you might expect from a grand hotel, is a unique experience. While excavating the indoor pool, the remains of a Roman villa were discovered, which are now on display in a mini museum, visible through glass panels in the floor. The setting is spectacular, with six hectares of parkland and a formal garden on one side and the water lapping the dining terrace on the other – a wonderfully romantic place to dine on a warm summer's evening.

Palo Laziale, 00055 Ladispoli,
Roma

Tel 06 9949501
e-mail
info@lapostavecchia.com
website
www.lapostavecchia.com
Food breakfast, lunch, dinner
Price €€€€€
Closed Nov to Mar
Manager Barbara Panzero

Borgo Pio 133, 00193 Roma

Tel 06 68801602
e-mail santanna@travel.it
website
www.travel.it/roma/santanna
Food breakfast
Price €€€
Closed never
Proprietor Viscardo Scialanga

Sant' Anna
Town hotel

On a cobbled street just outside the Vatican walls, this pretty hotel is ideal for those who want to beat the daily crowds. Its lobby is carpeted and plush, with faux marbling, 16thC-style portraits and antique mirrors. A marble-floored sitting area, with leather sofas, leads out to a charming courtyard, where white iron tables, orange trees in pots and a lion head fountain make an attractive backdrop for breakfast. Bedrooms, though comfortable and well equipped, lack character, with built-in furniture and dull colour schemes. Those with murals have more panache. The marble bathrooms are immaculate, and rooms facing the road have balconies. Murals of Roman scenes brighten the subterranean breakfast room.

Area introduction

Campania has four distinct parts: the frantic, magnificent, decaying city of Naples; the fabulous coastline between Sorrento and Ravello; the islands of Capri and Ischia; and the coast and countryside north of Naples.

Don't fight shy of Naples. Plunge down its central artery, Spaccanapoli, if you do nothing else. An authentic pizza for lunch, and a more refined dinner at **La Cantinella**, next door to the **Miramare** (page 270) and owned by the same family, makes a good combination. The owner of our other recommendation in Naples, the **Soggiorno Sansevero** (page 271), has opened a hotel, the **Palazzo Doria d'Angri** (tel 081 7901000) with its own dining room. Or, if you don't mind being some way from the centre, the **San Francesco Monte** opened in 2001 with 50 rooms in an impressive looking former convent on a hillside above the city (tel 081 2512461).

Unless you are there for its thermal baths, crowded Ischia is less appealing than Capri, whose natural beauty is liberally doused in glitz. Ischia is harder work for the seeker of small hotels than Capri, but we recommend two. If these are full, you could try the 85-room **Hotel Terme San Michele** above the little car-free village of Sant' Angelo (tel 081 999276). Capri has a good selection, and we can also recommend the **Luna** (tel 081 8370433) or, if money is no object, the exclusive **Scalinatella** (tel 081 8370633) and, at the other end of the spectrum, **Villa Helios** (tel 081 8370240), as a budget option. All our recommendations are in or just outside car-free Capri town (you walk to your hotel and your luggage is transported from the ferry by porter); we don't have any recommendations for Anacapri.

Hotels on the Sorrento and Amalfi coasts are well represented in the pages that follow. Sadly, the famous **Cappuccini Convento** in Amalfi has closed; and the **Caruso Belvedere** in Ravello (tel 089 857111) has new owners and has been closed for restoration for several years. We have been told that it will reopen in 2005. Positano, the famously pretty fomer fishing village has dozens of hotels; we believe that our selection is the best of the bunch. We haven't included the famous **San Pietro**, too plush for our purposes, but nonetheless a memorable place.

If you want to avoid staying in the tourist centres, you could opt for **Capo la Gala**, a neat modern hotel in Vico Equense below the Sorrento coast road (tel 081 8015758/fax 081 8798747), or the **Belvedere** at Conca dei Marini, once a stopover on the Grand Tour and with breathtaking views (tel 089 831282/fax 089 831439). Three discoveries on or near the still unspoilt Cilento coast south of Naples are they are **Domus Laeta** (page 268), **Palazzo Belmonte** (page 285) and **Albergo Il Castello** (page 287).

Along the coast and in the countryside north of Naples we have just two recommendations, one on the coast at Baia Domizia, and one in the medieval village of Dragoni.

Amalfi

84011 Amalfi, Salerno

Tel 089 871332
e-mail info@lidomare.it
website www.lidomare.it

Nearby cathedral and Paradise
cloisters; Ravello (6 km).
Location in *piazzetta* off Piazza
del Duomo; public car parking
nearby
Food breakfast
Price €–€€
Rooms 15 double and twin
with bath; all rooms have
phone, TV, air conditioning,
minibar
Facilities sitting/breakfast
room
Credit cards AE, DC, MC, V
Disabled not suitable **Pets**
accepted
Closed never
Proprietors Camera family

Lidomare
Seaside bed-and-breakfast

Locked in a time warp, you might sus-
pect this modest two star of being
fusty; in fact, it has its share of charm. Floor
tiles are burnished to such a gleam you can
see your reflection; huge bookcases are
bursting with battered leather-bound volumes; miniature figures are displayed in a
glass-fronted cabinet; and the large high-
ceilinged rooms are full of family antiques
and traditional hand-painted furniture.
From the entrance you can glimpse,
through the family's own parlour, the
charming old tiled kitchen where breakfast
is prepared. It is served in the only reception room, where guests sit at little wood-
en tables between a grand piano and potted plants. With the exception of the minibar and satellite TV in every bedroom, and
new Jacuzzi baths in every bathroom –
grating additions to our mind – little
seems to have changed at the Lidomare
for the last 100 or so years.

Though the entrance to the 15thC
house is off a little square, the front faces
the sea and the best rooms are on this
side. The others have no view to speak of
save the peace of the *piazzetta*. All are simple and spotless. This is not only a family
hotel but a home, and the warmth of the
owners resonates through the quirky old-
fashioned rooms and corridors.

Via P. Comite 33, 84011
Amalfi, Salerno

Tel 089 871002
e-mail info@lunahotel.it
website www.lunahotel.it

Nearby cathedral and Paradise
cloisters; Ravello (6 km).
Location 5 minutes walk
uphill from town centre, over-
looking sea; car parking
Food breakfast, lunch, dinner;
room service
Price €€€€
Rooms 45; 40 double and
twin, 2 single, 3 suites, all with
bath; all rooms have phone,
TV, hairdrier
Facilities sitting room, 2 din-
ing rooms, 2 bars, cloister,
swimming pool, disco
Credit Cards AE, DC, MC, V
Disabled not suitable
Pets not accepted
Closed never
Manager Signor Ciccone

Luna Convento
Converted monastery

Since the closure of the famous
Cappuccini Convento, the Luna
Convento has become the most appealing
Amalfi hotel. A five-minute walk uphill
from the bustling town centre, it occupies
two separate buildings, divided by the
winding coast road – one of them an old
Saracen tower perched right on the sea.

   The hotel opened in 1822 (it is the oldest in Amalfi), and has been in the same
family for five generations. But you only
have to step inside to see that the building's history goes back much further than
the 19th century. The unique feature is the
Byzantine cloister enclosing a garden and
ancient well. The arcade serves as a quiet
and civilized sitting area and breakfasts are
served within the actual cloister – a
delightful spot to start the day. You have
the choice of modern or traditional bedrooms, and for a premium you can have
your own private sitting room. Lunch and
dinner are taken either in the vaulted
restaurant in the main building, where
large arched windows give beautiful views
of the bay, or better still across the road
where the terrace and parasols of the
tower restaurant extend to the water's
edge. The swimming pool forms part of the
same complex. The hotel is well known for
its week-long cooking courses.

Baia Domizia

81030 Baia Domizia, Caserta

Tel 0823 721344
e-mail info@hoteldellabaia.it
website www.hoteldellabaia.it

Nearby Gaeta (29 km); Naples
within reach.
Location in S part of resort,
with gardens leading down to
long sandy beach; ample car
parking
Food breakfast, lunch, dinner;
room service
Price €€€
Rooms 50; 46 double, 16 with
bath, 34 with shower, 2 single,
1 with bath, 1 with shower; 2
junior suites; all rooms have
phone, TV, air conditioning
Facilities 2 sitting rooms, TV
room, dining room, bar, terrace,
garden, tennis, beach **Credit
Cards** AE, DC, MC, V
Disabled no special facilities
Pets accepted
Closed Oct to mid-May
Proprietors Elsa, Velia and
Imelde Sello

Hotel della Baia
Seaside hotel

Baia Domizia is a modern and quite
sophisticated seaside resort, stretching
along a splendid, broad, sandy beach north
of Naples. But at the Hotel della Baia you
are unaware of being in a resort at all. It is
a low-lying white building, standing well
away from the main development, and its
lush gardens lead straight past the tennis
court to the beach.

The hotel was opened about 40 years
ago by the three Sello sisters from Venice,
who have successfully reproduced the
peaceful atmosphere of a stylish, if rather
large, private villa. Spotless white stucco
walls, cool tiled floors and white sofas are
offset by bowls of fresh flowers and potted
plants, and the antique and modern furnishings blend well together. The house
feels lived-in, with books and magazines
around, and an interesting range of pictures on the walls.

Bedrooms are no less attractive; many
have balconies. A smartly furnished veranda links the house to the garden, and
deckchairs and extravagant white parasols
are set out on the lawn.

The hotel has traditionally aimed high
with its food, and new reports, praising
both the chef and the friendly restaurant
and bar staff, confirm it as a most congenial place in which to eat.

Capri

Via Fuorlorado 36, 80073
Capri, Napoli

Tel 081 8370044
e-mail
info@hotellapazziella.com
website www.apaziella.com

Nearby Capri town; monastery
of San Giacomo.
Location off Le Botteghe
Fuoriovado, 5 minutes' walk E
of Capri town
Food breakfast
Price €€€
Rooms 19; 17 double and twin
and suites, 2 single, all with
bath; all rooms have phone,
TV, air conditioning, minibar,
hairdrier, safe
Facilities sitting area, terrace,
garden, shared swimming pool
Credit cards AE, DC, MC, V
Disabled not suitable
Pets not accepted
Closed Oct to Mar
Manager Silvio del Pizzo

La Pazziella
Town villa

The scent of exotic flowers greets you on the path leading up to this low white bougainvillea-draped villa set in a romantic garden of lawns, lemon trees and classical statues. Despite being so close to Capri town, birdsong is the only sound likely to disturb you here. Our inspectors liked La Pazziella: a smart yet well-priced hotel (at the lower end of its price bracket) that has successfully side-stepped Capri's glitter and gloss and strikes all the right chords.

The decoration is fresh and bright. Plain white walls and blue-and-white-tiled floors set off attractive polished wood furniture. Moorish arches, a recurring theme both inside and out, link one area to another, form niches and alcoves and announce flights of steps. Plants and flowers add colour to the ground floor sitting area and arched picture windows frame the garden. Breakfast is served on a glorious covered terrace.

Decorated in the same vein, the bedrooms are stylish and comfortable. Even the standard doubles have dainty writing tables and large antique chests. The superior rooms have their own balcony or terrace. The icing on the cake is the large pool with plenty of sunbathing space – quite a rarity on this island.

Capri

Via Tragara 24a, 80073 Capri, Napoli

Tel 081 8370122
e-mail villabrunella@capri.it
website www.villabrunella.it

Nearby monastery of San Giacomo; Punta Tragara.
Location on lane leading to Punta Tragara, 10 minutes walk from Capri town
Food breakfast, lunch, dinner
Price €€€€–€€€€€
Rooms 20; 8 double, 12 suites, all with bath; all rooms have phone, TV, air conditioning, minibar, hairdrier, safe
Facilities sitting area, bar, restaurant, terrace, garden, swimming pool
Credit Cards AE, DC, MC, V
Disabled not suitable **Pets** not accepted
Closed Nov to Easter
Proprietors Vincenzo and Brunella Ruggiero

Villa Brunella
Town hotel

The Villa Brunella is a great find on Capri because it perfectly combines the warmth and friendliness of a small, family-run hotel with Capri-style glamour and all the services of a much larger establishment. The drawback is the very long flight of steps to and from the bedrooms; if you can face those, you are definitely on to a winner.

The hotel consists of a series of tumbling terraces, ending in a garden, with fabulous views of sea and coast across to Marina Piccolo. It begins with its restaurant, whose entrance is on narrow Via Tragara. With picture windows and a romantic atmosphere, it is staffed by friendly waiters and a characterful *maitre d'*, and the food is good. The hotel then continues down the hillside, accessed by the steps. Next comes the cosy, cluttered reception area, presided over by the charming and welcoming Ruggiero family. Then the glamour begins: first at the pool, with its spacious sun terrace where poolside lunches are served, and then, further down, in the bedrooms. These are a great surprise: very Capri, with silk materials, marble bathrooms, terraces, Jacuzzis, fancy bedheads and gladioli by the vaseful. A small, personal hotel, with all the advantages of the nearby Grand Hotel Quisisana, but much less formal.

Capri

Via Tiberio 3a, 80073 Capri,
Napoli

Tel 081 8370122
e-mail info@villasarah.it
website www.villasarah.it

Nearby Villa Jovis, Capri
town.
Location on lane leading to
Villa Jovis, 15 minutes' walk
from Capri town
Food breakfast
Price €€€
Rooms 19; 14 double with
bath, 5 single with shower; all
rooms have phone, TV, air
conditioning, minibar,
hairdrier
Facilities sitting area, bar,
breakfast room, terrace, garden
Credit Cards AE, DC, MC, V
Disabled not suitable
Pets not accepted
Closed Nov to Easter
Proprietors de Martino family

Villa Sarah
Town villa

It's a stiff uphill walk out of town (on the
road to Emperor Tiberius's palace, (Villa
Jovis) to Villa Sarah, surrounded by a large,
abundant kitchen garden. (As with all
Capri town hotels, you can arrange to
have your luggage carried by porter from
the ferry.) The reward is peace and simplicity in a calm family-run hotel far
removed from the bustle and vulgarity of
the town.

Villa Sarah, set back from the road, is a
spacious whitewashed villa whose bedrooms have old pictures and prints on
white walls, plain curtains on wooden
poles, dark wood furniture, tiled floors
and simple bathrooms. The best have balconies and sea views. Breakfast is served
in a no-frills dining room or on the terrace, with a good selection of rolls and
croissants, home-made jam, yoghurts,
cold meats and cereals. Afterwards, you
can lounge on the terrace, and then take
a turn around the garden. This is the pride
and joy of Signor de Martino: vine-cov-
ered paths skirt trees laden with fruit,
including oranges and lemons, as well as
beds stuffed with aubergines, peppers,
tomatoes and much more. The de
Martino's love to treat their guests, allow-
ing them to pick what they want themselves.

Dragoni

Via Ponti 30, 81010 Dragoni , Caserta

Tel 0823 866619
e-mail info@villadepertis.it
website www.villadepertis.it

Nearby Matese lake (30 km); Naples (55 km).
Location in small town of Dragoni, overlooking countryside; car parking
Food breakfast, dinner
Price €
Rooms 7; 5 double and 2 suites, all with bath; all rooms have phone; suites have TV and hairdrier
Facilities sitting room, dining room, billiard room, table tennis, terrace, garden, free bicycles
Credit Cards AE, V
Disabled access difficult
Pets accepted
Closed mid-Jan to mid-Mar, 2 weeks end Nov
Proprietor Nicola de Pertis

Villa de Pertis
Country villa

Originally a nobleman's country residence dating back to the 17th century, Villa de Pertis has been restored to provide plain but comfortable and very reasonably priced accommodation in the form of five bedrooms and two suites. Its owner, Nicola de Pertis, is a charming host and very knowledgeable about the area. This is a place in which to wind down: there is little to do other than to walk or bicycle (bikes provided) in the Matese mountains, or to wander around the medieval village of Dragoni with its fine church, and the nearby village of Baia e Latina. On your return you might be diverted by a game of billiards or table tennis. Dinner, featuring regional dishes in a firelit room, was 'special' according to one reader's report; others wrote that 'an excellent dinner was arranged, at short notice, almost exactly in line with our requests', and 'dinner was left to the chef and was simple but delicious'.

One of the same correspondents reports that her room was clean, cool and large, with a comfortable bed, a good bathroom and a wonderful view on to a small square in the centre of Dragoni where 'it seems time has stood still'. There is also a charming terrace overlooking the Matese hills.

Via Gioia 1, 84050 Giungano,
Salerno

Tel 082 8880177
e-mail info@domuslaeta.com
website www.domuslaeta.com

Nearby Cilento national park;
Punta Licosa; Agropoli (10
km); Paestum (10 km).
Location in centre of town;
with public car park nearby
Food breakfast; dinner on
request
Price €
Rooms 5; 3 double, one twin,
one suite, all with bath; one
room has air conditioning
Facilities dining room, sitting
areas, library, TV room, gym,
terrace, garden, swimming
pool
Credit Cards MC, V
Disabled not suitable
Pets accepted
Closed mid-Jan to mid-Mar
Proprietor Camilla Aulisio

Domus Laeta
Town bed-and-breakfast

Beside the main square and the church
in the small inland town of Giungano,
but with a distant view of the sea, Domus
Laeta has been the home of the aristocratic Aulisio family since it was built in the
17th century. The house is well preserved,
with watchtowers, walls punctuated by
loopholes, stables and mangers, a stone-
built oil mill, cellars and bread ovens. In the
lovely gardens a glorious swimming pool
(with hydromassage) has been created
from an old reservoir, fed by a spring-
water well.

Inside, the house is tasteful and cultured; the tiled floors and timbered ceilings of the public rooms, unchanged over
the centuries. The Aulisio family's heritage
is evident everywhere: in the antiques and
objets d'art, the portraits and other paintings, and the 3,000 rare books that fill the
library bookcases. Occupying the original
rooms, and some with historic names
('The Bishop's Antechamber' and 'The
Bishop's Chamber'), the bedrooms are
simple yet attractive.

Good value prices include a generous
continental breakfast, and the Aulisios,
always charming and accommodating
hosts, will organize dinner specially if you
request it in advance. There are also a
number of *trattorie* nearby, serving simple
local food.

Ischia

Via Giacinto Gigante 5. Porto
d'Ischia, 80077 Ischia , Napoli

Tel 081 991316
e-mail hotel@lavillarosa.it
website www.lavillarosa.it

Nearby Port of Ischia (500 m);
Castello d'Ischia (2 km).
Location 200 m from lido;
with limited car parking
Food breakfast, lunch, dinner
Price €€€
Rooms 40; 34 double and
twin, 20 with bath, 14 with
shower; 6 single, all with show-
er; all rooms have phone
Facilities sitting room, dining
room, TV room, bar, lift, ter-
race, swimming pool, sauna
Credit Cards AE, DC, MC, V
Disabled access difficult
Pets accepted
Closed Nov to Mar
Proprietor Paolo Amalfitano

La Villarosa
Town villa

This is a sharp contrast to our other
hotel on the island, Il Monastero (page
295), in every way: it is immersed in a jun-
gle of a garden right in the heart of the little town of Ischia, and its great attraction
– apart from the garden and pleasant thermal pool – is its series of delectable sitting
rooms, which are beautifully furnished
with comfortable armchairs and ornate
antiques. The bedrooms are furnished with
19thC pieces of Neopolitan, Sicilian and
French origin.

The light, welcoming restaurant upstairs
leads out on to a terrace overlooking the
garden and the rooftops of Ischia, and
meals are served there in summer. At one
time only full board terms were offered,
but we are pleased to report that Signor
Amalfitano now offers 'room only' and
half-pension terms as we have no evidence
about the standard of cooking: whenever
we have tried to send someone to stay, the
hotel has been fully booked. Readers'
reports would therefore be especially welcome.

Like many hotels on the island, the
Villarosa offers thermal treatments of various sorts – with a private 'thermalist
physician' on hand to supervise – but the
atmosphere is far removed from that of
the traditional spa hotel, and those not
seeking a *kur* will feel quite at home.

Via Nazario Sauro 24, 80132
Napoli

Tel 081 7647589
e-mail
info@hotelmiramare.com
website
www.hotelmiramare.com

Nearby Piazza dei Plebiscito;
Castel dell' Ovo; ferry ports.
Location on waterfront road,
10 minutes' walk from city centre, close to ferry ports; adjacent garage parking
Food breakfast; lunch and dinner available on request
Price €€€ **Rooms** 30; 27
double and twin, 3 single, all
with bath or shower; all have
phone, TV, video, air conditioning, minibar, hairdrier
Facilities sitting room, breakfast room, bar, lift/elevator,
roof terrace **Credit Cards** AE,
DC, MC, V **Disabled** access
difficult **Pets** not accepted
Closed never **Proprietors**
Enzo and Bibi Rosolino

Miramare
Waterfront hotel

There are two compelling reasons for
choosing the Miramare as your Naples
base. The first is its owners, Enzo and Bibi
Rosolino (attended by their comic-serious
Skye terrier, Gavroche), whose warmth
and charm filters through to their loyal,
attentive staff. The second is the rooftop
terrace, with sunloungers, capacious ham-
mock and terrific views across the Bay of
Naples to the Sorrento coast, Vesuvius and
Capri. You will have to ignore the roar of
traffic on the *lungomare* below; this is
Naples after all. In summer 'an abundant
and delicious' breakfast, according to a
reporter, is served here; you could also
have a romantic *dinner à deux*, with dishes
brought in from Cantinella, the excellent
Michelin-starred restaurant belonging to
Enzo's brother next door (discount for
hotel guests).

The building, dating from 1914, is a gracious Liberty-style villa which served as
the American Consulate before becoming
a hotel, well known for its piano bar, The
Shaker Club, in 1944. Nowadays the lobby
and breakfast room, in high romantic
Neopolitan style, are resplendent in green,
gold and red Venetian and Florentine silks.
Bedrooms, which have been carefully
redecorated in the same mood, are compact, but they have high ceilings and tall
windows. The best have sea views.

Piazza San Domenico
Maggiore 9, 80134 Napoli

Tel 081 7901000
e-mail prenotazione@alber-
gosansevero.it **website**
www.albergosansevero.it

Nearby Capella Sansevero;
Santa Chiara.
Location in heart of city at
Spaccanapoli; car parking at
Albergo Sansevero
Food none
Price €
Rooms 6; 4 double and twin
and triple, all with shower, 2
single with shared shower; all
rooms have phone, TV, air
conditioning, hairdrier
Facilities none **Credit cards**
AE, DC, MC, V
Disabled not suitable **Pets**
small dogs accepted
Closed never
Proprietor Armida Auriemma

Soggiorno Sansevero
Town guesthouse

Peace reigns in this no-frills guesthouse
circling the internal courtyard of an old
palazzo, but it hasn't always been so. In
1590, here in the home of the Princes of
Sansevero, the troubled madrigal composer Carlo Gesualdo murdered his wife and
her lover in a frenzied attack. But we did-
n't feel the presence of any ghosts in the
newly painted cream bedrooms or their
modern grey bathrooms. The decoration is
modest – mosaic floors, functional furniture – but the rooms are spacious and
prices rock-bottom. Our favourite is No.
6, 'Marechiaro', vast with a vaulted ceiling
and more character than the others, and it
only costs more. The owner, Armida
Auriemma, a kindly Italian woman who
speaks no English, is an unlikely property
magnate, but she owns three other guesthouses in Naples: Albergo Sansevero, similar in style, and Albergo Sansevero
(Degas), aimed at students, and her latest
acquisition, Doria D'Angri, in Piazza VII
Settembre, which occupies the *piano nobile*
of an 18thC *pal-azzo* and serves dinner in
a stunning frescoed dining room.

Breakfast is not provided, but you'll find
Scaturchio, one of the best known cafés in
the city, in the colourful *piazza* below.
Don't miss the Sansevero chapel next
door to (and once part of) the *palazzo*.

Positano

Via C. Columbo 141, 84017
Positano, Salerno

Tel 089 875382 **e-mail**
info@hotelcaliforniapositano.it
website www.hotelcalifornia-
positano.it

Nearby Amalfi (17 km);
Ravello (23 km).
Location on road leading
into/out of town, overlooking
town and sea, 10 minutes' walk
from waterfront; car parking
Food breakfast
Price €€–€€€
Rooms 15 double and twin
with bath; all rooms have
phone, TV, air conditioning,
minibar, hairdrier
Facilities terrace **Credit
Cards** AE, DC, MC, V
Disabled not suitable **Pets** not
accepted **Closed** mid-Nov to
Mar
Proprietors Antonio and
Francesco Cinque

California
Town bed-and-breakfast

Directly opposite the Sirenuse (see page 277), this is another Neapolitan nobleman's *palazzo*, built in 1677, but in all other respects completely different. Come here if you want atmosphere, a warm welcome and (for Positano) budget prices. The *châtelaine* is Mary Cinque (English first name, but 100 per cent Italian *mamma*) who now runs the hotel opened by her father-in-law in 1968 and named after his much-missed sister who had emigrated to California. "I want my guests to be happy," she says, and she means it. Mary tries hard to keep up with modern requirements and a programme of renovation has recently been completed. Luckily most of the rooms, though plain, still retain an old-fashioned charm, and all have a balcony or terrace. No. 54 is large, with green tiled floor and high painted ceiling. No. 55 is even bigger. No. 61 is one of the rooms in which Mary has proudly installed a Jacuzzi, and benefits from windows on two sides.

The hotel's star feature is the upper-floor terrace which stretches along the front of the building. It has a pure turn-of-the-century feel, leafy, elegant, dotted with wrought-iron and wicker furniture. There are no other public spaces; breakfast is served here or in your room. As the Eagles sang of another *Hotel California*, we thought it was 'a lovely place'.

Via G. Marconi 8, 84017
Positano , Salerno

Tel 089 875513

Nearby Amalfi (17 km);
Ravello (23 km).
Location on Amalfi road, 15
minutes' walk E of centre of
town; car parking
Food breakfast
Price €
Rooms 12 double and twin, 6
with bath, 6 with shower; 1
apartment for 4; all rooms have
phone
Facilities sitting area, terraces,
swimming pool, private beach,
fishing
Credit Cards not accepted
Disabled not suitable
Pets not accepted
Closed Christmas
Proprietor Costantino
Mandara

La Fenice
Seaside bed-and-breakfast

Guests should be issued with a health warning before arriving at this unusual B&B. Some 400 steps (and a main road) separate the beach from the breakfast terrace, reception-sitting area and main bedrooms. Only the fit should attempt the climb (though a section can be done by stair lift). The rest of the bedrooms are in cottages that cascade down the steep cliff, reached by little staircases and narrow paths, ending with a glorious salt water swimming pool and waterfall, hewn out of the rock face. The pool was built by Costantino Mandara, the enterprising owner, who gave up being a vet in 1982 to turn his family home into a hotel. But Solomon the myna bird, Asuaro the dog, Tiberius the cat and a flock of geese – mementoes of his earlier life – are still in residence.

Handsome antique beds, huge armoires and family heirlooms fill the modest bedrooms, whose white walls and vaulted ceilings keep them beautifully cool with no need for air conditioning. Some of the cottages have private patios (we liked the one belonging to No 2). The trek from here up to the flowery terrace for breakfast is well rewarded by Signora Mandara's delicious home-made jams and Solomon's cheery *'buon giorno'*.

Via Cristoforo Colombo 56,
84017 Positano, Salerno

Tel 089 875130
e-mail info@marincanto.it
website www.marincanto.it

Nearby Amalfi (17 km);
Ravello (23 km).
Location on road leading
into/out of town, overlooking
town and sea, 10 minutes' walk
from waterfront; car parking
Food breakfast
Price €€€
Rooms 25 double and twin,
triple and family, 3 suites, 2
with private terrace, all with
bath or shower; all rooms have
phone, TV, air conditioning,
minibar, hairdrier
Facilities sitting area, lift, ter-
races **Credit Cards** AE, DC,
MC, V
Disabled access possible **Pets**
accepted
Closed Nov to week before
Easter
Proprietor Celeste Vespoli

Marincanto
Town hotel

When we visited this unpretentious B&B a few years ago, we were utterly charmed by it. Now it has under-gone a dramatic transformation, emerging as a much sleeker, glossier and pricier three-star establishment. The entrance through the car park is unprepossessing, but once the lift has whisked you down to the main floor and a huge tiled room over-looking the sea across a flowery terrace, its charms become clear. From its stunning position, perched on a cliff on the out-skirts of Positano, there is a panoramic view stretching out to sea and of the whole little town as it clings to the cliff face. The delightful Vespoli family have owned and run the hotel for several gen-erations, and they and their friendly staff take great trouble to look after their guests, with small services such as turning down beds at night – a rare luxury even in much grander establishments.

Renovated in pale colours, with creamy curtains and attractive wooden furniture, bedrooms are divided between the main building, the best of which have balconies with sea views, and an annexe. The annexe rooms are larger and several have lovely secluded terraces. Steps lead down to the beach past a succession of terraces. Breakfast – outside in fine weather, inside if it's cold or wet – is an impressive buffet.

Via Trara Genoino 25-27,
84017 Positano, Salerno

Tel 089 875002
e-mail miramare@starnet.it
website www.starnet.it/mira-
mare

Nearby Amalfi (17 km);
Ravello (23 km).
Location 3 minutes' walk W
of main beach; car parking
Food breakfast
Price €€€
Rooms 15 double and twin
with bath; all rooms have
phone, TV, air conditioning,
minibar, hairdrier, safe
Facilities sitting room, dining
room, bar
Credit cards AE, DC, MC, V
Disabled not suitable **Pets**
accepted
Closed Nov to week before
Easter
Proprietors Attanasio family

Miramare
Town bed-and-breakfast

Whatever bedroom you are given at
the Miramare, an appealingly understated, discreet hotel and baby sister of
the Palazzo Murat (see page 276), it will
have a private sea-facing terrace, shaded
by vine or bougainvillea and furnished with
table and deckchairs. The rooms were
revamped a few years ago and look stunning with white walls, terracotta floors,
elegant fabrics and antiques; minibar and
safe kept well out of sight. Bathrooms
(Nos 209 and 210 with sea views themselves) are spacious, and decorated with
hand-painted tiles.

The sitting room is an attractive area
with a vaulted ceiling, more terracotta
tiles, antique and pale upholstered furniture and plenty of plants and flowers. The
breakfast room is a delight: a glassed-in
terrace with bougainvillea hanging from
the ceiling in great swathes, and views to
the beach far below.

Set on the steep hill to the west of the
beach, down seven or eight flights of steps
(more steps lead to the seafront), the
Miramare is a series of old fishermen's
houses joined to make what recent visitors call a 'positively gorgeous' hotel, but
they warn: 'It's not for people who can't
negotiate lots of stairs two or three times
a day.' This was less of a problem a few
years ago when it had its own restaurant.

Via dei Mulini 23, 84017
Positano, Salerno

Tel 089 875177
e-mail info@palazzomurat.it
website www.palazzomurat.it

Nearby Amalfi (17 km);
Ravello (23 km).
Location in heart of resort;
public car park nearby
Food breakfast
Price €€€
Rooms 30 double and twin
with bath; all rooms have
phone, TV, air conditioning,
minibar, hairdrier, safe
Facilities sitting rooms, bar,
terrace
Credit cards AE, DC, MC, V
Disabled access difficult
Pets small ones accepted
Closed early Jan to first week
Mar
Proprietors Attanasio family

Palazzo Murat
Town hotel

Most hotels in Positano are ranged up the steep hills on either side of the ravine leading down to the sea. The Palazzo Murat, in contrast, is right in the heart of things – just inland of the *duomo*, and on a pedestrian alley lined with trendy boutiques.

The main building is a grand L-shaped 18thC *palazzo*. Within the L is a charming courtyard – a well in the middle, bougain-villea trained up the surrounding walls, palms and other exotic vegetation dotted around – occupied by the gorgeous, but pricey Al Palazzo restaurant, recently taken over by the hotel and specializing in Mediterranean cuisine. Breakfast is served here (though in spring early risers will find it sunless) and it makes a romantic spot for dinner. Along one side of this court-yard run the interconnecting sitting rooms, beautifully furnished with antiques.

Bedrooms in the *palazzo* itself are attractively traditional in style – some pai-nted furniture, some polished hardwood – and have doors opening on to token bal-conies (standing room only). Rooms in the more modern extension on the seaward side of the main building have bigger ones.

Positano's many restaurants are mainly congregated behind the beach, a short stroll away. 'Excellent value, stunning loca-tion', was one visitor's verdict.

Via C. Colombo 30, 84017
Positano Salerno

Tel 089 875066
e-mail info@sirenuse.it **web-site** www.sirenuse.it

Nearby Amalfi (17 km);
Ravello (23 km).
Location on road leading
into/out of town, overlooking
town and sea, 10 minutes' walk
from waterfront; car parking
Food breakfast, lunch, dinner;
room service
Price €€€€€
Rooms 63 standard and de
luxe double and twin bedrooms
and suites, with or without
view; all rooms have phone,
TV, air conditioning, minibar,
hairdrier, safe
Facilities sitting room, dining
room, bar, lift, terraces, swimming pool
Credit Cards AE, DC, MC, V
Disabled not suitable **Pets** not
accepted **Closed** sometimes in
Jan **Proprietors** Sersale family

Sirenuse
Town hotel

We didn't include the famous Sirenuse in the first editions of this guide, believing it too grand, and with too many bedrooms for our purposes; but our latest visit made us think again. It is, simply, too beautiful to ignore, filled with so many lovely things that it feels like a mix between a living museum of decorative arts and the private home of an aristo-cratic family – which is exactly what it was. Though until recent times Positano was a simple fishing village, it was always a popu-lar summer destination for Neapolitan nobility, and this 18thC *palazzo* was the residence of Marchese Sersale. At the end of the Second World War, it was used as a rest house for a British guards regiment, some of whose members later wanted to return with their families. It became a hotel, still to this day owned and run by the Sersale family. Over the years, the *palazzo* has expanded to include more rooms, a web of public and private ter-races, a delightfully pretty pool (which can become crowded in summer), and a glam-orous restaurant with top-flight food.

The cool, white-walled bedrooms are heavenly. They are liberally endowed with family heirlooms – including fine paintings and delightful Venetian and Neapolitan fur-niture – which complement the original ceramics.

Positano

Via Pasitea 318,
84017 Positano, Salerno

Tel 089 875655 **e-mail**
info@villafrancahotel.it **website** www.villafrancahotel.it

Nearby Amalfi (17 km);
Sorrento (17 km); Ravello (23
km).
Location on main road above
town; car parking (paid valet
service)
Food breakfast, snacks, dinner;
room service
Price €€€€–€€€€
Rooms 28 double and twin
with bath or shower, 9 rooms
in annexe; all rooms have
phone, TV, air conditioning,
minibar, hairdrier, safe
Facilities sitting room/bar,
dining room, fitness centre,
lift/elevator, swimming pool
Credit Cards AE, DC, MC, V
Disabled access difficult **Pets**
small ones accepted **Closed**
Nov to Mar
Proprietor Mario Russo

Villa Franca
Town hotel

Provided you are not worried by
heights, this smartly traditional hotel
has much to commend it. The position,
high on the western side of the Positano
ravine, gives an excellent view of the
resort and the coast beyond from the windows and terraces – but does mean that
the walk down to the resort centre and
beach takes a few minutes and that the
walk back up is exhausting. Happily, there
is a private bus to and from the beach at
certain times.

If the hotel's panoramic position is its
first attraction, the second is its smart,
cool sitting area – a series of interconnecting spaces with white-tiled floors and
white-painted walls, linked by arched
doorways. Comfortable armchairs with
vivid blue covers are grouped around low
tables. The dining room has the same decorative style, and the food is 'fresh, unpretentious and really delicious', according to
our reporter. Bedrooms are fresh, pretty
and comfortable, though the standard
rooms are small; the best have their own
sea-view balconies. The glorious rooftop
pool and terrace share the view.

We've had very enthusiastic reports
about this friendly hotel, which has been in
Mario Russo's family for several generations. He is now helped by his niece and a
team of willing, welcoming staff, many of
whom have been here for years.

Via C. Colombo 127, 84017
Positano, Salerno

Tel 089 811955
e-mail
info@villarosapositano.it **website** www.villarosapositano.it

Nearby Amalfi (17 km);
Ravello (23 km).
Location on road leading
into/out of town, overlooking
town and sea, 10 minutes' walk
from waterfront; public car
parking nearby
Food breakfast
Price €€ **Rooms** 12 double
all with terrace, 11 with show-
er, one with bath; one apart-
ment; all rooms have phone,
TV, air conditioning, fridge,
hairdrier
Facilities sitting area, garden
Credit Cards AE, DC, MC, V
Disabled not suitable **Pets** not
accepted **Closed** Nov to Easter
Proprietors Franco and
Virginia Caldiero

Villa Rosa
Town bed-and-breakfast

Villa Rosa is the parent of the chirpy young Villa La Tartana (see following page), by dint of the fact that its owners, the Caldieros, are the parents of Beniamino, the chirpy young owner of La Tartana. Although it lacks the freshness and zest of La Tartana, Villa Rosa has plenty to impress, and makes an excellent choice for a very reasonably priced stay in Positano. Its greatest assets are undoubtedly its spacious private terraces, all with fabulous views over the town and the Mediterran-ean. Its drawbacks are the many thousands of steps (well it seems that way) that lead from the road up to the reception lobby. However, as long as you are averagely fit you will cope, and luggage is taken for you.

Bedrooms are arranged on three tiers looking out to sea. Four have particularly huge terraces, which feel like a second room. Our favourite, however, has a charming lime tree plum in the middle, shading the patio table and chairs. There is also one family room, with two extra beds and a large outside table, and an apartment with two double rooms and roof terrace.

Villa Rosa has the feel of a comfortable old house. Bedrooms are simply but pleasantly decorated. The Caldieros have opened a restaurant, Caffè Positano, with a breathtaking view, nearby.

Via Vicolo Vito Savino 6/8,
84017 Positano , Salerno

Tel 089 812193
e-mail info@villalatartana.it
website www.villalatartana.it

Nearby Amalfi (17 km);
Ravello (23 km).
Location beside the church of
Santa Maria Assunta, overlook-
ing the beach and sea; public
car parking nearby
Food breakfast
Price €€
Rooms 12 double all with
shower, 9 with sea view; all
rooms have phone, TV, air
conditioning, fridge, hairdrier,
safe
Facilities sitting area
Credit Cards AE, DC, MC, V
Disabled not suitable **Pets** not
accepted
Closed Nov to Easter
Proprietor Beniamino
Caldiero

Villa La Tartana
Town bed-and-breakfast

Deliciously fresh and clean, with simple bedrooms that feel good to wake up in and are a joy to come home to, this modern *pensione* has made a terrific addition to the hotel scene in Positano since it opened in 2000. The owner, Beniamino Caldiero, may be young, but he has the touch.

Villa La Tartana is pristine as well as admirably simple, and its good vibrations emanate from the fact that all the decorative elements have been chosen with attention to detail and an eye for quality, and all locally made, from the charming ceramic wall lights to the carved and painted bedheads and hand-painted bathroom tiles. Gaily tiled floors, white walls, floaty white curtains, a vase of flowers, a little terrace with pretty table and chairs overlooking the sea where breakfast is served ... delightful.

Villa La Tartana (*tartana* means fishing boat) can be found right at the base of Positano, near the main square and the beach. The sherbet lemon tiled reception lobby, reached via a flight of stairs next to the Caldieros' clothing and ceramics shop, sets the tone. The same zingy yellow tiles are continued throughout the corridors, which account for much of the place's feel-good factor. Charming staff, well presented, we could hardly find a fault.

Via S. Giovanni del Toro 16,
84010 Ravello , Salerno

Tel 089 857244 **e-mail** reception@hotelpalumbo.it **website** www.hotelpalumbo.it

Nearby Villa Rufolo; Villa Cimbrone; Amalfi (7 km).
Location perched on cliffs, close to town centre, 200 m from the main square; garage parking
Food breakfast, lunch, dinner; room service
Price €€€€€ **Rooms** 11 in main house; 8 double and twin, 3 suites, all with bath; 7 double and twin in annexe, all with bath, phone, TV, air conditioning, minibar, hairdrier, safe **Facilities** sitting room, dining room, bar, terrace, garden, swimming pool (by arrangement at nearby hotel)
Credit Cards AE, DC, MC, V
Disabled access difficult **Pets** accepted **Closed** never
Proprietor Marco Vuilleumier

Palumbo
Converted palazzo

Although it has long been in our guide, we have not perhaps done justice to this lovely hotel, very much our kind of place in the luxury bracket. It stands next to the much-vaunted Palazzo Sasso, but is in every way different: while the international-style Sasso could be anywhere, the Palumbo oozes individuality, panache and understated elegance. It feels like a private house – or rather a private Moorish-style 12thC *palazzo* – which is what it was until converted by its Swiss-Italian owners, the Vuilleumier family.

Public rooms focus on the core of the *palazzo*, an inner courtyard where Corinthian-topped columns, a dazzling deep blue-and-white tiled floor, imaginative modern wall ceramics and comfortable sofas and chairs create a strong first impression. The first floor-restaurant is equally elegant, graced by lovely antiques and paintings including a (school of) Caravaggio. Or you can eat on the terrace, with views over vineyards to the dazzling blue sea below. Half board is compulsory in high season, but this is no hardship. Bedrooms, accentuated by antiques and rugs, are elegant and unpretentious, as are the bathrooms, some with quite elderly fittings. We don't mind: if you want state-of-the art, go to Palazzo Sasso. Bedrooms in the annexe are much less appealing.

Viale G. d'Anna 5, 84010
Ravello , Salerno

Tel 089 857144 **e-mail**
info@hotelparsifal.com **website** www.hotelparsifal.com

Nearby Villa Rufolo; Villa
Cimbrone; Amalfi (7 km).
Location overlooking the
town and sea, 5 minutes' walk
from main square; parking in
street or public garage nearby
with parking metres
Food breakfast, lunch, dinner
Price €–€€
Rooms 19; 18 double and
twin, 1 single, 10 with bath, 9
with shower, 8 with sea view;
all rooms have phone, TV
Facilities sitting room, dining
room, bar, terrace, garden
Credit Cards AE, DC, MC, V
Disabled not suitable
Pets small ones accepted
Closed never
Proprietor Antonio Mansi

Parsifal
Converted monastery

The Parsifal (which Wagner composed in Ravello) retains a certain monastic simplicity along with its 13thC cloister. The former convent is still owned by nuns, but for many years now has been a family-run hotel. On a recent visit we discovered that the place has changed hands, and is now run by Antonio Mansi and his young family. Signor Mansi comes from Ravello, and worked at the Parsifal as a teenager. He went on to become manager of the famous Danieli in Venice, before returning home to pursue his dream of owning his own small-scale hotel. It couldn't be more different than the Danieli: though professional, the family are particularly friendly and willing to please.

While gradually upgrading the Parsifal (the hotel had become very tired), Signor Mansi wants to retain its simple feel. Certainly the panoramic but dowdy dining room could do with his attention, but it has heart-stopping views. Here, and on the creeper-clad terrace, honest food with creative touches is served (half-board is compulsory for three nights or less). Bedrooms are plainly furnished, and some are smallish: ask for the one with the terrace and sea view. Recent reports have been positive.

Via Santa Chiara 26, 84010
Ravello Salerno

Tel 089 857459/858072
e-mail info@villacimbrone.it
website www.villacimbrone.it

Nearby Monastero di Santa
Chiara; Convento di San
Francesco.
Location in Villa Cimbrone
gardens, 10 minutes' walk from
town centre; public car park in
town (luggage service)
Food breakfast, lunch, dinner
Price €€€€€
Rooms 19; 16 double and
twin, one single, 2 suites, all
with bath or shower; all have
phone, TV, air conditioning,
minibar, hairdrier, safe
Facilities sitting room, breakfast room, dining room, garden, tennis, pool **Credit Cards**
AE, MC, V **Disabled** access
difficult **Pets** not accepted
Closed Nov to Apr **Manager**
Giorgio Vuilleumier

Villa Cimbrone
Town villa

It's hard to imagine a more romantic setting than the Villa Cimbrone's, in the fabulous gardens laid out by English aristocrat
Lord Grimthorpe in the early 19th century. A formal network of paths and beds
with wilder landscaped areas, they boast a
belvedere, from where you can admire 'the
most beautiful view in the world', according to Ravello *habitué* Gore Vidal. The villa
is equally enchanting. A 12thC building,
revived by Grimthorpe and recently
restored again, it has kept all its period features including splendid stone fireplaces
and tiled floors, and is crammed with
knick-knacks, books, oil paintings and
antiques. Through white Gothic doors, the
comfortable bedrooms are all individually
and exquisitely decorated. It feels exactly
like a private house, and it's easy to see
why the famous, from D.H. Lawrence to
Greta Garbo and her lover Leopold
Stokowsky, have taken refuge here.

When we visited the Villa Cimbrone, we
felt that all it lacked was its own restaurant: it has now opened 'Il Flauto di Pan',
which must be a great addition to this
lovely place. Now guests don't have to
make the 10-minute walk into town for
dinner every night, and simply relish having
the gardens all to themselves once the
daytime visitors have left. Reports about
the restaurant would be welcome.

Ravello

Via Santa Chiara 2, 84010
Ravello , Salerno

Tel 089 857255 **e-mail** villa-maria@villamaria.it **website** www.villamaria.it

Nearby Convento di San Francesco; Villa Cimbrone.
Location on path leading to Villa Cimbrone, 5 minutes' walk from town centre; car parking
Food breakfast, lunch, dinner
Price €€–€€€€€
Rooms 23 double and twin with bath or shower; all rooms have phone, TV, air-conditioning, minibar, hairdrier, safe
Facilities sitting room, breakfast room, dining room, dining terrace, garden, swimming pool
Credit Cards AE, DC, MC, V
Disabled access difficult
Pets accepted **Closed** never
Proprietor Vincenzo Palumbo

Villa Maria
Town villa

Sit in the sunshine at one of the tables in the Villa Maria's lovely garden restaurant, sip chilled white wine, eat perfectly cooked pasta and enjoy the glorious vista of mountains sweeping down to a glittering sea. This is an understandably popular place. Inside, a charming medley of potted palms, busts, piano, inlaid furniture and silver arranged on wooden shelves lends the old villa a distinctly Edwardian feel. Up the marble staircase and through heavy wooden doors, the bedrooms strike the same note, with vaulted ceilings and solid furniture. Though almost double the price of a standard room, No. 3 is a cut above the rest, with its huge terrace, five sets of French windows and handsome *secretaire*. In a modern annexe there are six rooms with picture windows but little character.

Never far behind the scenes is the kindly Vincenzo Palumbo, who keeps a book of comments from his guests ('The food was superb – the best in all of Europe'), masterminds cookery courses and walking tours, and enjoys rubbing shoulders with the stars. Guests may use nearby Villa Eva's lawn (useful for kids) and the pool belonging to sister hotel, the Giordano.

A recent inspection revealed that little has changed at the Villa Maria, and the food is still 'delicious'.

Santa Maria di Castellabate

84072 Santa Maria di
Castellabate, Salerno

Tel 0974 960211 **e-mail** belmonte@costacilento.it **website**
www.palazzobelmonte.com

Nearby Cilento national park;
Punta Licosa; Agropoli (15
km); Paestum (40 km).
Location on the edge of town;
car parking
Food breakfast, lunch, dinner
Price €€€€ (half board
supplement of 45 euros per
person)
Rooms 47 double rooms,
suites and apartments with
bathroom or shower; all have
phone, TV, hairdrier; some
have air conditioning, kitchen
facilities, terrace **Facilities**
restaurant, meeting rooms, terrace, garden, pool, pool bar,
private beach **Credit Cards**
MC, V **Disabled** not suitable
Pets not accepted **Closed**
Nov-Apr **Proprietor** Principe
Angelo di Belmonte

Palazzo Belmonte
Seaside apartments

Just a step from the colourful houses and
brightly painted fishing boats of this
attractive resort, the Palazzo Belmonte
stands in complete privacy, surrounded by
a large park enclosed by high stone walls.
The *pal-azzo* has been in the Prince of
Belmonte's family since it was built in the
17th century as a hunting lodge, where
guests often included the kings of Italy and
Spain.

The Prince still lives here in a top-floor
apartment. The rest of the *palazzo* and
neighbouring Edoardo's House have been
converted into 20 guest suites and self-
catering apartments of different sizes.
Rooms are large and airy, with their original features untouched. Many have vaulted
ceilings; some private terraces. You can
choose to overlook the walled courtyard,
where the scent of jasmine perfumes the
air, or the beautiful gardens and the sea.
Despite the grandeur, the atmosphere is
relaxed. Within the park, Villa Belmonte
has 29 luxurious air-conditioned rooms,
many with private terraces and sea views.

A path through the garden leads to a
gorgeous pool, bordered by flowers, and
beyond to a gate, which takes you down to
the sandy gently-shelving beach, solely for
guests' use. Meals are served at the restaurant on the Belvedere terrace; breakfast
and drinks at the pool bar.

Via Nastro Verde 8, 80067
Sorrento, Napoli

Tel 081 878 1154
e-mail info@hotellabadia.it
website www.hotellabadia.it

Nearby Sorrento; Amalfi
coast.
Location in hills, 2 km by road
outside Sorrento, 10 minutes'
walk by path from town centre;
ample car parking
Food breakfast, lunch, dinner
Price €
Rooms 14 double and twin, all
with shower; all rooms have
phone, TV, hairdrier; some
have air conditioning
Facilities sitting room, dining
room, bar, lift, terraces, garden,
swimming pool
Credit Cards MC, V
Disabled access
possible
Pets accepted **Closed** Nov to
mid-Mar
Proprietor Marisa Picco

La Badia
Out-of-town villa

On first acquaintance La Badia, simple and old-fashioned, seemed a great new find, almost too good to be true, until we discovered at dinner that it was a base for package tours and not a find at all. Nevertheless, if you can overlook the mainly British babble at mealtimes, you will find other compensations, not least the lovely hilly setting in on the outskirts of town, set amid groves of olives and oranges, with stunning views across the Bay of Sorrento. Then there is the pretty, circular pool, surrounded by greenery, and the several terraces, both on the roof and at ground level.

Run by the Picco family for decades (mother oversees, daughter serves, granddaughter runs around), this handsome 16thC former monastery, has changed little. There are lace curtains, bamboo blinds, Edwardian family antiques, dark stained doors and wooden shutters. Rooms are plain and elderly but spacious, with simple bathrooms. A door at the end of the first-floor corridor leads to a charming, little-used *loggia* overlooking the olive groves. The dinner menu is limited and the food as old-fashioned as the house (tinned fruit salad for dessert), but all in all we felt we had value for money. A recent reader loved the tranquillity and the views, but also found the food disappointing.

Castellabate

Via Amendola 1, 84048 Castellabate, Salerno

Tel 0974 967169
e-mail
albergoilcastello@hotmail.com
website www.hotelcastello.co.uk
Food breakfast; lunch and dinner on request
Price €
Closed Nov to Apr
Proprietor Franca Di Biasi

Albergo Il Castello
Town hotel

The relatively undiscovered Cilento coast is dotted with sandy beaches and picturesque resorts. Perched above one of these, Santa Maria, is the medieval hill town of Castellabate and this friendly 17thC albergo, recommended to us by a reader. Bedrooms are fresh and simple: all white walls and linen, majolica-tiled floors and period furniture. Some have their own terrace or balcony with views over the Cilento national park. A breakfast of fresh croissants, homemade jam and buffalo mozzarella straight from the farm is served on the main terrace under the shade of a giant fig tree. Equally delicious lunches and dinners can be provided. The welcoming owner and staff quickly made our reader feel part of the family.

Ischia

Castello Aragonese 3, Ischia Ponte, 80070 Ischia , Napoli

Tel 081 992435
e-mail ilmonastero@castel-loaragonese.it
website www.castelloaragonese.it
Food breakfast, dinner
Price €€
Closed mid-Oct to Easter
Proprietor Nicola Mattera

Il Monastero
Converted monastery

Ischia Ponte gets its name from the low bridge to the precipitous islet on top of which stands the island's original settlement, known collectively as the Castello, although it consists of several buildings. One of these is an old monastery, run as a simple but captivating *pensione* with an amiable padrone. Paintings hang on the plain walls of the hallway and the neat little sitting room. Bedrooms, white with blue tiles, are the former monks' cells and correspondingly simple; some are reached from the spacious terrace, which gives a breathtaking view of the town and the island. Recent improvements mean that every bedroom now has its own shower or bathroom, half board is no longer obligatory, and simple snacks are served.

Sorrento

Piazza della Vittoria 5,80067
Sorrento, Napoli

Tel 081 87810241604
e-mail info@bellevue.it
website www.bellevue.it
Food breakfast, light or packed
lunch, dinner
Price €€€€
Closed never
Proprietor Giovanni Russo

Bellevue Syrene
Seafront hotel

Built as a count's summer retreat in 1750 in a magnificent clifftop position, this grande dame hotel opened in 1820, and has been carefully restored over the years. Well-proportioned reception rooms, corridors and bedrooms, painted in restful shades of yellow, are brought to life with attractive frescoes, trompe l'oeil, and fabrics ranging from brocades and Regency stripes to zebra prints. Public rooms are furnished with fine European antiques; the smart majolica-tiled bedrooms with wrought iron and marble. The airy dining room is staffed by an army of impeccable waiters and features a menu of mainly local specialities. One reporter encountered too many large groups here, though Giocanni insists this is no longer the case.

Sorrento

Via Califano 2, 80067 Sorrento,
Napoli

Tel 081 8073187
Fax 081 5329001
Food breakfast, lunch, dinner
Price €
Closed mid-Nov to Easter
Proprietor Giuseppina Ercolano

Loreley et Londres
Town hotel

A complete dump. Tatty, scruffy and seedy are just some of the adjectives that come to mind to describe the present-day condition of this once-dignified hotel. Why include it? If rock-bottom budget is what you require, and if you are a connoisseur of quirky time warps, then you may well forgive the shortcomings, at least for a night. The splendidly atmospheric façade and old sepia photographs in the lobby attest to its former status as a favoured stop-off on the Grand Tour, and it still has a few attractive old pieces of furniture, a (very) faded charm and an air of lingering regret. Bedrooms and service are absolutely basic, with prices to match. Ask for a 'room with a view'; some have a tiny balcony giving on to the sea.

Area Introduction

To say that charming small hotels in the heel and toe of Italy are difficult to find is a wild understatement. It would be nearer the truth to say that they don't exist. Much of the landscape is stony and barren, with imposing mountains, and a rugged, inhospitable western coastline. The exception is the area around the little resort of Maratea, where you will find two of our hotels. Most of our other recommendations are on the Strait of Otranto coast along the outside of Italy's heel. Here you will find almost deserted beaches, punctuated by small communities, and an interior that becomes more mountainous the further you go. The hotels which appear in the following pages are the best there are, but some alternative recommendations may be helpful, particularly in the heel.

The **San Nicola** (tel 080 3105199), a smart, 30-roomed hotel in the heart of Altamura is one possibility. To stay in *trulli* themselves (ancient stone dwellings), go to the **Trulli Country House** in Cisternino, which is a new entry to the guide. Or, in the *trulli* capital Alberobello, the **Dei Trulli** (tel 080 4323555), which also offers enthusiasts the irresistable opportunity to stay in one of these curious little stone bungalows, set here among pines and neat flower beds. If you want to make it right to the southern tip of the heel, you could aim for the **Terminal** (tel 0833 758242), a well-run seaside holiday hotel at Marina di Léuca.

For travellers in the 'toe' heading south with time to spare, the SS18 makes a slow-paced alternative to the A3 motorway, sticking to the eastern coast south of Lagonegro where the motorway takes a long detour inland. There are a few places further south than Maratea that are worth bearing in mind. At Diamante is the Mediterranean-style **Ferretti** (tel 0985 81428), with terraces overlooking the sea and a highly reputed restaurant. The 65-room **Grand Hotel San Michele** (tel 0982 91012) at Cetraro is rather more swish – a well-restored old house in an attractive informal garden on cliffs above the beach.

The main tourist attraction of the toe, however, is on the other side of the A3 – the magnificently wild landscape of the Sila mountains east of Cosenza and north of Catanzaro. Each of these towns has a handful of acceptable hotels.

Via Carlo Mazzei 4, 85046 Maratea, Potenza

Tel 0973 877487
e-mail info@mondomaratea.it
website www.mondomaratea.it

Nearby Monte San Biagio; Lagonegro (20 km); Rivello (20 km).
Location in village; car parking
Food breakfast, lunch, dinner
Price €€€
Rooms 29 double and twin, suites, all with bath; all rooms have phone, TV, air conditioning, minibar, hairdrier
Facilities sitting room, piano bar, restaurant, garden, swimming pool, private beach
Credit cards AE, DC, MC, V
Disabled access difficult
Pets accepted
Closed never
Manager Gabriella Labanchi

Loc. delle Donne Monache Village hotel

For years, Maratea was one of the most unspoiled seaside villages on Italy's west coast, its pink and white houses clustered on low cliffs above the harbour and its old quarter crammed with interesting buildings, including two medieval churches. In the last decade or so new hotels have been built and restaurants opened, but its essential character remains intact, and this locanda is an example of how past and present can be successfully combined. Originally an old monastery, it has been transformed into an elegant contemporary hotel.

The flamboyance of the entrance hall gives way to cool modern chic in the bedrooms, each slightly different, but all comfortable with tiled floors and smart Italian-designed furniture and lighting. White drapes hang at the windows, while patterned, red-striped ticking or coloured drapes encircle wrought-iron canopy beds.

Jasmine, bougainvillea and lemon trees grow in the lovely peaceful garden at the front which contains a fair-sized pool with a terrace and plenty of sunbeds. The beach is also conveniently close by. The locanda has been bought by a company, which owns two other hotels in the area, and will organize sporting activities such as scuba diving courses, rafting and pony trekking, as well as local excursions for guests.

Via Nazionale, 85041 Acquafredda di Maratea, Potenza

Tel 0973 878134
e-mail info@villacheta.it
website www.villacheta.it

Nearby Maratea (8 km); Lagonegro (20 km).
Location 1.5 km S of Acquafredda; car parking
Food breakfast, lunch, dinner
Price €€€
Rooms 23 double and twin with shower; all rooms have phone, air conditioning
Facilities dining room, TV/reading room, bar, terrace, garden
Credit cards AE, DC, MC, V
Disabled access possible
Pets small ones accepted
Closed never
Proprietor Stefania Aquadro

Villa Cheta Elite
Lakeside hotel

The remote and mountainous region of Basilicata does not possess much coastline. But the tiny stretch of shore on the west side, where a corniche cuts through wild and beautiful cliffs, is one of the most spectacular parts of Italy's deep south. Villa Cheta Elite is set high up on this precipitous coastline, with splendid views. If the villa enjoyed no other distinction, its position would be enough to attract many travellers to the south. But this gracious art nouveau building has other attractions.

The villa is a pleasure to behold: a confection of ochre and cream stucco, decorated with ornate mouldings that would look at home in a grand Edwardian living room. It lies among lush, flowery terraces, one of which is set out with café-style chairs and smartly-laid dining tables. Inside, lace tablecloths, chintz sofas, carefully-chosen period pieces and abundant pictures create the feel of a private house.

The beaches in the area are small, but the waters are clear, and reached in only a few minutes from the villa. The Aquadros are relaxed and charming hosts, who take great care over every aspect of their hotel, including the food, which is highly regarded, and Stefania has even introduced yoga lessons for her guests.

Via San Giovanni Vecchio 89, 75100
Matera

Tel 0835 331009
e-mail hotelsassi@virgilio.it
website www.hotelsassi.it

Nearby Strada Panoramica dei Sassi
(in town); Bari (65 km); Lago di San
Giuliano (12 km).
Location in centre of old town, just
N of Via Fiorentini; public car park
nearby
Food breakfast
Price €
Rooms 20 double and twin, single
and suites, all with bath or shower;
all rooms have phone, TV, air condi-
tioning, minibar, hairdrier
Facilities breakfast room, bar, meet-
ing hall, terrace
Credit cards AE, DC, MC, V
Disabled access difficult
Pets not accepted
Closed never
Proprietor Raffaele Cristallo

Sassi
Town bed-and-breakfast

In this city of caves (sassi), a Unesco world heritage site, where the inhabitants lived as troglodytes for centuries (the last were evicted as recently as the 1960s), it is appropriate to stay at this unique bed-and-breakfast, where many of the bedrooms are hewn out of the tufa, their floors, walls and ceilings all gently undulating. In a peaceful pedestrian-only part of the ancient city, it occupies a labyrinthine 18thC building, with spectacular views over the Sasso Barisano to the Romanesque cathedral from its terraces and balconies.

Committed owner, Raffaele Cristallo has recently refurbished the Sassi, keeping simplicity as the keynote. Plain wooden tables and rush-seated 'peasant' chairs furnish both breakfast room and bedrooms, each one of which is different, modestly comfortable and full of character. The excavated rooms are naturally cool and only need their air conditioning on the hottest of days. Staff are charming and friendly. There is a no smoking policy.

As the hotel doesn't have its own parking, there's a short walk (with your luggage) from the nearest public car park. If you have time, try to see the exhibition, telling the story of Matera's cave dwellings, in the Ridola Museum on Via Ridola.

Contrada Torricella 345, 70043
Monópoli Bari

Tel 080 6909030
e-mail melograno@melograno.com
website www.melograno.com

Nearby ruins of Egnazia; Castellana caves; Alberobello (19 km).
Location 3 km from Monópoli towards Alberobello; car parking
Food breakfast, lunch, dinner
Price €€€€€
Rooms 37; 31 double and twin, 6 suites, all with bath; all rooms have phone, satellite TV, air conditioning, minibar, hairdrier, safe
Facilities sitting rooms, dining room, bar, health centre, swimming pool, garden, tennis, private beach, helipad
Credit cards AE, DC, MC, V
Disabled access possible
Pets by arrangement
Closed February
Proprietors Guerra family

Il Melograno
Country villa

Sophisticated rooms, filled with fine antiques, paintings, fabrics and oriental carpets, give us a clue to the profession of the man who masterminded the transformation of this 16thC fortified farmhouse, used by the Guerra family as a holiday home, to a luxurious small hotel. Until the mid-1980s Camillo Guerra was an antiques dealer, and his special, personal touch is evident everywhere. The elegant reception rooms are housed in the main building. But for the individually-furnished bedrooms, he built a clutch of white Moorish houses around a piazza, overlooking orange and olive groves, lemon and pomegranate trees (the name 'melograno' means 'pomegranate').

Dinner, a Mediterranean feast, is usually al fresco on a canopy-covered veranda beside a wonderfully gnarled old olive tree. Breakfast is served beside the outdoor pool, bordered by prickly pear, almond and citrus trees, whose fruit is the basis for the juice and jams on the table.

If relaxing by the pool or on the private beach begins to pall, there is plenty to see in the area, including Frederick II's Swabian castles and the mysterious trulli of Alberobello.

Savelletri di Fasano

Litoranea 379, 72010 Savelletri di Fasano, Brindisi

Tel 080 4827769
e-mail
info@masseriasandomenico.com
website www.masseriasandomeni-co.com

Nearby Castellana Caves; Fasano (7 km).
Location 2 km S of Savelletri on SS379 to Torrecane; car parking
Food breakfast, lunch, dinner; room service
Price €€€€
Rooms 35 double and twin with bath; all rooms have phone, TV, air conditioning, minibar, hairdrier
Facilities sitting room, dining room, gym, spa, terrace, garden, swimming pool, pool bar, tennis, golf, private beach
Credit cards AE, DC, MC, V
Disabled access difficult Pets accepted
Closed Jan
Manager Antonio Polesel

Masseria San Domenico
Farmhouse hotel

On one of the sprawling agricultural estates with a fortified farmhouse at its centre that crop up all over Puglia, this masseria has its origins in the 14th century when the knights of Malta used it as a watchtower against the Turks. Set in 60 acres of orchards and olive groves, its metamorphosis into an impressive hotel was completed in 1996. The architecture is typically Moorish – pristine white walls, turrets and arched windows and doorways – with fitting decoration inside, where details like curvy wrought-iron bedheads and fabrics in vibrant colours or floral designs bring the rooms to life. The marble-floored bedrooms are attractively and individually furnished and equipped with large modern bathrooms.

Although the hotel is only 200 m from the sea, the huge salt-water swimming pool might have even greater appeal. It is skilfully built, with no straight lines, so that it looks like a huge, natural rock pool. Drinks and meals are served here at the pool bar and barbecue grill, while in the dining room seafood is one of the specialities in a range of delicious regional dishes.

It's little surprise that this peaceful hideaway with its understated luxury has been embraced by the glitterati, who – like Sven Goran Eriksson – come here for a total escape and some serious pampering.

Cisternino

Contrada Figazzano 3
Cisternino

Tel 335-60.94.64.7
e-mail hoteldeitrulli@inmedia.it
Food breakfast
Price €
Closed never
Manager Caroline Groszer

Hotel dei Trulli
Trulli accommodation

So laid back is the pace of life at Hotel dei Trulli that breakfast has been renamed break-slow: feast on fresh local pastries, home-made breads and jams at charming little tables spread under the old mulberry tree. No one is in a hurry at this intimate place, with its plain but stylish main rooms, and interesting black and white prints adorning the walls. The living room boasts a fantastic mosaic tiled floor.

Bedrooms are individually decorated, all with stone floors, and there is a well thought out lighting scheme throughout. A good value retreat, with plenty of individual charm.

Matera

Via Fiorentini, 71 75100 Matera

Tel 0835 256600
e-mail info@locandadisanmartino.it
website www.locandadisanmartino.it
Food breakfast
Price €–€€
Closed never
Manager Dorothy Louise Zinn

Loc. di San Martino
Converted caves

Owner Dorothy bought and restored a series of cave dwellings in the centre of Matera's historical district, and the result is this rather unusual hotel. Finding it hard to imagine that a former cave could be inviting, our reporter was amazed to find it spacious, comfortable and surprisingly light.

Rooms are sparsely furnished – their appeal lies instead in their interesting architecture: dramatic archways and high ceilings. Some may find it a bit like staying in a monastery, as much of the interior is white, but charming details such as bright blue chairs in the breakfast room give the place a fresh feel. 'Best breakfast in Italy' one reader comments.

Baia Paraelios
Resort village

Overlooking a picture-postcard bay of white sand washed by a turquoise sea, Baia Paraelios is not so much a hotel as an upmarket holiday camp with accommodation in 83 small bungalows sprawled across a wooded hillside. Each has a private terrace, a view of its own, one or two bedrooms and a sitting room in mellow colours. Communal areas are equally stylish. Prints add colour to plain walls; tiled floors and a scattering of plants bask in a cosy glow from artful lighting. There is a relaxing sitting room, open-air bar and terrace dining room beside the sea. Three swimming pools (one salt-water), flood-lit tennis courts, mini-golf, bowling, windsurfing, canoeing and child-minding make this a choice for families.

Fornaci, 88035 Parghelia, Catanzaro

Tel 0963 600300
e-mail info@baiaparaelios.com
website www.baiaparaelios.it
Food breakfast, lunch, dinner
Price €€€€
Closed Oct to Apr
Manager Adolfo Salabe

Area Introduction

Sicily, the largest and most populous island in the Mediterranean, has an extraordinary mix of sightseeing interest: spectacular scenery, ancient Greek ruins, medieval towns, splendid Baroque architecture, busy street markets, wonderful food and wine and even an active volcano. It enjoys a balmy climate and its tourist season runs from Easter through until October although July and August are particularly crowded. Taormina is the main resort and is well represented by hotels on the following pages. We have yet to find a hotel in the sprawling, chaotic city of Palermo that is 'charming' and 'small', but the **Grand Hotel Villa Igea** (tel 091 543744), set in gorgeous gardens on the edge of the sea, is a possibility if you are into old-world splendour at a price. Or there is the ornate **Grand Hotel et des Palmes** (tel 091 602 8111). We have a new entry in Siracusa (**the Gutkowski**) and another in the shadow of Etna, near Catania (**L'Olmo**).

If you plan a more peaceful holiday, you might do best to choose one of the Aeolian (or Lipari) islands. We have one entry on Panarea, **the Raya**, while on Lipari itself we suggest **Villa Diana** (tel 090 9811403), **Villa Meligunis** (tel 090 9812426), **Giardino sul Mare** (tel 090 9811004) and **the Oriente** (tel 090 9811493). On the neighbouring island of Salina, we have a new entry: the lovely **Hotel Signum** (see page 299). Or, try a clifftop hotel, **Punta Scario** (tel 090 9844139), or a restaurant-with-rooms, **L'Ariana** (tel 090 9809075). Off the north-west coast of Sicily near Trapani are the much quieter Egadi Islands, famous for their tuna fishing and canneries; we can recommend a simple but pleasant hotel on Favignana, **the Aegusa** (tel 092 922430).

Although about the same size as Sicily, Sardinia is completely different: its population is sparse; there are few major sightseeing attractions and no very large towns or resorts; and there are few crowds, even in the most developed area for tourists, the Costa Smeralda – which is where most of our recommendations are located. Development is gradually spreading along the coastline from there in both directions. On the north coast, the **Shardana** (tel 0789 754031) and the **Li Nibbari** (tel 0789 754453), both at Santa Teresa Gallura, are possibilities.

On the east coast, the **Hotel l'Oasi** (tel 0784 93111) at Dorgali is a well-equipped *pensione* set on a hill overlooking the sea, amidst gardens and pinewoods. But if you really want to get away from it all, a small island just off the south-west coast of Sardinia may appeal: the Isola San Pietro – try the **Hieracon** (tel 0781 854028) on the waterfront at Carloforte.

Isole Eolie o Lipari, San
Pietro, 98050 Isola Panarea,
Messina

Tel 090 983013
e-mail info@hotelraya.it
website www.hotelraya.it

Nearby Strómboli; Salina;
Sicily.
Location 400 m from port on
hillside; hydrofoil from Naples,
Milazzo, Reggio Calabria,
Palermo, Messina
Food breakfast, brunch, dinner
Price €€€€€
Rooms 36 double and twin,
duplex, all with shower; all
rooms have phone, air condi-
tioning, minibar, hairdrier
Facilities sitting areas,
bar/breakfast room, dining
room, disco, terraces, garden
Credit cards AE, DC, MC, V
Disabled access difficult **Pets**
accepted
Closed mid-Oct to mid-Apr
Proprietor Myriam Beltrami

Raya
Seaside hotel

This unique, stylish hotel was the creation of Myriam Beltrami and Paolo
Tilche, who came to the alluring, car-less
little island of Panarea in the 1960s, were
enthralled and never left. The Raya consists
of a cascade of pink and white bungalows,
linked by arches and whitewashed steps,
tumbling down the hillside through a
Mediterranean garden to the sea. At every
level bougainvillea-shaded terraces – for
dining, sunbathing or attached to bedrooms – look out to the uninhabited Lipari
islands with the threatening vision of the
volcano, Strómboli, in the distance.

Inside all is cool and white – from the
tiled floors to the sofas and chairs – a fitting background for the dramatic pieces of
ethnic art from Polynesia, Africa and Asia
that Myriam collects and loves to display.
She sells similar pieces in her boutique
(next door). Also predominately white,
some of the bedrooms have a slightly
dated feel, with Indian bedspreads and
rush ceilings.

Choose between a continental breakfast in the small bar or on your terrace; or
brunch in the airy dining room. In the
evening, this room is lit by oil lamps on
tables, which in summer are set out on the
panoramic terrace. No young children.

Salina

15 Via Scalo, Salina 98050

Tel 090 9844222
e-mail salina@hotelsignum.it
website www.hotelsignum.it

Nearby by hydrofoil: 1 hr 40
min from Milazzo, 2 hrs from
Messina, 3 hrs from Palermo
Location on sea front
Food breakfast, lunch,
dinner
Price €–€€
Rooms 30, mixture of superi-
or, deluxe and classic; all have
shower, hairdrier, safe, air con-
ditioning, telephone, minibar,
internet, television
Facilities bar, terrace,
solarium, swimming pool
Credit cards V, MC, DC, AE
Disabled suitable
Pets small pets on request
Closed never
Proprietor Clara Rametta

Hotel Signum
Seaside hotel

Clara Rametta and Michele Caruso
always dreamed of opening a hotel in
the village in which they were born.
However, local residents were far from
happy, and when the hotel first opened it
was shut down again, and the owners were
given a *sigillo* (the Latin derivation of which
is *signum*). Thankfully, Clara and Michele's
determination won through, and visitors
to Salina have been overjoyed to find this
gem of a hotel, with its fabulous views over
the island's two imposing peaks and on to
the sea.

Tourism on the island is carefully moni-
tored, and (perhaps more than can be said
for any other hotel in our guide), the owners have ensured that Signum does not
invade the landscape in any way – each
room has a separate building so as to
avoid the hotel look. Rooms are simple in
style, clean, and many have private
terraces.

Reports praise the fabulous setting (*Il
Postino* was filmed nearby), the lush vegetation surrounding the hotel and the views
(especially from the infinity pool). We
would welcome more reports about the
hotel itself, having received one about
noise from the breakfast area which the
guest's room overlooked.

Lungomare Valencia 1, 07041
Alghero, Sassari

Tel 079 981818
e-mail info@hotelvillalas-
tronas.it
website www.hotelvillalas-
tronas.it

Nearby Maria Pia, the best
nearby beach, is 4 km north.
Location in modern Alghero,
800 m S of old Alghero; with
car parking
Food breakfast, lunch, dinner
Price €€€€
Rooms 25; 20 double and 5
suites with bath; all rooms have
phone, TV, air conditioning,
minibar, hairdrier
Facilities sitting room, dining
room, bar, sea-water swimming
pool, gym, bicycles **Credit
cards** AE, DC, MC, V
Disabled not suitable
Pets accepted
Closed never
Manager Maria Teresa Masia

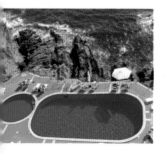

Villa Las Tronas
Seaside hotel

This castellated, 19thC folly lords it
over its own bare, rocky promontory,
and it stands aloof from the blocks of flats
that otherwise characterize this unattractive part of modern Alghero. The interior –
all marble floors and ornate chandeliers –
is as grand as you might expect of somewhere that was a holiday retreat for Italian
royalty until the 1940s. Yet the unstuffy and
businesslike staff ensure it is not intimidatingly formal.

Antiques abound, including in the luxurious bedrooms, which feature brass or
sleigh beds and grand canopies, along with
swanky marble bathrooms. Those billed as
having garden views in reality overlook
Alghero's apartment blocks. You pay extra
to open the shutters on a view across the
bay to the awesome cliff of Capo Caccia;
the priciest sea-facing rooms come with
balconies. Rooms were revamped in 2000.

There are no beaches in this part of
Alghero, but the hotel has a pool, and
many guests swim off the rocks and from
an old dockyard.

When we inspected, breakfast was dire.
For food, you may be better off making the
five-minute stroll along the seaside promenade into the magical backstreets of old
Alghero, where you'll find a wide choice of
restaurants. Bicycles are provided free.

Oliena

08025 Oliena, Nuoro

Tel 0784 287512
e-mail gologone@tin.it
website sugologone.it

Nearby Gennargentu mountains; Monte Ortobene (21 km).
Location 8 km NE of Oliena, in remote mountain setting, with private car parking
Food breakfast, lunch, dinner
Price €€
Rooms 65; 53 double and twin, 8 suites, 4 family rooms, all with bath; all rooms have phone, TV, air conditioning, minibar, hairdrier **Facilities** 5 dining rooms, 2 bars, meeting rooms, gym, health centre, swimming pool, tennis, mini-golf, bicycles, Land Rover and motorbikes for excursions
Credit cards AE, MC, V
Disabled no facilities **Pets** accepted **Closed** Nov-Feb, except Christmas **Proprietor** Giuseppe Palimodde

Su Gologone
Country hotel

The Barbagia is a mountainous inland region where the landscape is wild and spectacular. The hotel is a low-lying white villa, covered in creepers, surrounded by flowing shrubs and set in a landscape of rural splendour: wooded ravines, fields of olives, pinewoods and the craggy peaks of the Supramonte mountains. It feels isolated, and it is; but the Su Gologone is far from undiscovered.

Once, only a few adventurous foreign travellers found their way here; now, they come for the peace, or indeed for the food alone, which is typically Sard: cuts of local meats, roast lamb and the speciality of roast suckling pig – you can watch it being cooked on a spit in front of a huge fireplace. The wines are produced in the local vineyards. The dining room spreads in all directions – into the vine-clad courtyard, the terrace and other rooms, all in suitably rustic style. The bedrooms are light and simple, again in rustic style, in keeping with the surroundings. Walls are whitewashed, floors are tiled and there are lovely views. Despite its size, the Su Gologone still feels small and friendly, and, in most respects, still typically Sard.

Loc. Cala Capra, 07020 Palau

Tel 0789 702000

Nearby Maddalena and
Caprera islands; Costa
Smeralda.
Location 6 km E of Palau, car
parking
Food breakfast, lunch, dinner
Price €€€€ (3-7 night
miniumum)
Rooms 70 double, family and
suites, all with shower; all
rooms have phone, TV, air
conditioning, minibar, hairdri-
er, balcony or terrace
Facilities sitting room, 2
restaurants, bar, swimming
pool, tennis, boat trips, water-
sports
Credit cards AE, DC, MC, V
Disabled not suitable
Pets not accepted
Closed Oct to May
Manager Sig. Luca Cagliero

Capo d'Orso
Seaside hotel

This civilized yet unpretentious waterside hotel stands in marked contrast
to the flashy establishments on the nearby
Costa Smeralda. It's a place for slow-
paced, laid-back, water and beach-oriented
holidays. Basking in mesmerising views of
the verdant yet rocky coastline and off-
shore islands, its secluded setting – the
nearest centre, the humdrum port of
Palau, is a 10-minute drive away – could
hardly be prettier. For chilling out, choose
between two picturesque, sheltered slips
of sand, a lovely amoeba-shaped pool and,
in what amount to the focus of the hotel,
thoroughly romantic drinks and dining terraces shaded by olive trees and tamarisks.
The food is praised; breakfasts come in the
form of buffets, and there is also a
lunchtime and evening pizzeria. The hotel
is not suitable for anyone who finds steps
difficult.

The simple bedrooms, in low-rise
blocks, are lifted by cheerful paintings and
the fact that all face the sea and have a balcony or terrace. Suites suit families: the sitting room, connected to a bedroom by a
sliding door, has a sofa bed.

If boredom sets in, the hotel can
arrange diving and riding. Boat trips from
its jetty visit Maddalena and Caprera, and
the fleshpots of the Costa Smeralda's
Porto Cervo.

Porto Cervo

07020 Porto Cervo, Costa
Smeralda, Sassari

Tel 0789 976111
e-mail caladivolpe@luxurycol-
lection.com

Nearby Porto Cervo (8 km);
Olbia (25 km).
Location S of Porto Cervo,
Costa Smeralda; car parking
Food breakfast, lunch, dinner;
room service; half-board only
Price €€€€€
Rooms 121; 100 double, 9 single, 12 suites, all with bath;
Presidential suite has private
pool; all rooms have phone,
TV, air conditioning, minibar,
hairdrier **Facilities** restaurant,
bar, pool, terrace, garden,
beach, private harbour, jetty,
water-skiing, 9-hole putting
green, tennis, bike hire, boat
hire, fitness centre **Credit
cards** AE, DC, MC, V
Disabled not suitable **Pets** not
accepted **Closed** late Oct-Apr
Manager Marco Milocco

Cala di Volpe
Seaside hotel

Approached from the front, Cala di
Volpe has the slightly forbidding exterior of a Moorish fortification, with towers, crenellations and turrets. Viewed from
the sea, however, the hotel resembles a
simple fishing village, where clusters of little houses painted in shades of ochre and
amber are softened by arches and porti-
coes – a magical sight when lit up at night.
Simplicity of style is carried through into
the interior: niches, painted stairways and
modern stained glass insets in the hall-
ways; plain bedrooms (some with *trompe
l'oeil* embellishments), with terraces or
gardens overlooking the sea. Overall, the
effect of wooden beams, bamboo, terracotta floors, and orange, yellow and brown
colours, offset by cool white, creates an air
of Sardinian rustic chic.

The super-rich turn up by boat and
moor their vessels in the small marina. If
you don't have a boat, don't worry: a free
hotel launch leaves half hourly for a private beach – a little paradise, complete
with sunloungers, towels and crystal clear
water. Or it's just a short stroll away
along a wooded track.

Beware the veneer of simplicity at Cala
di Volpe: it belies discreet, understated luxury. Your credit card needs to be in good
working order.

Porto Cervo

07020 Porto Cervo, Costa
Smeralda, Sassari

Tel 0789 931111
e-mail cervo@Sheraton.com
website
www.sheraton.com/cervo

Nearby Olbia (30 km); Costa
Smeralda coastline; boat trips.
Location in middle of Porto
Cervo; car parking
Food breakfast, lunch, dinner
Price €€€€€
Rooms 108 all with bath and
shower; 6 suites with private
pool; all with air conditioning,
minibar, satellite TV
Facilities 5 restaurants, bars, 3
swimming pools, sports centre
and golf nearby
Credit cards AE, DC, MC, V
Disabled not suitable
Pets not accepted
Closed never
Manager Franco Mulas

Cervo
Seaside hotel

A stone's throw from the old quay, this
Mediterranean-style hotel overlooks
the *piazzetta* right in the heart of Porto
Cervo – an almost too perfect resort village, crammed with designer shops and
smart restaurants. It is part of the Costa
Smeralda development, started in the late
fifties by a consortium led by the Aga
Khan.

Within the hotel it is refreshingly airy
and simple. There are textured white walls,
terracotta floors, plain, bright fabrics and
wooden furniture. Ceilings are low and
windows are arched. Despite the fact that
the Cervo has a purpose-built conference
centre a short distance away and sometimes hosts large groups, the terraces and
shaded dining areas are small in scale and
intimate. There are several restaurants to
choose from: the Grill specializes in Italian
cuisine and has splendid views over the
marina; Il Pescatore serves fish and
seafood; and Il Pomodoro is informal and
rustic.

For sports enthusiasts, a short walk
over a little wooden bridge leads to the
sports complex where tennis, squash, a
fully-equipped gym and jogging track are
available. Sun worshippers and sea bathers
will appreciate the free boat service
(between May and September) that whisks
them away to a secluded beach.

Porto Cervo

07020 Porto Cervo, Costa
Smeralda, Sassari

Tel 0789 930111
e-mail pitrizza@luxurycollec-
tion.com **website** www.star-
wood.com/hotelpitrizza

Nearby Beaches of the Costa
Smeralda; Maddalena archipelago.
Location 4 km from Porto
Cervo, at Liscia di Vacca; parking
Food breakfast, lunch, dinner;
room service
Price €€€€€
Rooms 51; 38 double and
twin, 13 suites, all with bath; all
have phone, TV, air conditioning, minibar **Facilities** dining
room, bar, terrace, fitness centre, sea-water pool, beach,
water-skiing, boat hire, windsurfing **Credit cards** AE, DC,
MC, V **Disabled** no facilities
Pets not accepted **Closed** late
Oct to early May **Manager**
Pierangelo Tondina

Pitrizza
Resort village

The smart playground of the Costa
Smeralda is liberally endowed with
luxury hotels, but there is one that stands
out from the rest: the Pitrizza. What distinguishes it (apart from its small size) is its
exclusive, intimate, club-like atmosphere.
No shops, disco or ritzy touches here.
Small private villas are scattered discreetly
among the rocks and flowering gardens,
overlooking a private beach. Rooms are
furnished throughout with immaculate
taste, some of them amazingly simple. The
style is predominantly rustic, with white
stucco walls, beams and locally crafted furniture and fabrics. Each villa has four to six
rooms, and most have a private terrace,
garden or patio. The core of the hotel is
the club house, with a small sitting room,
bar, restaurant and spacious terrace where
you can sit, enjoying the company of other
guests or simply watching the sunset. A
path leads down to the golden sands of a
small beach and a private jetty where you
can moor your yacht. Equally desirable is
the sea-water pool, which has been carved
out of the rocky shoreline.

There is of course a hitch to the
Pitrizza. The rooms here are among the
most expensive on the entire Italian
coastline.

07020 Porto Cervo, Costa
Smeralda, Sassari

Tel 0789 977111
e-mail romazzino@luxurycol-
lection.com **website** www.star-
wood.com/romazzino

Nearby Hotel Cala di Volpe, a
jaw-dropping faux-Medieval
castle.
Location 11 km from Porto
Cervo; car parking
Food breakfast, lunch, dinner;
room service
Price €€€€€
Rooms 94; 78 double and
twin, 16 suites, all with bath; all
rooms have phone, TV, air
conditioning, minibar,
hairdrier
Facilities sitting room, 2
restaurants, bar, terrace, swim-
ming pool, tennis, watersports
Credit cards AE, DC, MC, V
Disabled access difficult
Pets not accepted
Closed mid-Feb to mid-May
Manager Bart Spoozenberg

Romazzino
Seaside hotel

Though fabulously stylish and expensive, the Romazzino is a little less
exclusive and pricey than its smaller sister,
the Pitrizza (see page 305). It's a better
choice if a beach is important in your
plans, since the whitewashed, terracotta-
roofed complex presides over one of the
biggest on the Costa Smeralda (as well as
an enormous pool). Families in particular
should be more at home here.

Make no mistake, however: this is still
one of Europe's most luxurious beach
hotels. The interior has the airiness and
understated elegance of a giant Moorish-
cum-Mediterranean mansion. For example, whimsical, painted ceramics adorn the
walls of the sitting room, while gay colour
schemes complement soothing Sardinian
fabrics in the tasteful bedrooms.

A veritable army of staff panders to
your every need. At dinner, it's hard to
know whether to be more impressed by
the creative Mediterranean cuisine, or the
zealously attentive, multilingual service.
Although the Romazzino exceeds our
normal room limit by a considerable mar-
gin, we continue to include it because it
has the feel of a much smaller place.

Santa Margherita di Pula

09010 Santa Margherita di
Pula, Pula

Tel 070 921171
e-mail info@ismorus.it
website www.ismorus.it

Nearby The sand-dune beach-
es at Chia; the Punic and
Roman ruins at Nora.
Location on the coast S of
Pula; car parking
Food breakfast, lunch, dinner;
room service; half-board
obligatory
Price €€€€
Rooms 85 double and twin,
single and suites, all with bath
or shower; all rooms have
phone, TV, air conditioning,
minibar, hairdrier
Facilities sitting room, restau-
rant; bar, terrace, swimming
pool, tennis, watersports
Credit cards AE, DC, MC, V
Disabled no special facilities
Pets accepted
Closed Nov to Easter
Manager Maurizio Maffei

Is Morus
Seaside hotel

Is Morus is one of several upmarket and
isolated hotels along a strip of flat coastline dotted with holiday homes and green-
houses, and backed by parched, rocky hills.

Secluded within a garden of oleanders
and a pine and eucalyptus wood, pantiled
and whitewashed Is Morus is a
Mediterranean rendition of a smart coun-
try-house hotel. In keeping with the fairly
formal service, an understated elegance
pervades the place, both in the cool, light
sitting rooms that are interconnected by
arches and furnished with squashy modern
soft furnishings, and in bedrooms that are
almost minimalist in style. Some of these
are in the main building (avoid those without a sea view or balcony), others in villas
sprinkled through the wood, with two or
three bedrooms per villa.

The sandy beach isn't one of Sardinia's
best (it can be weedy), but it is yards from
the main building, private and immaculately maintained, and the swimming pool is
large and inviting.

This is a civilized and peaceful corner of
Sardinia, bereft of bright lights or of even
anything amounting to a resort.

Carruba

Via Olmo 16, 95010 Carruba,
Catania

Tel 095 964920
e-mail info@lolmo.it

Nearby Etna; Taormina (20 km);
Catania (20 km).
Location exit the A18 motorway at
Giarre; ask the hotel for detailed
instructions from there. In own
extensive grounds with ample car
parking
Food breakfast
Price €€; mimimum stay three
nights
Rooms 8 doubles, all with bath or
shower; all rooms have hairdrier;
phone and TV on request
Facilities sitting rooms, dining
room, terraces, garden, pool
Credit cards not accepted
Disabled no special facilities but
ground floor rooms
Pets not accepted
Closed never
Proprietor Andrea and Marina di
San Giuliano

L'Olmo
Country villa

Immersed in the family's lemon grove
between Mount Etna and the sea,
L'Olmo is the home of Andrea, Marchese
di San Giuliano, and his wife Marina who
have recently converted part of their
property into guest accomodation; it lies
within easy reach of Taormina, Catania and
Siracusa.

The bedrooms are divided between the
main 'casale' and another pretty adjacent
building. A private house party atmosphere
prevails and, indeed, is encouraged; it's the
sort of place that would lend itself very
well to being taken over by a group of
friends. The houses are filled with family
antiques and pictures, but while quite
grand, the atmosphere is not at all stuffy.
There are plenty of books and magazines
to read and open fires burn in cooler
weather. Bedrooms are large and airy with
good fitted wardrobes and big, well-
equipped bathrooms.

The large pool is equipped with smart
red and white striped sun beds while the
beautiful gardens, filled with bougainvilla,
jasmine and antique roses, provide plenty
of shaded spots for relaxing with a book;
views are of Etna in one direction and the
sea in the other. Activities can be organised on request such as expeditions to
view Etna's craters, fishing trips, cooking
courses, water skiing and sailing.

Erice

Via Vittorio Emanuele 63, 91016
Erice, Trapani

Tel 0923 869300
e-mail modernoh@tin.it
website www.hotelmodernoerice.it

Nearby Greek temple and theatre at
Segesta; Trapani (15 km); Egadi
islands.
Location in town centre; public car
parking nearby
Food breakfast, lunch, dinner
Price €–€€€
Rooms 40; 32 doubles and 8 singles,
all with bath or shower; all rooms
have phone, TV, minibar, hairdrier
Facilities sitting areas, dining room,
bar, roof terrace, lift
Credit cards AE, DC, MC, V
Disabled no special facilities
Pets accepted
Closed never
Proprietor Giuseppe Catalano

Moderno
Town hotel

Erice is an enchanting medieval town,
encircled by high walls and suspended
2,500 feet above Trapani. It makes a good
base for a couple of days and most tourists
leave in the evening making way for a
rather eerie atmosphere often enhanced
by swirling fog. The family-run Moderno is
situated at the top of the narrow main
street (park in the public parking near
Porta Trapani and walk up to the hotel); it
occupies a 19th century building, but as
the name suggests, it is decorated in modern style, although 'modern' in this case
means rather dated 70s décor mixed with
traditional Sicilian elements. There are
fresh flowers, pictures, ornaments and
bright, locally-woven rugs everywhere and
public rooms are simply firnished with
groups of chairs, sofas and tables.
Bedrooms (about half of which are housed
in a nearby annexe) are simple and fresh
with whitewashed walls and tiled floors;
some are furnished with antiques while
others have modern pine or bamboo
pieces.

The restaurant enjoys a good reputation for its traditional Sicilian fare, and the
roof terrace provides spectacular views of
the tiled roofs of Erice and beyond. A
recent visitor was enthusiastic about the
Moderno; 'it has not lost its individual
touch'.

Contrada di Gangivecchio, 90024
Gangi, Palermo

Tel 0921 689191
e-mail paolotornabene@interfree.it
website
www.tenutagangivecchio.com

Nearby Gangi (6 km); Madonie
region.
Location 130 km SE of Palermo.
Exit the A19 autostrada at Tre
Monzelli, follow the SS120 to
Petralia and then Gangi. Just after
the town sign for Gangi, turn right
and follow signs for Tenuta
Gangivecchio; the Tenuta is after 5
km on the right; car parking
Food breakfast, lunch, dinner
Price €
Rooms 10, 9 double and triple with
shower and 1 suite with bath; all
rooms have phone **Facilities** dining
room, restaurant, sitting rooms,
swimming pool, table tennis, moun-
tain bikes, horse riding **Credit cards**
AE, MC, V **Disabled** not suitable
Pets not accepted **Closed** July
Proprietor Paolo Tornabene

Tenuta Gangivecchio
Country guesthouse

If you want peace and seclusion, then
look no further than this converted
13thC monastery, reached after a long
drive through the beautiful Madonie
region. The home of the Tornabene family
for generations, the monastery lies at the
bottom of a steep valley, hidden behind tall
wooden doors that open to reveal a magnificent courtyard and magical buildings.
First came a restaurant in the monastery
itself whose reputation for marvellous
Sunday lunches soon spread far and wide;
the restaurant and its reputation are still
thriving. Some years later, the stables were
converted into guest accomodation, now
run by Paolo Tornabene. If you expected
to be sleeping in the monastery, you will
be disappointed, but the good-sized, simple
rooms with their red-tiled floors, country
antiques and pretty bedspreads are not
without rustic appeal. Recently a suite has
been added in the monastery building
itself. The guest wing has its own dining
room looking on to the garden where
imaginative variations on typical Sicilian
dishes using mainly home grown ingredients are served. There is no choice on the
menus, so warn the 'laconic' Si. Tornabene
in advance of any individual requirements.
Our reporter found that the Tenuta was, in
many ways, 'a very special place' and
offered excellent value for money.

Contrada Giubliana, S.P. per
Marina di Ragusa, 97100 Ragusa

Tel 0932 669119
e-mail info@eremodellagiubiliana.it
website
www.eremodellagiubiliana.it

Nearby Ragusa (7 km); private
beach (8 km).
Location signposted off the road
from Ragusa to Marina di Ragusa;
ample car parking
Food breakfast, lunch, dinner
Price €€€
Rooms 13; 10 double, 3 suites and 5
self-catering cottages, all with bath
or shower; all rooms have phone,
TV, hairdrier
Facilities sitting room, dining room,
terrace, garden, swimming pool,
mountain bikes, shuttle to Ragusa
and the beach
Credit cards AE, DC, MC, V
Disabled one adapted room Pets
accepted
Closed never
Proprietor Salvatore Mancini Nifosi

Eremo della Giubliana
Country hotel

If you are touring by car, this small, elegant hotel is well worth a detour. Alternatively, you can fly to the hotel's private airfield, from where you can also take sightseeing trips as far away as Malta or Tunisia.

The setting - far away from major roads in a pastoral landscape of rolling farmland cut by white lanes and stone walls where the dominant sound is birdsong - is idyllic. The hotel has been the home of the Nifosì family since the 18th century. Built as a fortified convent in the 15th century, it was later used by the Knights of the Order of St John on their way to Malta. In converting the convent, Signor Nifosì, an architect, has made every effort to preserve the building's original structure, retaining the original pitch and limestone floors and transforming the monks' cells into comfortable and stylish bedrooms with modern bathrooms. A recent addition is a delightful little walled garden filled with exotic Mediterranean trees and shrubs; there is small pool and bar - bliss in the summer heat.

Food is important at the Eremo; the restaurant serves unpretentious dishes from the Sicilian highlands using home grown organic produce and accompanied by a fine selection of local wines.

Lungomare Vittorini 26, 96100
Siracusa

Tel 0931 465861
e-mail info@guthotel.it
website www.guthotel.it

Nearby sights of Ortigia; ginnasio
Romano.
Location on north east part of
island; on road with limited parking
Food breakfast
Price €
Rooms 25; 3 singles, 19 doubles and
twins, 3 triples, all with bath or
shower; all rooms have phone, TV,
air conditioning, minibar, hairdrier
(some)
Facilities sitting room, breakfast
room, small terrace
Credit cards AE, DC, MC, V
Disabled 2 adapted rooms
Pets accepted
Closed never
Proprietors Paola Pretsch

Gutkowski
City guesthouse

The thriving metropolis of Magna
Grecia, Siracusa was one of the most
important cities in the Western world for
over a thousand years. The spiritual heart
of the city still lies in the island of Ortigia,
today joined to the mainland by two
bridges. Occupying an old fisherman's
house overlooking the sea on the north-
east corner of the island, the delightful
Gutkowski makes a great base for exploring and is a refreshing change from sometimes heavy-handed traditional Sicilian
style. It is painted sea blue (the only blue
building on the island) with white trim
around the tall windows; inside, the same
summer colours prevail and all is fresh,
clean and airy. The breakfast room has a
pretty tiled floor while a fire burns in the
sitting room in cool weather. Reports
praise the 'fabulous' breakfast which features home made almond granita in summer plus all sorts of home made jams, preserves and cakes served on fine china. The
bedrooms are quite spartan yet stylish and
comfortable. Again, natural colours dominate enhanced by the sun filtering through
filmy white curtains; the five at the front of
the house have small balconies overlooking the sea. Eleven rooms in an annexe
have been added, though perhaps the
word annexe is not appropriate – it is now
really a hotel with two main buildings.

Siracusa

Via del Platano 3, 96100 Siracusa

Tel 0931 717352
e-mail limoneto@tin.it
website www.limoneto.it

Nearby Siracusa (9 km); Noto (25 km).
Location 9 km W of Siracusa, off route 14 to Palazzolo, in own grounds; with car parking
Food breakfast, lunch, dinner
Price €
Rooms 10; 4 double, 3 triple and 3 family rooms all with shower or bath; all rooms have phone
Facilities sitting room, dining room, terrace, garden
Credit cards not accepted
Disabled no special facilities
Pets accepted
Closed never
Proprietors Norcia family

Limoneto
Country guesthouse

If you want to visit the fascinating city of Siracusa but stay in the countryside, we can recommend this simple agriturismo. Run by the Norcia family, Limoneto is an organic farm producing citrus fruits, vegetables, olive oil and wine. The solid, white-painted main house is set among orange and lemon groves; the scent from the citrus blossoms in spring is quite intoxicating.

The welcome here is very Southern Italian; warm and genuine with guests being treated as part of the family. Some of the bedrooms are in the main house while others are in a renovated barn; some are large enough for a family. Though modern rather than characterful, they are 'comfortable, fresh and spotlessly clean'. The main focus of any stay at the Limoneto, however, is definitely the food which, judging by reports, is fabulous; 'the best we had'. Adelina Norcia's no-choice Sicilian menus change daily and feature much of what is grown on the farm. Finish off your meal with a glass of ice-cold home-brewed limoncello.

We would welcome more reports about this hotel; although we have included it for some years now (urged by reader's recommendations), we have not yet managed a personal visit. But we like the sound of it very much.

Taormina

Via Bagnoli Croce 79, 98039
Taormina, Messina

Tel 0942 23791
e-mail info@villabelvedere.it
website www.villabelvedere.it

Nearby Greek theatre; Corso
Umberto, public gardens.
Location next to the Belvedere of
the Via Roma, close to public gardens and old town; with car parking
Food breakfast, light lunch
Price ⓔ–ⓔⓔ
Rooms 52, 50 doubles and 2 garden
suites, all with bath or shower; all
rooms have phone, satellite TV, air
conditioning, safe, hairdrier
Facilities 2 sitting areas, 2 bars,
breakfast room, TV room, terrace,
garden, swimming pool, poolside
snack bar
Credit cards MC, V
Disabled no special facilities
Pets accepted
Closed late Nov-end Feb
Proprietors The Pécaut family

Villa Belvedere
Seaside villa

The Belvedere is a refreshingly unpretentious, discreet and welcoming hotel, one of the first to be built in Taormina (in 1902). It has been in the Pécaut family ever since, and subsequent generations have managed to make their changes without altering the inherent charm of the place, Currently in charge are brother and sister Silena and Christian and their mother, all helpful and friendly.

As you would expect from its name, the Belvedere's greatest asset is its position. Close to the centre of town, it commands a spectacular panorama of the bay and the slopes of Etna to the south. Flowery gardens lead down to a small, delightful pool where the setting and the poolside bar (serving light meals and Sicilian regional dishes) tempt guests to linger all day and postpone the more serious business of sightseeing. Arrangements can also be made to take guests to local beaches.

There is no proper dining room, but plenty of choice amongst restaurants in Taormina. And the hotel does have two prettily furnished sitting rooms, and a sunny breakfast room. A sound choice for a reasonably priced family hotel, warmly endorsed by a recent reporter who also mentioned the 'slick valet parking and the 'clean bright bedrooms with stunning views from the balconies'.

Taormina

Via Leonardo da Vinci 60, 98039
Taormina , Messina

Tel 0942 28153
e-mail villaducale@tao.it
website www.hotelvilladucale.it

Nearby Greek theatre; Corso
Umberto; excursions to Etna.
Location above town centre, on
road to Castelmola; limited car park-
ing
Food breakfast, light snacks
Price €€€
Rooms 18; 13 double and twin, 5
suites, all with bath; all rooms have
phone, TV, air conditioning, mini-
bar, hairdrier
Facilities sitting room, library, bar,
breakfast room, terrace, hot tub, free
shuttle to beaches
Credit cards AE, DC, MC, V
Disabled access difficult
Pets accepted
Closed early Dec-mid Feb
Proprietors Dr Andrea and Rosaria
Quartucci

Villa Ducale
Hilltop villa

It's hard to fault Villa Ducale. Originally a
coaching inn, it was converted into a
patrician home at the turn of the century
by the great-grandfather of the present
owner, Andrea Quartucci. In 1993, he and
his wife opened the house to guests and
their new venture was an instant success.
Why? Because of the wonderful terrace,
the feel of a family home, the unexpected,
special touches and the friendliness of the
staff.

No two rooms are alike (try for one
with a private terrace), but they all have
fine linen on the beds, billowing curtains
and terrazzo floors, painted furniture and
pretty bedheads; in one junior suite is the
painted bed, inlaid with mother-of-pearl, of
Andrea's grandparents. Many walls are
decorated with trompe l'oeil or with fruit,
a symbol of richness in Sicily.

Perhaps the real quality of Villa Ducale
comes through best at breakfast, served
until 11.30 am. You won't easily forget sitting on the broad balcony, the table before
you laden with fruit, local cheeses, specially baked bread and Sicilian iced cakes, with
its amazing view across the town, the bay
and Mount Etna. Sipping a drink there at
sunset is pretty romantic, too. A recent
ecstatic report from a reader only con-
firms our enthusiasm.

Taormina

Via Roma 2, 98039 Taormina , Messina

Tel 0942 23921
e-mail hotelparadiso@tao.it
website www.hotelvillaparadiso-taormina.com

Nearby Greek theatre, Corso Umberto and public gardens; excursions to Etna.
Location on SE edge of town; small public car park next door, paying garage nearby
Food breakfast, dinner
Price €
Rooms 37; 21 double and twin, 13 junior suites, 3 singles, all with bath; all rooms have phone, TV, air conditioning, hairdrier
Facilities 2 sitting rooms, dining room, bar, terrace
Credit cards AE, DC, MC, V
Disabled access possible
Pets accepted
Closed never
Proprietor Salvatore Martorana

Villa Paradiso
Seaside hotel

Next to the public gardens and close to the heart of historic Taormina, the Villa Paradiso also has the advantage of a glorious panorama along the coast and across to the hazy cone of Etna. The only drawback to the location is that it is on a main road, which means some noise for back rooms and major problems with parking in high season.

The hotel is a well-maintained white building, and the public rooms have all the style and atmosphere of a private villa: white arches, patterned carpets on tiled floors, stylish sofas and an imaginative collection of prints, paintings and watercolours. The restaurant makes the most of the views, and the food is distinctly above average. Every bedroom has a balcony, and inevitably the most sought-after are those at the front with sea views. The majority are larger than you would expect from a *pensione*; some have attractive painted furniture. You can reach the beaches by cable car or – more conveniently – the hotel minibus, which takes you to the Paradise Beach Club in Letojanni (free facilities for guests from end of May till the end of October).

Agrigento

For. Baglio della Luna
Country Villa

Situated at one end of Agrigento's Valle dei Templi, the Foresteria Baglio della Luna occupies a Baglio dating from the 13th century, dominated by a sturdy square tower. Recent restoration has rendered the interior a little characterless, but the public rooms, contained in the tower, are furnished in traditional Sicilian style as are the bedrooms. The banal suites are over-priced for what they are while standards are unpretentiously decorated with floral prints and coloured ceramic floor tiles; bathrooms are fairly basic. Creative rendi-tions of Sicilian and regional Italian dishes are offered in the restaurant; in summer, meals are served on a terrace overlooking the temples.

Contrada Maddalusa, 92100
Agrigento

Tel 0922 511061
e-mail info@bagliodellaluna.com
website www.bagliodellaluna.com
Food breakfast, lunch, dinner
Price €€
Closed never
Proprietor Ignazio Altieri

Agrigento

Villa Palocla
Country hotel

A recent arrival to the Sicily hotel scene, this is a useful address at the NW end of the south coast recommended by a reader. Purpose built as a hotel in 2000 in the 'late Baroque' style, it is comfortable enough. The rooms are decorated in neu-tral but smart off-whites, beiges and pale yellows. Antiques here and there lend char-acter. It's about 3 km from the centre of Sciacca, with a pool that 'could be a holiday destination in itself' according to one reporter. He also noted the 'good restau-rant' and 'very nice rooms' all at fairly rea-sonable prices – 140 euros for a double and 80 for a single as we went to press.

Contrada Raganella, 92019 Sciacca,
Agrigento

Tel 0925 902812
e-mail info@villapalocla.it
website www.villaplocloa.it
Food breakfast, lunch, dinner
Price €€
Closed October
Proprietor Accurfio Marciante

Costa Dorata

Porto San Paolo, Costa Dorata,
07020 Vaccileddi, Sassari

Tel 0789 40006/4007
e-mail hoteldondiego@tiscali.it
website hoteldondiego.com
Food breakfast, lunch, dinner
Price €€€€€
Closed Oct to Apr
Manager Luigi Mennella

Don Diego
Resort hotel

Despite a reader's report criticizing the pool and beach for being dirty, the Don Diego keeps its place in these pages on account of its sheer charm. It stands in a secluded position south of Olbia on the Costa Dorata, a quieter stretch of coastline than the Costa Smeralda, with many coves and beaches. The hotel, of typical Sardinian design, consists of airy, comfortable and stylish single-storey cottages scattered amongst the macchia and pine trees. Double bedrooms are located further away from the main building than the junior suites, which enjoy sea views (though they may be obscured by vegetation). From the lovely curving sea-water swimming pool there are views across to the islands of Molara and, close by, Tavolara.

Erice

Via Vittorio Emanuele 75, 91016
Erice, Trapani

Tel 0923 869377
e-mail booking@hotelelimo.it
website www.charmerlax.com
Food breakfast, lunch, dinner
Price €€
Closed never
Proprietors Tilotta family

Elimo
Town hotel

Situated in the same street as the Moderno (see page 309) the Elimo makes an excellent alternative. One of our reporters described it as 'a happy mixture of traditional and modern, with attractive public rooms, individual bedrooms, a rooftop terrace and a pretty courtyard'. A more recent visitor endorses this view. The Elimo is a simple, straightforward hotel with no pretensions – but well run. Public rooms consist of a combined lobby, bar and small sitting area with a homely feel, and a dining room where fairly plain dishes are served (breakfast is basic). Bedrooms are clean, modern and simple, not too small, with functional but acceptable bathrooms. Some have views over the roof to the sea beyond.

Modica

L'Orangerie
Town Guest House

Among the faded Baroque splendour of Modica bassa and housed in an elegant 19th century *palazzo* is the delightful Orangerie. Elegant, stylish simplicity are the watch words here; the 3 self-catering apartments and four double rooms all have hard wood floors and strong colours on the walls. They are sparingly but comfortably furnished with fine antique or déco pieces; several have painted ceilings. Some rooms have a pretty, flower-filled terrace while others look over a garden filled with lemon trees. Breakfast is served in the old-fashioned kitchen around a big table. For dinner, try the imaginative food at the Fattoria delle Torri just around the corner.

Vico de Naro 5, 97015 Modica, Ragusa

Tel 347 0674698
e-mail info@lorangerie.it
website www.lorangerie.it
Food breakfast
Price €
Closed never
Proprietors Dott. Guglielmo Antonio Cartia

Noto

Monteluce
Country house hotel

With only four suites and one double room, this is an intimate hotel. Built in the early 1900s deep in the hills surrounding Noto, Monteluce is surrounded by olive, orange and carob trees. The suites are more than comfortable, and each has a private terrace – the Blue suite's terrace has a table and chairs: a perfect spot to escape from the midday heat whilst admiring the Iblei mountains. If your budget doesn't stretch to a suite, the Pilot room is nonetheless a treat – the walls are covered with beautiful stencils of old planes.

A relaxing base from which to explore Sicily. Reports welcome.

Contradda Vaddeddi - Villa del Tellaro, 96017 Noto

Tel 0335 6901871
e-mail info@monteluce.com
website www.monteluce.com
Food breakfast, self catering option
Price €; apartments
Closed never
Managers Claudio and Imelda Rubiano

Siracusa

Viale Mazzini 12, 96100 Siracusa

Tel 0931 464600
e-mail info@grandhotelss.it
website www.grandhotelss.it
Food breakfast, lunch, dinner; room service
Price €€€
Closed never
Manager Signor Bambara

Grand Hotel
Luxury town hotel

Situated in the old part of Siracusa on the island of Ortigia, the Grand Hotel is a splendid example of a luxurious, but not exorbitant, Mediterranean hotel. You are greeted by a cool and elegant reception area with circular marble stairs and bronze sculpture. Other public rooms are clad in marble, stained glass, and crystal, mixing modern art and furnishings with antiques. Bedrooms, are luxurious and thoughtfully equipped. There is a bar in the old pale stone-walled cistern and a sophisticated roof garden restaurant, with magnificent views of the Grand Harbour and seafront. It may not be charming and small, but the Grand makes a good base in the centre of Siracusa.

Valderice

91019 Valderice, Trapani

Tel 0923 891111
e-mail baglio-santacroce@ibero.it
website www.bagliosantacroce.it
Food breakfast, lunch, dinner
Price €–€€
Closed never
Proprietors Cusenza family

Baglio Santacroce
Country hotel

Located in the Erice foothills, on the outskirts of Valderice, this is a family-owned and run hotel set in a predominantly stone farmhouse dating back to 1636. With its central courtyard, thick bare stone walls (in both bedrooms and bathrooms), terracotta tiled floors and beamed ceilings, the hotel has a rustic, countrified feel – except for the annexe bar and dining room. Our original inspector liked this hotel, at least the old part, but we have had one report from someone who was disappointed by the plumbing. Breakfast is standard hotel fare, but the dinners, especially the fish, are above average. There is a small swimming pool, with superb views to the Gulf of Cornino and Mount Cofano, and the gardens are very peaceful.

Index – Hotel names

In this index, hotels are arranged in order of the first distinctive part of their names. Very common prefixes such as 'Hotel', 'Albergo', 'Il', 'La', 'Dei' and 'Delle' are omitted. More descriptive words such as 'Casa', 'Castello', 'Locanda' and 'Villa' are included.

Index – Hotel names

Index – Hotel locations

In this index, hotels are arranged in order of the names of the cities, towns or villages they are in or near. Hotels located in a very small village may be indexed under a larger place nearby. An index by hotel name precedes this one.

Index – Hotel locations

Index – Hotel locations

Other Charming Small Hotel Guide Titles:

Austria
Britain & Ireland
France
Germany
Greece
Mallorca, Menorca & Ibiza
New England
Paris
Southern France
Spain
Switzerland
Tuscany & Umbria
Venice and North-East Italy

Special offers

Buy your *Charming Small Hotel Guide* by post directly from the
publisher and you'll get a worthwhile discount. *

Titles available:	Retail price	Discount price
Austria	£10.99	£9.50
Britain & Ireland	£14.99	£13.50
France	£13.99	£12.50
Germany	£11.99	£10.50
Greece	£10.99	£9.50
Italy	£14.99	£13.50
Mallorca, Menorca & Ibiza	£9.99	£8.50
New England	£10.99	£9.50
Paris	£10.99	£9.50
Southern France	£10.99	£9.50
Spain	£11.99	£10.50
Switzerland	£9.99	£8.50
Tuscany & Umbria	£10.99	£9.50
Venice and North-East Italy	£10.99	£9.50

Please send your order to:
  Book Sales, Duncan Petersen Publishing Ltd, C7, Old
  Imperial Laundry, Warriner Gardens, London SW11 4XW
  enclosing:
  1) the title you require and number of copies
  2) your name and address
  3) your cheque made out to:
  Duncan Petersen Publishing Ltd
  *Offer applies to this edition and to UK only.

The perfect accompaniment to the *Charming Small Hotel Guides* is the *On Foot City Guides* series.

These books feature unique aerial-view maps, which show not only the city's street layout but the look of your surroundings too.

Following these walks is like being shown around by an exceptionally knowledgeable friend.

They're fun and they'll help you fit it all together. And you'll discover plenty of interesting things you never knew about the city.

Friendly accompanying text, full of personal insights and advice, including food, drink, and shopping along the way. Introduces you to all the must-see areas.

Most of the routes take an hour; or, with stops for sightseeing, two or three hours. Or interlink the routes for longer expeditions.

Titles in the series:

London Walks

Paris Walks

New York Walks

Visit charmingsmallhotels.co.uk

Our website has recently been completely rebuilt. Please take a look - it includes fantastic entries from all over Europe with up to four colour photographs for each entry as well as our independent reports.

It's the best research tool on the web for finding our kind of hotel.

Exchange rates

As we went to press, $1 bought 0.74 euros and £1 bought 1.47 euros